VALIANT WINGS

Valiant Wings

The Battle and Blenheim Squadrons over France 1940

by
Norman L.R. Franks

WILLIAM KIMBER

First published in 1988

British Library Cataloguing in Publication data

Franks, Norman L.R. (Norman Leslie Robert),
1940–
Valiant wings : the Battle and Blenheim
Squadrons over France 1940.
1. France 1939-1945. Air operations, by
Great Britain, Royal Air Force. Bomber
Command
I. Title
940.54′21

ISBN 0-7183-0697-X

*William Kimber Limited is part of the
Thorsons Publishing Group, Wellingborough,
Northamptonshire, NN8 2RQ, England.*

Photoset in North Wales by
Derek Doyle & Associates Mold, Clwyd
and printed in Great Britain by
Redwood Burn Limited, Trowbridge, Wiltshire

1   3   5   7   9   10   8   6   4   2

Contents

In Memory of

Leading Aircraftman

Lawrence Royston
REYNOLDS

WOP/AG
12 Squadron RAF

and to others whose bravery
during the Battle of France went
unrewarded

Acknowledgements

Once again I have been able to call on the help of a number of former RAF aircrew whose activities encompass the ambit of the period of Air Force history I have chosen to cover.

Considering the terrible losses inflicted upon Battle and Blenheim squadrons in the Battle of France, it is amazing that people who flew in that campaign survived in the first place, let alone survive a further five years of war. Yet they did, and I am grateful to the following men who have been so generous with their recollections.

Obviously any book of history can be written, but it takes the memories of those 'who were there' to make this history come alive. Gentlemen, I thank and salute you.

Squadron Leader G.N. Patterson DFM	12 Squadron
Wing Commander W.H. George DFC	15 Squadron
Group Captain G.M. Wyatt DFC	57 Squadron
Wing Commander E.F. Nind DFC	57 Squadron
Group Captain G.H.D. Evans DSO DFC	59 Squadron
Air Commodore W.P. Sutcliffe CB DFC	82 Squadron
Group Captain R.D. Max DSO DFC	103 Squadron
Wing Commander M.C. Wells	103 Squadron
Squadron Leader J.R. Havers DFC	103 Squadron
Air Marshal Sir Gareth Clayton KCB DFC*	107 Squadron
Flight Lieutenant L.S. Fearnley (MID)	107 Squadron
Group Captain H.P. Pleasance DSO DFC*	107 Squadron
Wing Commander R.C. Rotheram OBE DFC	107 Squadron
Flight Lieutenant J.R. Paine DFM	139 Squadron
Air Vice Marshal J.F. Hobler CB CBE	142 Squadron
Squadron Leader J.M. Hewson DFC	142 Squadron
Air Vice Marshal A.D. Frank CB CBE DSO DFC	150 Squadron
Squadron Leader F.H. Gardiner BEM	150 Squadron

I should also like to record my sincere thanks to my good

friends (and authors) Chaz Bowyer and Martyn Ford-Jones. Also to Mrs Judith Tait, Mrs Gillian Crews and Mr George Whitehead, the latter formerly of 82 Squadron. To Eric Munday and the staff of the Air Historical Branch, Fred Lake of the RAF Library, MoD., Ministry of Defence, Gloucester, and to the Keeper of the Public Records, Kew. Also to Jacques De Vos, of Ghent.

Also to Amy Myers, and all at William Kimber & Co, who help to make an author's life easier than most publishers, and not least to my darling wife Heather, who has brought me into the twentieth century by way of a word processor.

Lastly to my two sons, Rob and Mike, and the taxman, who help make it all so necessary.

N.F.

CHAPTER ONE

Off to the War

At 11.15 a.m., on Sunday, 3 September 1939, Britain's Prime Minister, Neville Chamberlain, made a radio broadcast from the Cabinet Room at 10 Downing Street in London. Earlier that morning, the British Ambassador in the German capital of Berlin had handed to the German Government a final note stating that unless Britain heard from them, by 11 o'clock that same day, that they were prepared to withdraw their troops from Poland immediately, a state of war would exist between Britain and Germany.

Much of Mr Chamberlain's speech was hardly taken in after his second sentence: 'I have to tell you now that no such undertaking has been received, and that consequently this country is at war with Germany.'

Britain had been holding its breath for two days, ever since the news was received that Germany had attacked and invaded Poland on 1 September. In contrast to Germany, Britain was ill-prepared for war and fortunately, despite its 'sabre rattling', Britain was not immediately challenged in a full-scale conflict at that moment. Both sides hoped the other would see sense and neither wanted to open a full-scale assault on the other. Germany wanted to finish off Poland first, while Britain was hardly capable of hurting its 'new' enemy without possibly provoking serious retribution.

Indeed, at that moment Britain's only offensive arm was its Royal Air Force. Her Army was largely at home, her Royal Navy either in port or on patrol – waiting for something to happen.

War with Germany, to many, had seemed inevitable for some considerable time, certainly since the Munich Crisis of 1938. Some advances had been made to re-arm and strengthen Britain's forces following years of stagnation but time had always been against her. Her air force, the mightiest in the world in 1918, was poorly equipped and far below the strength its commanders required. For them it had been an uphill struggle to expand and to have produced the modern aircraft types it desperately needed.

Some improvement had been achieved. Many of the obsolete biplanes which equipped its fighter and day bomber squadrons at the time of Munich had been or were being replaced with modern all-metal monoplanes. Open cockpits and unretractable undercarriages were almost a thing of the past. The new and exciting Hurricane and Spitfire fighters gave encouragement to Fighter Command. Bomber Command was delighting in its new twin-engined Wellingtons, Hampdens and Whitleys for long-range work, while the Blenheim seemed good news for light day bomber operations. In fact, the Bristol Blenheim caused quite a stir when it began to equip RAF squadrons in early 1937, for its high performance enabled it to outpace the contemporary biplane fighters of the day! With a crew of three, pilot, observer and air gunner, it could carry a bomb load of 1,000 lb, had a range in excess of 1,100 miles, had a service ceiling of 27,000 feet, and an endurance of over 5½ hours.

In 1939, the 'short-nosed' Blenheim I, as it was then called, was superseded by the Mark IV, which with an extended nose was inevitably known thereafter as the 'long-nosed' Blenheim. Its bomb load was still 1,000 lb internally but it could carry an additional 320 lb externally. Its range was now nearly 1,500 miles, endurance 8½ hours although its ceiling was reduced to around 22,000 feet.

The other light bomber in Bomber Command's new arsenal was the Fairey Battle. After years of two-seater biplane day bombers, looking very little different from their predecessors from World War One, the RAF were more than pleased with the new Battle concept. A single-engined, low-winged monoplane of clean design, with enclosed cockpits for its three crewmen, it also carried a 1,000 lb bomb load, and had a range of 1,050 miles at 23,500 feet. Its speed of 241 mph maximum or 210 at cruising was a little below that of the Blenheim – 260 mph maximum, but in 1937 when the Battles too entered RAF squadron service, that wasn't bad.

Both the Blenheim and the Battle had defensive armament. The Blenheim IV carried one fixed .303 machine gun in the port wing firing forward for use by the pilot and a Vickers Gas Operated (VGO) 'K' .303 gun in a dorsal turret. The Battle had one forward firing .303 Browning and one VGO 'K' gun, fired by the wireless operator/air gunner from his rear cockpit.

In the 1930s, the RAF had begun to believe that their modern bombers would easily be able to look after themselves in the event of war. With their metal fuselages, self-sealing fuel tanks, armour plate and defensive guns, the phrase 'the bomber will always get through' quickly became law. Compared to the silver biplane fighters of the 1930s this concept was undoubtedly true. However, Germany possessed a modern, fast and heavily armed single-engined monoplane, the Messerschmitt 109. Like the new Hurricane and Spitfire, the Me109 was far superior to all the biplane fighters of either side. Although few in number, the Me109 had proved superior to the Republican forces' aeroplanes in the Spanish Civil War. There can be little doubt that the RAF fighter pilots, in their new fighters, could see that the doctrine of the bomber being invincible was open to doubt, but the RAF were committed to its new bomber types. You just cannot change types, policy and ingrained thinking, overnight. Like all tactical theories, only real action can tell you if you've got it right! Now with a real war to fight, the myth of the bomber would soon be tested.

*

When war was declared, the RAF had already been mobilised. Plans to send an Expeditionary Force to France should war come had long been made. This Force would be provided with air support, an Air Component which was attached to the British Army and which would come under the operational direction of the British Commander-in-Chief, Viscount Gort VC, and an Advanced Air Striking Force (AASF).

The AASF would remain part of Bomber Command and under its control from Command HQ in England, although later this was changed and it had its own commander in France.

No sooner had the RAF been mobilised for war, than immediate preparations were made to send RAF units to France. Tinged with apprehension, sadness and doubts, the men and especially the pilots and aircrews, were undoubtedly excited at the prospect of action. All peacetime members of any armed forces while working for peace constantly prepare for war. In the first half of the twentieth century, wars, however unwanted, were part of life. The Big War of 1914-1918 was only twenty years in the past, and there had been any number of minor wars in various parts of the world since then. The RAF had been involved in skirmishes against Afghan rebel tribesmen on the North-West Frontier of India for much of the time and in Waziristan. Now the present generation of airmen had a new war and whatever their feelings about it, it could not be ignored. They were trained and hopefully they were ready. Only time would tell if all their training and preparedness, not to mention their equipment, were up to the tasks that lay ahead. Unless, of course, as had been the fear in 1914, it would be all over by Christmas!

Pilot Officer Roy Max, from New Zealand, was with 103 Squadron and remembers:

> We moved to Benson from Abingdon in 1938 as the airfield was finished. I well recall at Benson the officers' mess wasn't finished – the accommodation wasn't completed so we had to live in tents right outside the mess. We were able to have our meals in the dining room but the bedrooms hadn't been built. As we got nearer and nearer to the start of war, rumours and things were floating around and there was terrific activity in getting all the equipment together and making up the convoys. We had to be mobile so we had a great number of lorries and being a very junior pilot officer I was doing what I was told. I remember we were doing a good deal of practice flying, doing formation flying – we had to practise getting the 12 aircraft up together and we would do cross-country runs. It was very cold for we had no useful heating in the aircraft. I also remember doing practice low level bombing at a target on the airfield and one poor observer, while we were dropping smoke bombs, leaned over too far and fell out, which was ghastly.
>
> *Pilot Officer R.D. Max, 103 Squadron*

*

Above Fairey Battles of 103 Squadron at RAF Benson before the war. In the foreground is K9372 which flew on the first recce mission flown by the squadron on 17 September 1939, and later by Blackie Wells on the 27th when attacked by Me109s. Aircraft 'G' (K9271) was flown by Arthur Vipon on the 27th when his observer was mortally wounded. (*R.D. Max*)

Below A vic of Battles of 40 Squadron. They were soon to exchange them for Bristol Blenheims. (*R.D. Max*)

Bottom Swinging the compass – a 15 Squadron Battle at Abingdon before going to France. 15 Squadron too were soon to re-equip with Blenheims. (*R.D. Max*)

The Advanced Air Striking Force was comprised initially of ten squadrons of Fairey Battles, Nos. 12, 15, 40, 88, 103, 105, 142, 150, 218 and 226. In addition it had two Hurricane-equipped fighter squadrons, 1 and 73. The Air Component consisted of two Blenheim squadrons for strategic reconnaissance, Nos. 53 and 57 Squadrons, four corps squadrons equipped with Westland Lysanders – 2, 4, 13 and 26 – and two Hurricane squadrons, 85 and 87. Two other Blenheim squadrons, 18 and later 59, also flew reconnaissance missions in France as part of the Air Component, and were also called on to fly bombing sorties.

Most of these squadrons had been mobilised in late August or certainly by 1 September. On the 2nd, while war was still hopefully being avoided, the AASF began to leave for France.

First away was 15 Squadron based at Abingdon. Sixteen Battles took off for France at 10 a.m. for Bétheniville. Next away, at noon, were 16 Blenheims of 40 Squadron also from Abingdon, although some of the ground crews took off at 0940 by civil aircraft. They too landed at Bétheniville, situated 15 miles to the east of Rheims. All, that is, except for Flight Lieutenant W.G. Moseby. Bill Moseby developed engine trouble over the Channel and had to ditch 15 miles north of Dieppe. He was slightly concussed as the Battle hit the sea and the machine sank in two minutes. However, he and his crew, Sergeant P. Cody and ACl W. Furly, both unhurt, were rescued by a cross-Channel steamer.

After lunch 226 Squadron at Harwell flew 15 Battles to Rheims, led by its CO, Wing Commander S.L.G. Pope DFC AFC. 'Poppy' Pope had been a fighter pilot in WW1 with 60 Squadron, so France was no stranger to him.

Also away in the early afternoon were 12 and 105 Squadrons from Bicester and Harwell. 12 Squadron's 16 Battles and one Miles Magister landed at Berry-au-Bac, near Rheims, at 4.45 p.m. while 105's 16 Battles headed for Rheims too. However, one pilot, Sergeant Phillips, had to force-land in a field near Poix when a broken connecting rod went through the engine sump, effectively putting out his engine. Battle K9197 was a write-off but the crew were unhurt.

As the afternoon progressed, 103, 218, 150 and 142 flew out. 103 flew their 16 machines out from RAF Benson, in three formations of six, four and six, crossing the English coast at Shoreham and the French coast at Le Tréport. They landed at their base at Challerange in the Ardennes at 5.30 p.m.

John Havers led out the ground party:

> I took the ground party out, going by train to Southampton. We got stuck there for quite a long time. We disembarked, boarded our ship and then came those terrible French trains. I remember we had biscuits and bully beef to eat.
>
> We moved from Challerange to a nearby village. I was billeted in the butcher's shop. I was meant to be lucky but there was no bath in the place. We used to drive down to the aerodrome by truck or bus, the aerodrome being quite a long way away.
>
> *Flying Officer J.R. Havers, 103 Squadron*

No. 218, at Boscombe Down, took off at 3 p.m. and landed at Auberieve, while 150 from Benson also landed at Challerange at 6.15. 142 Squadron from Bicester put their 16 Battles down at Berry-au-Bac without incident. All squadrons had sent out advance ground parties by civil or RAF transport aircraft, but the main squadron personnel travelled out by sea by various routes.

Roy Max recalls:

> Then we started having vaccinations before going to France and we all had to queue up, it was awful – I hate needles and things. Much to my horror, the chap who had his after me died the day after the injections which put us all in a terrible flap.
>
> *Pilot Officer R.D. Max, 103 Squadron*

The one squadron that did not fly out was 88. It did not make the move to France until 12 September, when Squadron Leader T.C. Dickens, in charge of flying, led the 16 Battles to Mourmelon-le-Grand, south-east of Rheims.

Squadron Leader John Hobler was with 142 Squadron, and remembers:

> I was posted to 142 Squadron at Bicester a few weeks before September as my war station. 12 and 142 Squadrons shared

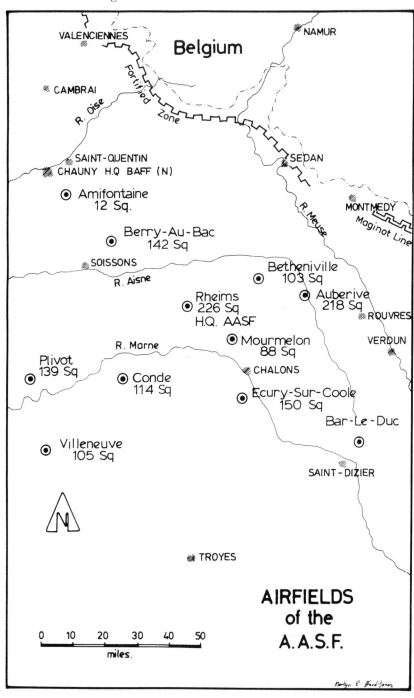

VALENCIENNES

Belgium

NAMUR

CAMBRAI

Fortified Zone

R. Oise

SAINT-QUENTIN
CHAUNY H.Q BAFF (N)

SEDAN

⊙ Amifontaine
12 Sq.

MONTMEDY

Maginot Line

R. Meuse

Berry-Au-Bac
⊙ 142 Sq

SOISSONS

Betheniville
⊙ 103 Sq

R. Aisne

Auberive
⊙ 218 Sq

Rheims
⊙ 226 Sq
H.Q. AASF

ROUVRES

VERDUN

R. Marne

⊙ Mourmelon
88 Sq

Plivot
⊙ 139 Sq

⊙ Conde
114 Sq

CHALONS

⊙ Ecury-Sur-Coole
150 Sq

Bar-Le-Duc
⊙

⊙ Villeneuve
105 Sq

SAINT-DIZIER

N

TROYES

0   10   20   30   40   50
miles.

**AIRFIELDS
of the
A.A.S.F.**

Martyn E. Ford-Jones

Bicester and from there both units received instructions to move to France on 2nd September.

The squadron was commanded by Wing Commander A.L. Faulkner. I was the Squadron Leader Flying, responsible for flying, and the two flight commanders were Flight Lieutenant K.R. Rogers and Flight Lieutenant W.B. Wight. We flew over in two formations to our French war station at Berry-au-Bac, just north of Rheims – a great cathedral city.

On going across the Channel I was reminded of the books I had read about WW1 when squadrons flew over to France and of the thoughts of the pilots then recorded, which were very much in line with mine now. We were going over and perhaps wouldn't see England again.

We were welcomed at Berry by the French air force, represented by a junior officer and some NCOs. There was nothing there by way of infra-structure, so we just parked our Battles where we could for the moment, dispersed as far as possible and the French were as kind as could be. They took us into the local village where lunch was prepared in a large cafe, and there, for the first time, the 'troops' encountered French food. A lot of them had not seen anything like it before and were not very impressed by it!

The squadron set to work to disperse its aircraft in and around the wood adjacent to the airfield. The airfield itself was simply a cleared space of ground with a windsock, and it ran along the famous, or infamous, Chemin des Dames, the scene of some very bloody fighting in the First War. There were many relics in the ground from that conflict, as we were soon to discover.

We cleared space, cutting down small trees, and made hard standings as best we could. We strung nets over the aircraft to camouflage them; it wasn't much but it was the best we could do. Inside the wood we found many relics of WW1 including an underground telephone exchange some 50–60 feet into the ground, with all the equipment intact. It was as if the Germans had just walked out, intending to return the next day.

The airmen were billeted in various places in and around the village while the officers made their mess at the Château de Guignicourt, the very attractive home of the Marquis de

Above Left Squadron Leader John Hobler, 142 Squadron. Photo taken on his wedding day in August 1939. Three weeks later he was in France. (*J.F. Hobler*)

Above Right Flying Officer L.H. Trent of 15 Squadron, when it still flew Battles. (*R.D. Max*)

Below Officers' mess at Auberive, France. The RAF pilot standing left, is Pilot Officer H.D. Wardle, a Canadian, who was taken prisoner 20 April 1940. Flying Officer C.A.R. Crews is seated far right in background. (*via Mrs G. Crews*)

Guignicourt. We were very comfortable and went to and fro in a bus driven by one of our officers.

As we expected to go into action straight away, we maintained an acute state of Readiness, but the whole lot of us hadn't much practice on the Battle. I for one had very little experience of it, having only joined the squadron a few weeks before war broke out. As time went on and no action came, or seemed even imminent from the enemy, we established ourselves more comfortably, made up an operations room, squadron headquarters and our communications became better with our neighbours and Wing HQ. Then we began to settle into a training programme. We had a lot of training to do. Many of the crews hadn't dropped bombs or fired their guns for a very long time. We practised bombing on the Mourmelon range near Rheims. This was an area contaminated by mustard gas in WW1, so nobody went onto the range, so we bombed it as often as we could.

Squadron Leader J.C. Hobler, 142 Squadron

Accommodation in France, as both air and ground personnel found, was not always ideal and certainly not what they had been used to with their purpose-built permanent RAF stations in England. For instance, 103 Squadron's aircrews at Challerange had to sleep under their aircraft as their billets had not been prepared. A few days later the squadron officers were put into various private houses in the local village, while the airmen slept in a large barn. The officers' mess was set up in the Café du Centre, in Challerange, which it shared with the officers of 150 Squadron. Roy Max:

When we got to France I found it all very amusing. Nothing happened, it was all phoney war but the weather was absolutely marvellous. However, we had to go round in gas capes and carrying gas masks, it was absolute murder. But having arrived at this place, we were all billeted around and I was billeted with a most charming woman. Her husband was up at the Maginot Line and she was very attractive, very pleasant. I was about 20 and a bit immature, to put it mildly, and the chaps all wanted me to move and wanted to take over my billet. She was absolutely gorgeous and very friendly but it was all wasted on me! She was a marvellous cook too, her scrambled eggs and omelettes were fantastic. Later on I moved into the mess, which was a small château with eight or nine rooms on top, one of which I was able to get eventually.

We none of us had any baths available in those billets, and with it being so hot we longed for a shower or bath. So they began to run a weekly trip into Rheims. A lorry would go in in the morning, having an arrangement with an hotel. The Endor, I think it was called. They'd give us a room where we'd have a bath, then most of the chaps would head off to the nearest brothel. They'd drag me off there and I was absolutely horrified.

We'd had lots of pep talks, how useless the Germans' aircraft were etc., nothing to worry about! We thought we'd be straight in right away but then it was such a let down. We were just sitting around and nothing happened at all. That's why our trips into Rheims were so popular.

I remember during one visit to this brothel they put on a blue show and I sat with all my buddies who were supposed to be looking after me, and watching this ghastly film – a most awful thing – and there was this wretched female sitting beside me and she said, 'Now we go and do even more than that.' I very quickly declined. To visit this establishment was the thing to do, it being the one place where one could go and sit and have a drink in the nice bar there, where pleasant girls would come and sit and chat to you. There was no pressure, of course, and I always made sure there were some of my buddies sitting alongside to protect me. It was just the way to fill in an hour or two.

Pilot Officer R.D. Max, 103 Squadron

At Rheims, 105 Squadron, the officers were billeted at the Hôtel du Nord, while NCOs and other ranks were put into French barracks on Rheims aerodrome. 218 Squadron had their officers billeted in local houses, with their mess at the Café du Commerce in Aubérive; the men were housed in houses and barns, and ate on the aerodrome.

Possibly in anticipation of great things to come, 12 Squadron had two of its Battle aircraft bombed-up and taxied out to the take-off point at two o'clock on the 3rd, but although war had by now been declared, it failed to start – in France anyway. At home it had started, albeit somewhat tentatively.

One observer with 150 Squadron was Sergeant Frederick Gardiner, but known to everyone as Joe. He recalls:

Our squadron took off from Benson on 2 September to land in France; war was declared on the 3rd. The AASF was concentrated around Rheims in the Marne Department.

Our arrival in France might well have been a continuation of the 1914–18 shindig – it was all so primitive. To start with we slept under the aircraft's mainplanes for the first two or three nights. Fortunately it was beautiful weather that September. Some of the food had been stored in last war underground posts. I don't mean it had been there that long, although the bread, I remember, was stale enough to have been fossils of that era.

Sergeant F.H. Gardiner, 150 Squadron

The RAF in England were ordered at the beginning of the war to search out and attack only German naval targets. Under no circumstances was anyone to risk dropping bombs on land with the risk of killing civilians. The German navy was known, of course, to be in or around its naval bases, especially at Kiel and Wilhelmshaven. On 3 September, 139 Squadron, which as we shall see became heavily involved alongside the AASF in 1940, gained the distinction of having one of its Blenheims being the first RAF aeroplane to cross the German frontier.

At noon, just an hour after the opening of hostilities and only 40 minutes since Mr Chamberlain's speech, Flying Officer Andrew McPherson took off in Blenheim N6215 to fly a photo-reconnaissance of the German fleet. With a Royal Navy man, Commander Thompson, flying as his observer and with Corporal V. Arrowsmith as his WOP/AG, McPherson completed his historic mission, bringing back 75 photographs of the enemy's fleet. He landed back at RAF Wyton at 4.50 p.m. The weather had been terrible and the camera had then become frozen, as had the Blenheim's radio. A force of Blenheims were waiting for the sighting report in order to launch an attack but, of course, without the radio nothing could be relayed back to base.

The next day McPherson again flew out, again in bad weather, but he returned with more sightings and immediately

15 Blenheims, five each from 107, 110 and 139 Squadrons, led by Flight Lieutenant K.C. Doran, took off to attack. Making their attack in severe weather, only two of the squadrons found targets and met heavy defensive fire which accounted for five of the ten bombers. McPherson and Doran were both awarded Distinguished Flying Crosses the following month, presented to them at a ceremony at RAF Wyton on 2 November, for their work on these first flights of the war.

For the squadrons of the Advanced Air Striking Force in France, there were to be no early chances of action and glory, which was probably just as well. But their time would come.

CHAPTER TWO

The Adventure Begins

The Battle squadrons in France quickly settled in to their new bases and new surroundings. The men of the Royal Air Force, while undoubtedly grumbling about their lot wherever they were sent, nevertheless always made the best of it, and under their experienced and long-serving senior NCOs, got things organised.

On many of the French airfields the Battles had to be dispersed, in order not to be shot up or bombed by an enemy that just might attack at any moment. The September weather was good but obviously if things continued into the coming winter months, the aeroplanes would need to have some protection from the elements, and accommodation for the men would need improving. There was much to be done.

The flyers too needed to prepare. They were now away from their well-established bases, in a foreign country where the countryside was unknown. A first priority was to gain as much knowledge of the lie of the land as possible. To this end the aircrews were quickly making local flights to assimilate their new localities. Most of the AASF's bases were within a radius of Rheims where its cathedral was a good landmark, and, as 103 Squadron at Challerange found, the Forêt D'Argonne was a good landmark for them.

One of the UK-based Blenheim squadrons, 114, made a flight to France on 6 September, visiting French fighter squadrons in the Rheims area, to show them what their aeroplanes looked like, in the air and on the ground. This would be useful if the Germans attacked, for the Blenheims would be flying over France in support of British and French forces.

Also on this day, the first of the Air Component's Blenheim

units began to leave for France: 57 Squadron left Upper
Heyford for Roye, although it would be several more days
before the aircraft were flown out. These squadrons were larger
in personnel and equipment than the normal Blenheim
squadrons because they had all their own photographic cara-
vans, vehicles, etc, and, being totally self-contained in case of
moves, had their own cooks and kitchens, as well as petrol
supplies. 53 Squadron, for example, who would also be arriving
in France during the month, had a total strength of 313 officers
and other ranks, 12 aircraft, 48 vehicles and five trailers! Little
wonder it took time to move all these across to France by sea. 57
Squadron's advance party sailed from Southampton for
Cherbourg.

Then came the first operational flights by the AASF. There
can be little doubt that all were keen to get on with it. This is what
all the training had been for, all the work. They would show the
Germans what it meant to inflict war on Europe for the second
time in 20-odd years. However, it was a case of 'slowly does it'. No
great bombing raids, no sky dark with avenging eagles; nobody
wanted to hurt each other – yet.

On 9 September 1939, 105 Squadron put up three Battles
which carried out a reconnaissance to within 15 miles of the
French/German border. Heady stuff! The three pilots were

F/Lt C.R. Mace	F/O S.G. Wise	Sgt H.J. Houghton

The next day, 105 Squadron repeated the exercise with

S/L G.C.O. Kay	W/Cdr D.McFadyen	F/Lt H.C. Samuels

At Challerange 150 Squadron flew its first operation; A
Flight sent out three Battles at 2.35 p.m.:

Pilot	Observer	WOP/AG	Aircraft
S/L W.L.M. Macdonald	Sgt F.H. Gardiner	AC A. Murcar	K9283
F/O F.M.C. Corelli	Sgt L.B. Webber	AC K.V. Gay	K9387
P/O M.A. Poulton	Sgt T.A. Bates	AC H.E.A. Rose	K9389

Then 218 Squadron sent three Battles for a familiarisation
recce over the route Rheims-Nancy-Bitche-Sierck:

W/C L.B. Duggan	Sgt R. Hazell	AC Gill	K9254
F/O E.V. Hulbert	Sgt Dewar	AC Wiltshire	K9252
F/Sgt Herring	Sgt Butt	AC Davies	K9325

Joe Gardiner recalls this first sortie, his pilot, and the move of 150 Squadron the next day:

> I had been with Squadron Leader, later to be Air Marshal Sir William Macdonald, for some time at Boscombe Down and Benson, where we opened that, then, new RAF station. I suppose I could say we became rather a star turn (in spite of that right Irish temper; crikey, Mac could be red hot). One such experience was the occasion of navigating 70 Battles out across the North Sea, then running back for the benefit of the 'infant' radar, radio locations, then, probably the early CH stations. Then 150 Squadron, with Mac out in front and me the navigator (air observer in those days) to take 140 Battles out over France when we were showing the flag to 'reassure' our allies of our strength should war come. Hmmm!
>
> It can be imagined the tension I went through to get that lot across to landfall at Le Tréport then over Paris, Lyons and other large towns, and for good measure on one of these occasions, the Albert Hall was to be our target on the return. And the strain was really intense to line up the target from 16,000 feet. I was cocky then and got a good picture, so I can boast that I 'bombed' the Albert Hall!
>
> We did a little flying practice once in France, and, as recorded, 10 September saw the first op. official, which consisted of a low flying effort over parts of the frontier. I think that both A and B Flights did this in turn but I cannot recall any significant results, or reaction from the Hun.
>
> *Sergeant F.H. Gardiner, 150 Squadron*

*

Following this flurry of activity, the 11th and 12th saw activity of another kind as some squadrons moved their bases. On the 11th, 150 Squadron moved to Ecury-sur-Coole, south-east of Rheims, and 88 Squadron began its move to France – Mourmelon-le-Grand, also south-east of Rheims. 15 Squadron left Bétheniville and relocated at Condé-Vréaux, south-east of Rheims. 105 Squadron moved to Villeneuve-les-Vertus, near Paris, while 142 Squadron moved to Plivot, to the south of Rheims. Joe Gardiner again:

Then we moved to Ecury, a small village near Châlons-sur-Marne, and is today that town's local airport. We SNCOs were billeted in a hayloft of a local farm, though we did share a mess with the French in the school. I am uncertain which of the perfumes I enjoyed most, the horses or the cows who lived below our bedroom!

However, we eventually moved completely *dans l'école*. Those early days were to reveal how unprepared the whole show was. For example the starter trolleys were late arrivals. Imagine starting a Merlin engine, swinging the prop. with a canvas bag on a rope!

There were, of course, quite a lot of Battle squadrons about. Our 'sister' 103 was nearby and so was 218. Social life was little but we did get a night out in Châlons, I remember. We met up with other types for what turned out to be an almighty thrash followed by terrible fat heads. *C'est la Guerre.*

Sergeant F.H. Gardiner, 150 Squadron

A second Air Component Blenheim recce squadron, 18 Squadron, began its move to France on the 12th; its advance party, Flight Lieutenant G.P.L. Weston and one airman, travelled out via Southampton. Five days later, the squadron, together with 57 Squadron (both had been based at Upper Heyford) sent their road convoys to Southampton while the rail parties left on the 22nd.

The Battles of 12, 15, 103, 150 and 218 Squadrons operated on the 17th. No. 15 sent three aircraft to within ten miles of the German frontier, while 103 made its first war flights with three aircraft to the border area between Bouzonville and Lauterbourg, at a height of 3,000 feet, taking off at 11 a.m.:

S/L J. Coverdale	Sgt V.A. Pengilley	AC Mitchell	K9372
F/Lt C.E.R. Tait	Sgt Dowling	AC J.E. Summers	K9871
Sgt C.D. Perry	Sgt Davidson	AC P.J. Lamble	L4957

At five minutes past one o'clock, 150 Squadron sent three aircraft to the border:

F/Lt A.E. Hyde-Parker	Sgt L.F.L. Cole	AC D.E. Jones	N2093
P/O A.R. Gulley	Sgt Berry	AC D. Phillips	L4945
P/O J.R. Saunders	Sgt C. Wall	AC D.L. Thomas	K9483

Then later, 218 Squadron sent three machines out at 2.45 p.m.:

Above Three Battles of 103 Squadron return from a recce sortie. The three pilots are F/O D. Kelly, F/Lt C.E.R. Tait and F/O M.C. Wells. (*via Mrs J. Tait*)

Below P2199 of 142 Squadron. Note new camouflage paint partly obscuring peacetime yellow surround to RAF roundels. (*J.F. Hobler*)

Bottom 'Modern' French transport taking guns to the front. (*J.F. Hobler*)

F/Lt H.C. Daish	Sgt Young	AC Jones	K9329
F/Sgt Mitchell	Sgt R. Hazell	AC L.D. Davies	K9355
P/O H.G.K. Waring	Sgt W.H. Harris	AC H.B. Jones	K9256

Finally, 12 Squadron sent three crews of A Flight out at 4 p.m., flying a recce five miles behind the frontier:

F/Lt J.R. Gillman	Sgt Willis	AC Bunker
F/O A.L. Pitfield	Sgt Jones	AC G.N. Patterson
F/O P.H.M.S. Hunt	Sgt C. Shelton-Jones	AC H. Cooke

No. 53 Squadron's Blenheims joined the AASF briefly on the 18th, arriving at Rheims at 2 p.m. before moving on to Plivot at 4 p.m. 53 Squadron was commanded by Bill Murray and one of its flight commanders was Flight Lieutenant Bill Clements, one of the first Canadians to go to France with the RAF. 18 and 57 Squadrons were supposed to be used by the AASF as bomber units but had yet to fly to France, so 53 joined the AASF for some weeks.

Both 103 and 105 Squadrons flew recce missions on the 18th, 103 being led by Flight Lieutenant C.E.R. Tait (in K9264) taking off at 8.30 a.m. The squadron personnel were now billeted at Monthois, about one mile from the aerodrome and two miles from the village of Challerange, while still using the café in the village as the officers' mess.

The weather on the 18th was bad and the three Battles got lost somewhere between Saarlautern and Saarbrucken. They were fired on by German flak gunners but none was hit. The recce had then to be abandoned. Meanwhile, 105 Squadron flew three sorties to within three miles of the German border but without incident.

Further recce missions were flown on the 19th, by 142 and 226 Squadrons, but a flight by 150 Squadron brought the first fatality to the Battle squadrons in France.

At 11.15 a.m. Pilot Officer J.L. Calvert with his crew of Sergeant T.B. Woodmason and AC1 J.L. Marsh, took off in L5225 for a local photo flight. Soon after take-off the Battle developed engine trouble and in trying to force-land, James Calvert crashed and the aeroplane caught fire. His crew died in the crash and Calvert was badly injured, dying in a French hospital at Châlons that evening.

Most squadrons were now actively flying recce missions to the

German border. Most were uneventful, and almost all were unescorted which was the policy. Still with the theory of bomber aircraft looking after themselves, if any fighter effort was made it was generally in the shape of a fighter patrol to the area of the bomber sortie rather than direct, close escort. Occasionally someone tried something different, but for a reason.

The reason, on the 20th, was because German fighters were encountered for the first time. 88 Squadron chose this day to fly its first war flights but the excitement quickly turned to grim reality. The usual three aircraft section took off at 10 a.m. with the following crews:

F/O L.H. Baker	Sgt F.A. Letchford	AC1 C.A. Edwards	K9243
F/O R.C. Graveley	Sgt W.S. Everett	AC1 D.J. John	K9242
F/Sgt D.A. Page	Sgt A.W. Eggington	AC1 E.A.W. Radford	K9245

The mission was not helped when the three Battles came under French AA fire south-east of Bitche, although it did cease as soon as the British aircraft fired off the colours of the day. Then, at 11.47, three Messerschmitt 109 fighters, flying in a vic formation, attacked when over Aachen. The Battles closed up but almost immediately Flight Sergeant Douglas Page's Battle went down in flames.

Flying Officer Baker began to lose height in a series of diving turns and on levelling out, he could not see his Number Two aircraft. During the fight, Baker's observer had fired at one of the 109s and claimed it destroyed, which was later confirmed by the French. This was the first German aircraft shot down by an Allied airman in WW2.

The second Battle was also hit and brought down. Flying Officer Reg Graveley crash-landed and suffered severe burns being flown to the RAF's Halton Hospital in England. His gunner had been killed outright, hit in the head by the German fighter in the air. Sergeant Everett had to have a leg amputated, but he too died later. Graveley later received the OBE (Military Division).

Thus the day had seen the first air battle between the AASF and the Luftwaffe, each side having lost aircraft. This was why, that afternoon, when 218 Squadron's CO, Wing Commander L.B. Duggan, led six Battles on a high reconnaissance mission

(23,000 feet), ten miles over the German frontier, they were promised an escort of French fighters. However, they failed to make rendezvous with the French Moranes.

On the return flight, 10/10ths cloud obscured the ground, making it impossible for the Battles to find their base, so they landed at the Aero Club at Gray, 20 miles north-east of Dijon, where they stayed the night. Two of the Battles collided while descending through the cloud, but although both machines were damaged, nobody was hurt and both aircraft landed safely.

Now that the air war had hotted up slightly, it was a problem when 103 Squadron found its Vickers 'K' guns would not fire in the air. Investigation found that it was due to too much oil on the moving parts. Oil-free guns were flown, tested and found to fire satisfactorily.

The Battles of 150 Squadron met some high flak on the 25th when Wing Commander A. Hesketh DFC (in L4948) led six of his aircraft on a high level photo recce at 23,000 feet. At this height over Deuxponts–Zweibrucken, in mid-morning, several of the aircraft were hit by shell splinters.

The next day, the ill-fated 88 Squadron sent six aircraft on a visual and photo recce over enemy territory east of Saarbrucken, also at 23,000 feet. This time they met their French fighter escort—eight in number. They too experienced German flak, as Flight Lieutenant A.J. Madge led them over the area.

Six battles of 226 Squadron also met AA fire on the 27th, a day that also was to prove eventful for 103 Squadron. However, the day began with the first operational sorties by a UK-based Blenheim squadron, No. 82, based at Cranfield, also operating from the satellite airfield of Horsham St. Faith. The squadron was commanded by Wing Commander S.H. Ware.

At 6.29 a.m. the first of three machines took off, the other two following at approximately ten minute intervals:

F/O R.J. McConnell	Sgt L.E. Stack	AC M.C. Cleary	P4862
F/O G.F. Hall	Sgt T.S. Weightman	AC I.T. Harris	P4863
P/O D.A. Fordham	Sgt F. Fearnley	Cpl A.G. Richards	P4828

McConnell's route took him to Emden Harbour, and the aerodromes of Vechta and Oldenburg. Hall flew to Midluiy, Stade, Wenzendorf and Fassberg aerodromes, while Fordham's course was Celle, Langenhagen, Detmond and Münster aerodromes. Running short of petrol he had to land at Albert to refuel before returning to England.

No. 103 Squadron had flown recce sorties over Germany almost daily for the previous few days. It will be noted that since 88's air battle on the 20th, recces had been flown by six aircraft (two sections rather than the usual one). This, one assumes, was for mutual self-protection. However, on the 27th, 103's mission to the German frontier between Bouzonville and the Rhine shortly after midday, was by three Battles:

F/Lt M.C. Wells	Sgt Whitelam	AC T.H. Bowen	K9372
F/O A.L. Vipan	Sgt J.H. Vickers	AC J.E. Summers	K9271
P/O G.B. Morgan- Dean	Sgt Warren	AC H.B. Sewell	K9265

Nearing the frontier, three French Curtiss Hawk fighters attacked the British aircraft from out of some clouds. Maurice 'Blackie' Wells quickly fired off recognition signals as he took his section down from 3,000 feet to ground level. After a single pass, the three Frenchmen turned away. Had they stuck around they might have proved far more useful than they had just been, for at the moment they disappeared, three Me109s, previously unobserved, carried out a surprise attack.

In the first attack, Sergeant John Vickers was badly wounded, when a bullet pierced his bladder. The Battle's engine was also hit and began to splutter. Sergeant Vickers, in great pain, asked to be landed as soon as possible and Flying Officer Arthur Vipan quickly selected a field and made a forced landing. Only one undercarriage wheel came down resulting in some slight damage to the aeroplane.

> The mission was one of several undertaken by squadrons of the AASF. Our orders were to take oblique photographs at 2,000 feet along the Siegfried Line. At the completion of our task and turning for home we observed three Me109s about to attack us. I took evasive action and led the formation of three aircraft down to ground level so that they could not get underneath us. The Me109s got one attack on us as we were diving in which they hit Arthur Vipan's aircraft and one bullet entered Sergeant Vickers' body. He was in considerable pain so Arthur Vipan broke away from the formation and landed at a French airfield on the Maginot Line where

medical attention was given to Sergeant Vickers, but he died. Arthur Vipan returned to the squadron a few days later who then told me that three French Moranes arrived on the scene and chased the Me109s away and said they shot one down and another one crashed which they attributed to one of our air gunners.

I never actually saw the Moranes.

Flight Lieutenant M.C. Wells, 103 Squadron

Sergeant Vickers was removed to the nearest hospital and then a French *poilu* (soldier) pointed out to Vipan a column of smoke rising from the centre of a nearby wood. The Frenchman told him that one of the Battles had shot down one of the attacking Messerschmitts which they could now see burning. Later a French report confirmed the destruction of one Me109.

The other two Battles returned unscathed. The victorious gunner had been Leading Aircraftman (LAC) John Ernest Summers. He had held his fire until the 109 attacking his Battle had closed right in before giving it a burst from his Vickers gun, whereupon the 109 had fallen into the wood. He was later awarded the Distinguished Flying Medal.

The next day, Group Captain R.T. Leather, Officer Commanding No. 74 (Bomber) Wing, made a search for the crashed 109 but it was unsuccessful due to the impenetrable area of woodland into which the German fighter had fallen. The badly wounded Sergeant Vickers died of his wound on 7 October, just before he was awarded the French Medaille Militaire by General Gamelin – the first French decoration bestowed upon a member of the BEF.

*

Two days after this action, on the 29th, six aircraft of 105 Squadron, led by Flight Lieutenant H.C. Samuels (K9485) encountered flak at 21,000 feet over the frontier, five of the machines being hit by shrapnel. That night, 53 Squadron began to fly night recce missions over Germany. They were to watch for troop movements towards the Siegfried Line. The pilots had little night flying experience and the flares that they might have used were deemed too heavy and with a brighter burning capacity than those they used in peace-time. There was

Above Officers of 57 Squadron at Roye-Amy, October 1939. *Front row, (l to r)*; F/O E.E. Nind, F/Lt G.M. Wyatt, S/L A.H. Garland, W/C H.M.A. Day (POW 13 Oct), Maj Jock Fielden, F/Lt J. Roncoroni, F/Lt D.S.M. MacArthur (Doc); *Middle row*: P/O H.G. Graham-Hogg, P/O R.L. Saunders (killed 22 May 1940), F/O J.R.D. Hird, P/O A.D. Morton (killed 6 Nov 1939), F/O M.J. Casey (POW 16 Oct 1939 and later murdered in the Great Escape from Stalag Luft III), W/O W.H.G. Hampshire (Armt Off). *Back row*: P/O O.C. Hume (KIFA 23 Nov 1939), P/O J.R. Grant, P/O A.C. Stewart, P/O F.A. Buckingham (Equip Off), F/O W.W. Adam (KIFA 1 March 1940), P/O H.R. Bewley (POW 7 Nov 1939), F/O C.T. Norman, F/Lt J. Foulsham. (*G.M. Wyatt*)

Below 53 Squadron Blenheims at Odiham in 1939. TE-N (L4841) was lost in action 17 May 1940. (*J. Butterworth, via R.C. Bowyer*)

a danger of one falling on the roof of some sleeping German civilians and causing an incident!

The crews selected for the first night ops had to fly from Plivot to Metz and they would land back at Vitry which had a radio D/F from which they could receive a homing signal. The French had organised a night flying aid by providing a series of little lamps that flashed various letters into the night sky, thereby helping navigation. As the lights could not be seen above 1,500 feet and the Blenheims were told to operate at 20,000 feet, they did not prove too useful!

First away was the Canadian, Bill Clements (in L4842), followed later by Pilot Officer J.A.A. Read (L4840). Neither saw very much and upon their return, the French D/F operators wouldn't reply, thinking they were Germans. Clements eventually force-landed at Essertaux, ten miles south-west of Amiens, while Jasper Read did get down at Vitry, only accidentally to retract his wheels when he went to pull up the flap lever.

On the last day of September, 18 Squadron's Blenheims arrived in France, being based at Beauraignes, on the Somme. Commanded by Wing Commander W.A. Opie, the squadron, after some local flying, began to operate in conjunction with 57 Squadron, each taking alternate 48-hour duty periods.

The advance party of 57 Squadron had established its base at Roye by the 24th, and six days later the aircraft were flown out. Its commanding officer was Wing Commander H.M.A. Day, a Royal Marine in the First War who had later joined the RAF. He was known as 'Pricky' Day, or P.D. One of his pilots was Geoffrey Wyatt:

We flew to France (Roye/Amy) on 30/9/39: I believe P.D. had gone on a week or so before with the surface advance party. I can only recall this accommodation as being rough to the point of squalor – and the troops' was that much worse. I remember one large billet in the loft of some stables, and the coincidence of one corporal reservist, with a Croix de Guerre from the First War, who had been billeted in exactly the same spot during that earlier contest.

Shortly after we arrived, 18 Squadron and ourselves, together forming 70 Wing, were lined up on the airfield and addressed by the AOC Air Component, BEF (AVM Blount, I believe). I can't recall the details but the gist was that we would be going straight in to long-range recces, deep in Germany. I don't think we were surprised or unduly dismayed at this news; with the exception of P.D. himself, the emotions of war were unknown to us, but we had always understood our likely role to be 'Strat.R.' from when we had been re-equipped with Blenheims in 1938. I think our morale at this early stage was pretty good, despite the depressing living conditions. P.D. held a 100% squadron parade every morning, detailing off working parties and officers' duties, etc., as apart from local flying on air tests, etc., there were no facilities for realistic operational training. (Later on in the campaign air firing ranges, and long-range navigational areas did become available, but initially we were, I believe, severely restricted).

Flight Lieutenant G.M. Wyatt, 57 Squadron

The last action of the month went to 150 Squadron. The AASF had encountered Me109s on two previous occasions in the latter half of September, and it was only going to be a matter of time before they met again. After 30 September, if anyone even thought the war was a new and exciting adventure, they would only have to ask someone in 150 Squadron what he thought.

CHAPTER THREE

The Winter of Discontent

On 30 September 1939, 150 Squadron was ordered to fly a photo op, to Auve-Pont a Mousson-Puttelange-NW of Saarbrucken-NW of Neunkirchen-SE of Wittring and back. At 11 a.m., the six Battles that had been detailed took off and headed east:

S/L W.L.M. MacDonald	Sgt F.H. Gardiner	AC A. Murcar	K9283
F/O F.M.C. Corelli	Sgt L.B. Webber	AC1 K.V. Gay	K9387
F/Lt A.E. Hyde-Parker	Sgt L.F.L. Cole	AC D.E. Jones	N2093
P/O M.A. Poulton	Sgt T.A. Bates	AC H.E.A. Rose	N2028
P/O A.R. Gulley	Sgt Berry	AC D. Phillips	L4945
P/O J.R. Saunders	Sgt G.J. Springett	AC D.L. Thomas	K9484

Before reaching the frontier, Pilot Officer Gulley's machine began to drop behind as it developed engine trouble. He finally turned for home and landed at 1.20 p.m.

The others flew on and by midday were over the Saarbrucken area. They began to be fired on by German anti-aircraft fire. A sliver of shrapnel hit MacDonald's aircraft, injuring Joe Gardiner over his right eye. Then, in between these bursts, they were suddenly assailed by no fewer than 15 Messerschmitt 109 fighters.

The five Battles were at 23,000 feet or more when the attack came, diving in in sections before each section concentrated on individual targets. They made repeated attacks, picking off Battles despite a spirited return fire from the gunners. Joe Gardiner relates:

The operation was to be a high level flight, photo recce, five aircraft with cameras for line overlaps and thus a resultant mosaic from Saarbrucken towards Mannheim. If I remember right, B Flight had had a go at this but, perhaps it was the weather, they didn't make it. So off we went, climbing steadily for the old Battle, crossing the frontier at 26,000 feet in bright, clear sunlight, cloudless sky. For the Nav. the Battle had a sliding trap for the bombsight giving quite a wide span of view at this height ... we did have oxygen, that hadn't been forgotten. We had not got far when I could see puffs of smoke below which was to be German ack-ack and very accurate it was too, for I got a bit of shrapnel cut over my right eye although it was reported a 'slight gunshot wound'. But we pressed on regardless, and it wasn't long before I then spotted a formation of black aeroplanes below, way down. Very quickly they were up and recognisable as Me109s – 15 of them and then the fun started, and I was to survive the longest half hour of my life.

William MacDonald held his formation together in an effort to bring the maximum defensive fire to bear, and indeed, one Me109 was seen to go down on fire and another spin away apparently out of control.

Sergeant T.A. Bates, observer to Mike Poulton, later made the following report of the battle:

We were flying in a box formation on a course into Germany when we were attacked by enemy fighters. The enemy aircraft attacked us from behind (and it was not until later I had some indication that the Air Gunner was wounded) when they immediately tried quarter attacks which in each case were fatal. When changing magazines the Air Gunner kept his gun trained on the enemy, and when the enemy were making an attack and obviously firing upon us, the Air Gunner sheltered behind the armour plating beneath and then kept the gun pointing towards the enemy with one hand.

Believe the enemy aircraft commenced their attack from the starboard side but I'm not sure. I was completely drenched (in petrol); the Air Gunner for some reason did not get so much petrol over him. Petrol came from the lead to the engine in the nose of the aircraft, which was severed by an enemy bullet. The enemy were firing incendiary bullets which repeatedly struck the stem behind the camera. The bullets made a loud report which could be heard above the roar of the engine and were accompanied by a flash as big as an orange. It was one of these bullets which set the aircraft on fire.

I passed the Air Gunner his parachute and then put on my own, immediately petrol started flooding the cockpit. As the flames started spreading, Rose climbed out over the right hand side of the aircraft and hesitated for a few seconds, then with one foot in and one foot out, I seized him by the inside foot and heaved him over. He went over the left side. I sat over the edge of the cockpit, facing the inside of the aircraft, lifted my legs and slid over backwards.

I dropped for 2-3,000 feet before pulling the ripcord. The falling sensation was very pleasant. My fall prior to opening my parachute, was all on my back, but as the parachute opened I was just turning overhead downwards. I pulled the ripcord with my left hand as I'd put the parachute on the wrong way round, although not intentionally. I pulled the ripcord with my left hand automatically; I never thought of using my right hand.

The only rotten moments were when watching the parachute of another airman, presumably Sergeant Spring-ett, burn away from him and watching his body drop like a stone the remaining 6-7,000 feet to the ground. On landing I slightly sprained my ankle and bruised my side. I landed on my heels and fell over backwards. I was picked up immediately by French soldiers who were waiting for me and taken to hospital by ambulance.

As the four Battles behind him were all shot down, MacDonald began to take violent evasive action while three 109s concentrated on him. The Battle was repeatedly hit but he was able to keep these to a minimum by his avoiding action.

On two occasions, 109s overshot the Battle, giving MacDonald a chance to fire his front gun but he found the mechanism frozen. The fight lasted half an hour and then the 109s broke away, but not before his aircraft had been seriously damaged, having been hit more than 40 times. The auxiliary and port petrol tanks were punctured and fuel was flowing into the fuselage. The boost pressure gauge, rev counter, and other instruments on the right hand side of the instrument panel were wrecked. The control for the elevator trimming tabs was immovable and flaps and undercarriage levers inoperative. Despite this, MacDonald flew towards home.

Joe Gardiner continues:

I suppose we weren't terribly well organised – intercom and R/T were so inadequate. The first I realised they were among us was that awful sound of slashing bursts of fire hitting us. I have always thought of it as gravel thrown on corrugated iron. And we were being picked off. Young Alec Murcar, our gunner, was banging away and in fact he was credited with shooting down two of the blighters. Still, we were still there, but the others were not so lucky. I could see Bill Cole, a real old mate of mine, hanging from his aircraft, harness obviously caught on the bombsight spigot. This instrument had to be kicked to jettison it if you escaped through the hatch. But there he was shot to pieces, before disappearing. Our aircraft was riddled. I remember now, seeing the morse key disappear as another burst caught us, rattling through; above me was the auxiliary tank, now punctured, and I was nicely sprayed with 100 octane. I thought Mac had 'got it' at one time and was preparing to make my own exit when luckily I heard his voice, as nose down we screeched. I thought we'd surely break up, but no and eventually sanity returned and I was able to identify Metz and give Mac a course for home. But alas, as we landed, so she went up in flames. Mac was OK, for it was all aft of the driving seat.

MacDonald brought the lone Battle into land, having coaxed his damaged machine back 130 miles; the engine had failed when the damaged fuel tanks emptied, but picked up again when they switched to the starboard tank. As he touched down, a punctured tyre caused the Fairey Battle to slew round 360 degrees, then it caught fire.

Joe Gardiner, despite his own clothes being set alight, succeeded in extinguishing the burning clothes of Aircraftman Murcar, by rolling him on the ground and beating out the flames with his hands. The aircraft was destroyed.

As Joe Gardiner remembers it:

'Midst the scramble to get free I realised that Alec was a bit dazed from a blow, but he was to suffer further, for at one

Top K9264 of 103 Squadron over France. Note unusual position of code letters in relation to RAF roundel.
(*via Mrs J. Tait*)

Above Pilots of 218 Squadron prepare for a sortie to the German frontier. The two Flying Officers far right are Alan Rogers and Charles Crews.
(*via Mrs G. Crews*)

Left Sergeant Joe Gardiner of 150 Squadron receives the BEM from the King, December 1939.

moment I thought him in such agony I knocked him out, but at the crucial moment he moved and got a terribly busted up mouth for good measure. He never forgave me!

Off we went to hospital in Châlons, with very red faces from burns. I've a lovely scar on one of my knees as a memento, and a smooth upper lip as proved when in later times I entered a joke in the mess on the best moustache and mine was likened to straw in a dustbin.

Sergeant F.H. Gardiner, 150 Squadron

It had been a massacre. Although two 109s had been claimed as shot down (one being credited to Alexander Murcar having been confirmed by Gardiner) four Battles had been shot out of the sky, and the fifth shot to ribbons and lost when the petrol-soaked machine had landed with a shredded tyre. Flying Officer Corelli had been killed and his gunner had been killed by a bullet through the throat. The observer, Sergeant Webber, had baled out but was injured. Tony Hyde-Parker, OC B Flight, had baled out and fractured an ankle, while his gunner, who also baled out, had received burns. He landed between the lines but was rescued by French soldiers. The observer was dead, having been shot in the head early in the fight.

Mike Poulton and his crew had all baled out, but all had some degree of injuries, mostly burns. Of Pilot Officer John Saunders and his crew there was no immediate news and they were posted as missing.

In November, Sergeant Frederick Henry Gardiner was rewarded with the BEM, presented to him by the King at Plivot on 8 December. In February 1940, MacDonald and Murcar received the DFC and DFM respectively. It was the first time in WW2 that the whole of one crew had been decorated.[1]

It is not surprising to read in 150 Squadron's diary that early in October the crews were flying evasive action practice.

*

This air fight effectively halted all offensive operational flying by the AASF Battle squadrons. If it had not been obvious to the Battle crews already that they were highly vulnerable when up

---

[1] MacDonald later became Sir William MacDonald GCB CBE DFC. Alec Murcar was later reported missing over the North Sea, flying in a Hudson.

against German fighters, it was now. Presumably the cessation of operational sorties ordered by AASF HQ also acknowledged this fact. Yet the aircraft could not be changed overnight, even if that course of action was considered. The AASF had a front line strength, on paper, of 160 Battles. To take these from the Western Front would have caused concern not only to the British Government and the Air Council, but our French allies. What was agreed was that the value of constant reconnaissance was obviously not worth sending the Battles out over Germany. Oddly, there does not seem to have been any effort to provide direct fighter escort. The myth of the bomber aircraft's invincibility had been dented but not smashed.

Even so, there was soon to be further evidence of the bomber's vulnerability when up against German day fighters. Just the day prior to 150 Squadrons' disastrous day, a formation of five Hampdens of 144 Squadron had all been shot down by Messerschmitts over Heligoland. On 14 December, Bomber Command despatched 12 Wellingtons for an attack on German ships in the Schillig Roads, north of Wilhelmshaven. Engaged by flak and by fighters, five were shot down. The RAF were very reluctant to concede that it had been fighters rather than the flak that had accounted for the missing aircraft.

However, just four days later, a force of 24 Wellingtons were sent out on a shipping search of roughly the same area. Picked up by German radar, German fighters attacked the 22 bombers (two had already had to abort) and shot down 12 for the loss of two fighters. As if to add insult to injury, on 21 December 24 Hampdens and 18 Wellingtons were again sent across the North Sea in search of shipping but failed to locate any targets. On the return flight, a squadron of RAF Spitfires spotted some of the Hampdens and promptly shot down two!

Some of the lessons must have filtered to the other squadrons however. In 103 Squadron, for example, the vulnerable central fuel tank situated in the fuselage was removed, retaining just the wing tanks.

*

If the Battle squadrons' activities were being restricted, the reconnaissance Blenheim units now took on the main reconnaissance role. In England, this period was beginning to be called the 'Phoney War'. The men of the Air Component reconnaissance squadrons would not call it phoney at all. They began to take quite heavy casualties.

> Talk of the Phoney War in the British Press sounded pretty sour to us: it was anything but phoney, and the 'remounts' coming out from Andover were very skimpily trained – about 10-12 hours on Blenheims. One was reminded of the First World War 'at the front' and we'd only just started this one!
>
> The onset of one of the severest winters for years all but stopped flying. Poorly maintained French roads started to crumble, and on Rosières airfield a complete First War trench system opened up which added to the interest of take-off and landing.
>
> We re-equipped with Mk. IV Blenheims (long-nose) during the winter, which provided a few welcome days home on the ferrying trips. I think most of us preferred flying the Bristol-built I's to the 'shadow' factory IV's, although the latter had 9 lb boost, long-range tanks, and better navigational facilities. Freddie Foulsham and I took one on a 7-hour 'jolly' round France, admiring the Pyrenees on the southern leg.
>
> *Flight Lieutenant G.M. Wyatt, 57 Squadron*

Eric Nind was also with 57 Squadron; in fact at one time, Geoff Wyatt was his flight commander:

> Most of our casualties were incurred during the eight months of the 'cold war' prior to 10 May 1940. Very few happened between then and 19 May when we evacuated France. An example of the casualties incurred during the winter of 1939/40 is that of the 21 pilots who went to France in September 1939 only three returned in May 1940, and that takes no account of the numerous casualties among our replacement pilots. Of course, in referring to 'pilots', I should refer to complete crews, as each aircraft lost accounted for three casualties, pilot, observer and wireless operator/air gunner.
>
> Our main task during the eight-month period was high-level photographic reconnaissance of the German

border with Belgium, Luxembourg and Holland, to try and find out what measures the Germans were taking to extend the Siegfried Line up these borders. To do this we were required to fly high level (i.e. 20,000 feet or thereabouts) in clear weather when the opportunity arose. Although the Blenheim was a very pleasant aircraft to fly, it soon became apparent that, operating singly, if you met up with German fighters you didn't come back, and if you didn't meet up with them you were lucky.

Flying Officer E.F. Nind, 57 Squadron

At the beginning of October missions were undertaken by the few Blenheim squadrons with the Air Component. After their try at night recces, 53 Squadron switched to day sorties on the 1st and shortly afterwards began to operate from Poix. 57 Squadron began flying from Metz, while 18 Squadron at Beauraignes would soon become operational. Bad weather was stopping their working up period and their aircraft from operating from Metz.

For some of the AASF men came the chance of a period of leave. In 103 Squadron, six pilots and six airmen were given three days' leave in Paris which, it was believed, was the first such given to any AASF unit, if not the whole of the BEF. (Later, Paris leave was cancelled.)

Social diversions consisted of visiting the various estaminets in Rheims and nearby towns of consequence. There we met some of our colleagues and exchanged views, although we were all very much in the same boat, finding our way about and considering what was going to happen.

We had access to the local village where we could buy champagne for the equivalent of about 3/6d a bottle. Makes one grieve heavily when one thinks of it these days.

We had our morale raised considerably by being given leave and we could go home for a fortnight at a time. Mail too was coming through regularly. People would worry about their private affairs at home, their family's situation, etc., but when the leave roster started, it made all the difference.

Squadron Leader J.F. Hobler, 142 Squadron

On the 12th, three Blenheims of 114 Squadron flew from RAF Wyton to Villeneuve in order to carry out a recce mission over the Ruhr the next day. Two of the crews were detailed:

F/Lt F. Harrison	Sgt Lutwyche	AC Alves	N6232
P/O K.G.S. Thompson	Sgt G.W. Marwood	AC A. Lumsden	N6160

They took off shortly after midday and Harrison met heavy AA fire and then two Me109s attacked. One was seen to go down during the brief skirmish, but no claim was made. Harrison landed back at 4 p.m. but Pilot Officer Thompson failed to return and his crew were later reported killed.

Another Blenheim was lost this same day, this from 57 Squadron. It was the squadron's first operational mission and was flown by the squadron commander:

W/C H.M.A. Day	Sgt R. Hillier	AC F.G. Moller	L1138

Harry Day took off at 11.40 a.m. to fly a recce over north-west Germany but was not happy at such a mission in a short-nosed Blenheim I, and was hoping at least to re-equip with Mark IVs. The other thing was that the 13th was a Friday!

Fifty miles inside Germany, they ran out of cloud, finding themselves in a very open and vulnerable position. The weather men had promised cloud all over Germany. As Day was debating whether to call it off, they were attacked by three Me109s. His Blenheim was set on fire and he and his crew quickly prepared to bale out. No sooner had he struggled out of the top hatch than the aircraft exploded.

Day was quickly taken prisoner and taken to the village of Langweiler. Here, in the back of a lorry, lay the bodies of his two crewmen. Both had baled out but their parachutes had caught fire as they left the burning aeroplane. Harry Day stood and saluted his fallen men, and was then taken off to captivity. 'Wings' Day became an ardent and persistent escaper and escape organiser and it became a costly day when they took him prisoner.

Three days later, 57 Squadron lost another crew on a reconnaissance of Wesel-Bocholt, north-west of Essen:

F/O M.J. Carey	Sgt A.G. Fripp	AC Nelson	L1151

They too were believed to have been attacked by fighters and all three were later reported prisoners of war.

Flight Lieutenant Geoffrey Wyatt of 57 Squadron flew a reconnaissance operation on 17 October. This time, however, it was a case of third time lucky.

Our tasks, it seems, were a fair summary of wasted effort and life, although I suppose you could say that what we were doing was the start of PR. In retrospect, it was asking for trouble and losses to send unescorted relatively slow aircraft which were gasping at 20,000 feet (as were their occupants!) in fine weather on loosely defined tasks deep inside Germany.

However, I think I was about the first to bring back any reasonable photographs of German airfields (Osnabrück, Gütersloh) and rail activity.

That trip was part of about the most bizarre 24 hours of my young life. I flew down to Etain on the 16th with my usual crew (Sergeant 'Rocky' Gardner, who'd been with me since the open air days on Hinds in 1936, and LAC 'Jack' Russell with us since re-equipment with Blenheims in early 1938. I was billeted out for the night in a local farmhouse also occupied by a pair of brothers or cousins named Kain ('Cobber' and Bill, both achieving early fame on Hurricanes). I joined in a bit of the evening's drinking in the mess (73 Squadron) but retired early in view of the next day. Sleep was short lived, however: in the early hours, those mad Kains introduced a live pig into the billet and I had to come the heavy flight lieutenant to get a bit of peace.

Briefed previously at 70 Wing HQ in the most general terms to look at 'road and rail movement' up as far as Bremen, we cracked off at first light and climbed into the overcast, coming out at about 10,000 feet above 10/10ths., and getting on to a northerly course. We soon ran out of this cover and I clearly recall coming into the open as if off a shelf with a hell of a lot of Germany ahead in a beautiful, cloudless autumn day.

With a general idea of our whereabouts (no sophisticted navigational aids in those days!) we pressed on, photo-graphing anything of interest, until we arrived at Bremen where we encountered our first flak – frighteningly accurate at about 20,000 ft. I'd decided by then to go home to UK over the North Sea. On these trips, it was left to the pilot's discretion whether he would return to France back through hostile territory or go out 'over the top' and the North Sea to England. We went out over Emden – more flak, plus some probably from the Dutch (then neutral) whose territory I had undoubtedly clipped in my haste to leave the scene. Going rapidly downhill, with several eyes open for 109s, we made it across the sea and eventual landfall, without being engaged by our own defence forces (a slight hazard in those early days), landing finally at Honington.

After de-briefing and photo assessment at Honington, an understanding Station Operations Officer gave permission for us to go on to our old base at Upper Heyford, which we made at dusk. After seeing to crew and aircraft, I rang up some local farmer friends, and we all beat it up to one of our favourite pre-war haunts – the Whately Hall at Banbury.

Came the morning, and I checked with Heyford to learn that the aircraft was U/S with a cracked stern frame (Mk.I Blenheims had a weakness there) and I recalled hitting a ridge at Etain a hell of a thump on landing and take-off. However, I was quite happy to remain in the area for the necessary repairs until 22nd October, when we returned to Rosières-en-Santerre. (The squadron had moved there from Roye-Amy during my absence.)

Flight Lieutenant G.M. Wyatt, 57 Squadron

Geoff Wyatt received the DFC in the New Year.

*

The Battle squadrons were now well aware of the lack of defensive armament but an observer in 150 Squadron, Sergeant H. Beddell, had made and fitted a third gun to one of their aircraft. On 21 October, Air Chief Marshal Sir Robert Brooke-Popham, a former Inspector General of the RAF, together with the present Inspector General, Air Marshal Sir Charles Burnett, visited the squadron.

They were particularly interested in the third gun installation. It was another VGO 'K' gun fitted on a moveable mounting in the bombing aperture and gave an excellent field of fire both fore and aft, below the fuselage. When it was trained aft, the gun was turned upside down and for this reason it was fitted with a second set of sights.

Three days later, Battle L4948, with the third gun fitted, was flown to Rheims by Flying Officer H.R. McD. Beall, along with Beddell and AC1 R.H. Hinder, for inspection by Air Chief Marshal Sir Edgar Ludlow-Hewitt, Air Officer Commander-in-Chief of Bomber Command, and Air Vice Marshal Philip Playfair, AOC-in-C of the AASF. Both found favour with the mounting and Playfair instructed that the aircraft be flown to the Fairey Aviation works at Stockport, England, for a demonstration.

Obviously something happened, for that same month 142 Squadron were fitting a third gun mounting to their Battles followed by 103 Squadron. The Fairey company must have worked fast for by 26 October, 103 were receiving gun mountings from them, fixed to fire back and down from the observer's bombing hatch. As 103 Squadron noted, the aircraft was not designed for it but it seemed all right: 'Although there is no way of sighting it and the observer has to be in an unnatural position to fire it, it should deter underneath attacks.' It seems that Faireys had made some adjustments to Beddell's original conception.

Although he had now left 150 Squadron, Joe Gardiner remembers some of these changes:

> The 'powers that be' later decided in their doubtful wisdom to try the Battle out in many ways in order to try to get some usefulness out of that terrible, inadequate aeroplane. Even dive bombing – a disaster for over 60 degrees she went over on her back. Then there was the installation of two Vickers guns swivelled by the bombsight so that the poor b ... navigator could hang out and fire backwards underneath, to try to overcome the blind spot under the tail. The WOP/AG could easily, and did, shoot his tail off, our 'opposition' knowing this fault.
>
> *Sergeant F.H. Gardiner, 150 Squadron*

At this time we had an improvised position for a VGO gun so it could be fired under the navigator's compartment. It was mounted on a swivel with a mirror attached, and the navigator got down on his stomach, opened the trap, pushed the gun through, tipped it upside-down and through the mirror, was able to fire. This gave some small lift to morale but we didn't really believe in it, I suppose, but it was another bit of aggression we could mount from our own little platform.

Squadron Leader J.F. Hobler, 142 Squadron

A couple of days earlier, on the 22nd, 103 Squadron had been alerted to prepare for a bombing raid on Germany! Six Battles were to attack a tank park, 15 miles the other side of the Siegfried Line. This caused some excitement, as can be imagined, and six crews of B Flight stood ready: then it was disclosed that the whole thing was a practice! One can only hope everybody was suitably impressed!

It was the Blenheims again that completed October's war flying. Earlier that month, on the 16th, four aircraft had taken off from Metz to fly photo recce sorties, two flying over Germany, two over the Siegfried Line, then flown directly back to England with their photos.

As 53 Squadron had already discovered, it was faster for the films and safer for the crews, to fly direct to England after flying recce missions. It enabled the crews to take an alternative course 'home' so that Luftwaffe aircraft would not be able to lie in wait for returning aircraft.

Now on the 30th (the squadron having meantime moved to Meharicourt in Picardy), 18 Squadron made repeat sorties but this time flown by two aircraft to Germany but only one, Flight Lieutenant Alan Dilnot, to the Siegfried Line:

F/O D.F. Elliott	Sgt K.B. Crew	AC1 J.A. Garrick	L1415
F/Lt A.A. Dilnot	Sgt E.H. Crellin	AC1 J.S. Burrows	L6694
P/O G. Howden	Sgt K.N. Shrosbee	AC A.G. Harmer	L1416

All took off from their advance base at Metz but only George Howden returned, to Bircham Newton. All were Blenheim Is. The missing airmen were all believed killed, Dilnot and his crew were indeed dead.

October 30 proved a busy day, for 2 Group in England sent a force of Blenheims of 139 Squadron on a recce of airfields in north-west Germany, where intelligence reports suggested the Luftwaffe were massing aircraft, in addition to stories of the assembly of merchant ships and barges at the mouth of the River Ems.

Despite bad weather, six Blenheims went off at 10.26 a.m., although one was delayed a quarter of an hour when it got stuck in mud on the airfield:

F/O N.E.W. Pepper	Sgt T.E. Hyde	AC Cronin	N6236 'G'
Sgt N.J. Price	Sgt R.J. Stanley	AC Pickering	N6224 'F'
F/O A. McPherson DFC	Sgt Woolnough	AC G. Sweetman	N6219 'N'
S/L T.G. Tideman	Sgt G. Thomas	AC1 T.M. Rodwell	N6217 'R'
P/O W.G. McCracken	Sgt S.R. Mitchell	AC R.B. Smith	N6234 'E'
Sgt T.C.R. Harrison	Sgt N.S.D. Jones	AC H.T. Garbett	N6227 'M'

Flying Officer Pepper was attacked and his aircraft shot up by German fighters and flak, and his air gunner was badly wounded. Sergeant Price too was caught by flak and his Blenheim damaged, his air gunner being wounded in the wrist and thigh. Pilot Officer McCracken failed to return.

Squadron Leader Tideman and Flying Officer McPherson failed to take any photos because of the bad weather, while Sergeant Harrison was engaged by six German fighters but evaded in the cloud. Neville Pepper later received the DFC for his determination on this mission, while Sergeant R.J. Stanley received a Mention in Despatches.

The next day, 18 Squadron were ordered to fly the Germany recce again, and again by a lone Blenheim I:

Sgt E.E.B. LeVoi	Sgt G.W. Buchner	AC1 G. Hawkins	L1430

In March 1940, George Hawkins, by then promoted to sergeant, was awarded the DFM, mainly for this mission. The citation read:

> This airman was the Air Gunner of an aircraft which carried out a highly successful reconnaissance over north-west Germany on 31st October. His aircraft was subjected to intense and accurate AA fire over the Siegfried Line and in the bad weather conditions was forced to descend to a low altitude over Central Germany, in order to carry out the recce allotted.
>
> LAC Hawkins observed enemy activity and movement which had escaped the notice of both the pilot and observer and successfully and accurately pinpointed this activity. While leaving the German coast, despite intense cold, he

quickly established communication with a D/F Station in the UK which enabled his pilot to bring the aircraft home successfully.

He has been an outstanding member of the squadron for the past 2½ years, during which time he has proved himself to be an Air Gunner and Wireless Operator of exceptional ability. Since the outbreak of hostilities he has taken a very great part in the training of Wireless Operators and Air Gunners posted to the squadron and been a never ending encouragement.

*

In addition to the curtailment of operational flying by the Battle squadrons, the wintry weather also began to restrict even practice flights. November found the AASF beginning to feel the effects of the beginning of what was to prove a severe winter. What recce missions were called for were all carried out by the Component Blenheim squadrons with varying degrees of success and failure.

What flying 12 Squadron did, for example, was all practice or affiliation with the French.

On 6 November, the Siegfried Line recce duty claimed another crew, when 57 Squadron was assigned the job. They took off from Metz at 10.30 a.m. and failed to return:

P/O A.D. Morton	Sgt G. Storr	AC F.A. Twinning	L1145

Alexander Morton, Geoff Storr and Fred Twinning were all killed.

Never wanting to be bested, Air HQ ordered 57 Squadron to try again on the 7th:

P/O H.R. Bewley	Sgt S. McIntyre	AC T.P. Adderly	L1325

They took off at 11.45 a.m. and also failed to return.

During the increasingly bad weather, the Battle squadrons did try to get airborne whenever possible. On the 13th, 218 Squadron organised a practice dive-bombing programme, with the aerodrome as the target. However, it was cancelled when the very first pilot dived into the ground. He and his crew were all killed instantly:

P/O R. Thynne   Sgt R.C.L. Pike   AC1 V.W.L. Richardson   K9356

Poor 57 Squadron continued its run of bad luck on 17 November. One crew were ordered to fly a recce over the Ruhr, but owing to severe icing, they were forced to land in Holland and were interned:

Sgt Gilmore   Sgt Turnidge   AC T.J. Jervis   L1148

As if this wasn't enough, the squadron had a Blenheim at Orly which had been repaired following damage received by enemy fighters (the occasion is not known). A crew was sent to fly it back to Rosières but the aircraft crashed into the River Seine shortly after take off due to engine failure. All three men were killed:

Sgt S.J. Farmer   Sgt Bowden   AC R.T.W. Partlow   L1246

Exactly a week later (on the 23rd) Pilot Officer Hume of 57 Squadron was killed in a flying accident over the aerodrome. Hume flew low over the field and struck a tent, which damaged the starboard wing. Hume, struggling with the controls, managed to get the Blenheim up to a safe height which enabled his crew to bale out, but then the aircraft went into a steep spiral, hit the ground and burst into flames.

At the end of the month, 103 Squadron moved to Plivot, near Epinay. There were a few hostelries in the local village where both officers and men would depart when they could.

> Wing Commander Gemmel used to go round at night to the pubs and anyone who was caught in his torch beam had to go home. Charlie Tait and Blackie Wells became quite renowned for hiding in a chicken house next to the pub.
> *Flying Officer J.R. Havers, 103 Squadron*

*

We had terrible trouble starting the aircraft during that winter. They were all standing out in the open, of course. I well recall our efforts when we'd help the ground crew. The only way we could start them was to make a sort of glove that

Above Battles of 142 Squadron at Berry-au-Bac with canvas cover to cockpit area, netting strung from the trees and branches leant against the wings to add to the camouflage. (*J.M. Hewson*)

Below Similar scene but winter's grip making work difficult for the poor groundcrew. (*J.F. Hobler*)

Bottom Battle with engine tent over the nose and cowling into which warm air is blown to help stop the oil from freezing. Note damage to wing-tip, caused when P/O Taylor of A Flight turned too close to the ground. (*J.F. Hobler*)

fitted on the end of the prop to which you'd have a rope attached, and we'd pull like mad and give it a flick over; it was too big a job to do by hand. It often took two or three tries to get it started.

Flying Officer R.D. Max, 103 Squadron

Winter's icy grip increased during December 1939 and January of the new year. Anyone who had thought that the war might end by Christmas need not have worried. Operations were almost non-existent and even the Blenheims stopped flying recce missions.

John Hobler recalls the weather, and that terrible winter of 1939–40:

With the onset of the colder weather, we had to work out a plan for being ready at all times, to cope with the call to operate. We had quickly realised we were going to be very uncomfortable.

We had to make taxi-ways from the woods onto the airfield, that would take our aircraft in any weather, so we had metal scrim for the hard-standings and the taxi-ways so we could get out from these camouflaged positions when necessary. When the snow melted, it was extremely dicey taxiing the Battles onto the airfield on this scrim for they would slide from side to side. A number of times we got our wheels stuck in a rut and found it very hard to move.

The winter was so severe that it had its effect on the airmen. They went about in balaclavas and swathed in woollen mufflers all the time. The problem too was to start the engines in this bitter cold. At one period we had teams of men going round the aircraft during the night, starting the engines to warm the oil and to keep some warmth in the metal to ensure they would start the following morning, if they had to.

The fact that no enemy challenged us at this stage, made this task a little difficult, because the airmen couldn't see the point of it. Yet there was a definite point: if we had had to go, and if we hadn't organised something, then the aircraft would not have started.

Squadron Leader J.F. Hobler, 142 Squadron

Early in December, 12 Squadron relocated to a new base at Amifontaine, but two significant moves came for 40 and 15 Squadrons. These two Battle units returned to England to re-equip with Bristol Blenheim IVs, both going to RAF Wyton.

No 40 Squadron was relieved by the Blenheim IV-equipped 139 Squadron, who by the 4th were at Bétheniville. Shortly afterwards, 114 Squadron flew to Vraux in France to replace 15 Squadron. The 16 Blenheims left Wyton at 10.10 a.m. on 9 December, landing at Vraux at 1.10 p.m. Vraux is on the north bank of the River Marne, midway between Châlons and Epernay, the airfield being three quarters of a mile north of the village.

His Majesty King George VI was in France at the end of the first week of December and visited a number of RAF bases. Those who he could not visit sent a handful of officers and men to represent their units. A number of recently awarded decorations were presented to recipients by the King. Geoff Wyatt recalls how interested the King was in talking to anyone who had actually flown over Germany, as Geoff had. There were comparatively few who had – and returned.

A Blenheim of 18 Squadron crashed at Champigny on 27 December, and all four men on board were killed, including one of the squadron's fitters, flying as a passenger:

| Sgt L.J. Sabin | Sgt V. Harvey | LAC W.S. Martin | LAC J. Job |

The AASF squadrons continued to suffer in the bitter cold of the French winter, where the weather was far worse than in England that year. Practice flights were made whenever possible and the hard-working, long-suffering ground crews struggled to keep the aircraft, often dispersed at the edges of nearby woods or under camouflage netting, in operational readiness – just in case.

The first operational flight in the new year was flown by 18 Squadron of the Air Component, on 3 January. It ended in failure. The Blenheim I took off at 7.55 a.m. to carry out a photo op:

| F/O C.M.P. Kempster | Sgt F.L. Smith | LAC P.B. Harris | L1410 |

On their way to the frontier they were attacked by a RAF Hurricane but were not hit before the British pilot realised his error. Crossing into Germany they were then intercepted by the inevitable Messerschmitt fighters. With the Blenheim crippled by the enemy's fire, Kempster was forced down out of control over neutral Belgium. His gunner attempted to bale out and was killed. The other two men were interned. Later Charles Kempster wrote the following letter to his CO, Wing Commander Bill Opie, from the military hospital in Liège, Belgium:

Undoubtedly you will already have heard of the disastrous end to our trip yesterday and the extreme good fortune of Sergeant Smith and myself. We were attacked by Messerschmitts over Emmerich and eventually shot down in flames, two kilometres over the Belgian frontier. At 5,000 feet the rudder controls were shot away and I gave the order to jump. Sergeant Smith experienced difficulty in getting out and it was impossible to get away with sufficient height for a safe jump and he stayed in. Apparently, poor Harris met with the same difficulty and he was killed when he hit the ground.

The last thing I remember was hitting some trees. Engine and aileron controls had completely gone and we went in at something like the speed of 140 mph. Both Smith and I lost consciousness and I eventually woke up to find him dragging me away from the remains of the aircraft. He put up a most terrific show and so did Harris. He was still firing when I gave the order to jump.

We have been treated with the utmost kindness and consideration here and our only injuries are bruises, other than a sprained ankle and a small cut in the head which I managed to collect when we hit the ground.

If possible I should like our personal kit to be forwarded to the above ... Please remember me to everyone and forgive this letter for being so scrappy.

On the 12th, a 114 Squadron Blenheim was fortunate to escape from the clutches of the Luftwaffe. A crew took off to fly a recce over three German Advance Landing Grounds, at Greimerith, Loshiem and Wahlen, taking off at 11.30 a.m.:

| P/O G. Turner | Sgt W.J. Paul | AC S.G. Peplar | L8859 |

Climbing up to 20,000 feet the crew set about their task, but before they could complete it, four Me109s attacked them at 12.45. The 109s approached from underneath so the gunner was unable to bring his gun to bear on them. The Blenheim was badly hit by machine gun, and it was thought, cannon fire. The starboard engine was knocked out but the aeroplane's armour plating saved them. Even so, one bullet went through the observer's flying suit while another pierced his flying helmet and knocked him out. George Turner then managed to evade further fire and flew back on one engine to Metz, returning to Vraux the next day.

The bomber squadrons maintained a schedule of practice flights during January, low dive-bombing, fighter co-operation, etc. On 23 January, a 218 Squadron Battle was airborne (K9329), piloted by Flying Officer I.G. Richmond. Coming in to land he had his flaps fail and floated down the runway and when he finally got the aircraft to touch down, he saw the danger of hitting parked aircraft. He quickly opened up and then tried to lift the starboard wing over the nearest Battle, but just failed to make it. The wing hit the engine of Battle K9327 and broke off, causing considerable damage to both aeroplanes. Two fitters working on the parked machine, which was covered by an engine tent to protect it and the fitters from the weather, had narrow escapes. However, Aircraftman Anderson was injured, and in the subsequent crash, Richmond sustained a sprained ankle but his crew were uninjured.

No. 57 Squadron lost yet another Blenheim on the 25th during a reconnaissance over north-west Germany. Their deaths in action were confirmed three days later:

| P/O J. Blackwood | Sgt D.J. Bendall | AC Hunter | L1280 |

*

One change in January, was the formation of the British Air Force in France (BAFF) under Air Marshal Sir Arthur Barratt. This gave Barratt full control of all RAF affairs in France. He could of course, call on Bomber Command (2 Group) for any support he required.

If December and January weather had proved bad, February was even worse and flying was again severely restricted. At Bétheniville, 103 Squadron recorded bad weather from the 1st to the 12th, while No. 12 Squadron recorded their airfield as snowbound from the 15th to the 27th. They had only recently returned from Perpignan in the south of France, on the Côte Vermeille. This was a detachment to No. 1 Air Training School, which all AASF squadrons began to visit during the first months of 1940. Here they could fly in the comparative warmth of the south of France, practise their low bombing sorties, as well as relaxing from the rigours of the cold north.

Meanwhile, 18 Squadron, who did manage to fly a few recce ops during the month, had their first encounter with the much publicised Me110 twin-engined fighter on the 11th, during a recce over Germany:

| P/O A. Hughes | Sgt A.E. Craig | LAC Fisk | L6983 |

They were over the town of Düsseldorf when they sighted three of the 110s, one of which made a quick pass, then flew off and disappeared. The Blenheim was also subjected to AA fire but returned safely.

It was 18 Squadron again that saw action on the 22nd, during another recce over Germany. The crew took some valuable photographs but their machine was badly damaged by enemy action. Pilot Officer Joseph Monette brought his damaged Blenheim back to England, but crashed at North Coates. He broke both legs in the crash and his observer was killed:

| P/O J.A.E. Monette | Sgt J.A.H. Potter | LAC A.C. Whitehall | L1444 |

This again was a short-nosed Blenheim I, but 18 Squadron was now beginning to exchange its aircraft for the long-nosed Blenheim IV, which it did over February and March.

A Blenheim IV of 114 Squadron was lost on the 27th. During a cross-country navigation exercise, the crew became lost in cloud and when fuel ran low, the order to bale out was given. Both rear men got out and landed safely but the pilot left it too late and died in the subsequent crash:

| P/O H. Dodgson | Sgt Hawkins | AC Barrow | L8838 |

*

During February, Barratt had re-grouped his ten squadrons into three Wings as follows:

71 Wing: *Group Captain H.S. Field*
             HQ Château Fagnières, Nr Châlons
105 Squadron   Villeneuve
114 Squadron   Condé
139 Squadron   Plivot
150 Squadron   Ecury

75 Wing: *Group Captain A.H. Wann*
             HQ St. Hilaire le Grand
 88 Squadron   Mourmelon
103 Squadron   Bétheniville
218 Squadron   Aubérive

76 Wing: *Group Captain H.S. Kerby, DSC AFC*
             HQ Neufchatel
 12 Squadron   Amifontaine
142 Squadron   Berry-au-Bac
226 Squadron   Rheims-Champagne

CHAPTER FOUR

The Spring of Anticipation

March 1940 began with a series of crashes. The squadrons were flying practice low level bombing attacks on the Rheims Road and cross country navigation flights, on the 1st. On one of the latter, Flying Officer Hulbert of 218 Squadron, ran into bad weather and crashed 40 miles north of Dijon. He suffered a broken ankle but both his crewmen were killed. They had been one of the crews that had flown on the squadron's first operation back in early September:

| F/O E.V. Hulbert | Sgt Dewar | AC Wiltshire | |

That night, 57 Squadron flew a night recce mission which left the ground at 11.45 p.m. Details of what happened are not recorded except that the Blenheim crashed at Orzy; the observer escaped by parachute but the pilot, William Adam, and his gunner died:

| F/O W.W. Adam | Sgt Park | AC Mantle | L9249 |

The following day, again during a night flight, a 114 Squadron crew became lost. After flying around for some time they thought they were over the aerodrome so dropped a parachute flare to ascertain if this was correct. It was later thought that the sudden change from bright light to sudden darkness when the flare went out, confused the pilot and he lost control of the Blenheim. He quickly gave the order to abandon the machine but the observer was in difficulty owing to the aircraft then being on its back. He was pushed out by the pilot, Robert Farrow, who then followed. Unfortunately Farrow came into contact with one of the propellers and was killed, while the air gunner had no time to get away and died when the aircraft hit the ground:

| P/O R.W. Farrow | Sgt Wallis | AC Sanders | N6157 |

There were a number of awards for some of the Blenheim squadrons in early March. To 18 Squadron went a DFC for Squadron Leader K.W. Niblett, and DFMs to Sergeants F. Miller and G. Hawkins. George Hawkins's decoration was mentioned in the previous Chapter.

Ken Niblett was one of the squadron flight commanders and he received his DFC for flying a number of recce missions in difficult weather conditions. His usual observer was Frank Miller and his DFM was a reward for his work in reconnaissance work with Niblett over Germany. It was noted that on one occasion, despite enemy aircraft being in the vicinity and under fire from flak, he photographed objectives, making two runs over one target, and no less than five over another.

The complete crew in 53 Squadron received DFC and DFMs: Flying Officer A.D. Panton, Sergeant W.J. Cronin and Aircraftman Ferre. Alastair Panton was a product of RAF Cranwell and had joined the squadron in December 1937. Cronin had been awarded his Observer Badge in November 1939, having been, like so many observers and gunners, a former member of the ground crew personnel who volunteered for flying duties. He was considered to be one of the best navigators on the squadron.

It will be noted that in both Battle and Blenheim squadrons, the air gunners, who also operated the wireless, were virtually all aircraftmen – either AC1, AC2 or leading aircraftmen (LAC) and just occasionally, corporals. Prior to December 1939, air gunners and wireless operator/air gunners (WOP/AG) wore the famous 'winged bullet' on the upper right arm of their tunic. This was replaced at the end of 1939 by the introduction of the now-familiar 'AG' cloth brevet sewn above the left breast tunic pocket. Although sergeant rank for air gunners was also approved, subject to qualification, there were virtually no sergeant air gunners in AASF or even 2 Group squadrons by the time the Battle of France began.

The third squadron to receive decorations was 57. A DFC

went to Flight Lieutenant G.M. Wyatt, DFMs to Sergeant A.C. Thomas and LAC S. Culver.

*

It was still very cold as winter retained its grip on the Western Front. It was difficult to keep warm when on the ground let alone in the air. There was no heating in the aircraft, and no heated flying clothing at this early stage of the war. Only fleece-lined leather flying jackets and trousers, and fur-lined boots protected the airmen from the elements. For the ground crews who had to service and keep the aircraft ready it was even worse. A greatcoat and balaclava and gloves were their only protection and when delving into the insides of an engine, gloves had often to be discarded in order to grip the tools and spanners.

Flying, however, still occurred whenever possible. On 11 March, 103 Squadron co-operated with the Hurricane pilots of No. 1 Squadron and the crews 'profited from the criticism by the Hurricane pilots'! All knew they would be up against it if they had again to face the Messerschmitts in their Battles.

Then in March came action – of a sort. With slightly improving weather the RAF felt they should be a little more aggressive. 'Higher Authority' too felt some aggression might be appropriate. It was decided to bomb the enemy – with leaflets! That would show 'em.

The first 'raids' were flown on the 18th. At Mourmelon, 88 Squadron sent off a Battle at 7.46 p.m. to drop the deadly paper over Mannheim and Saarbruchen – noted also as a recce mission:

F/Lt A.J. Madge	Sgt J.R. Jones	LAC J.H. Gegg	P2247

This was followed by a sortie by 226 Squadron at 8.35 p.m.

F/Lt B.R. Kerridge	Sgt D.I. Anthony	Cpl G.H. Dixon	L5247

Brian Kerridge flew his Battle through corridor 'P' (there were set corridors for excursions into Germany, safe from French anti-aircraft guns), then turned due east to a point 23 miles south-west of Mannheim where eight bundles of *Darem Krieg* were dropped at 10 p.m., from 9,000 feet. They then flew a recce of the River Rhine from Speyer to Karlsruhe, although low cloud proved a problem. No traffic was seen on the river and the German black-out was excellent. Some searchlights probed for them and some AA shells were fired at them, but they returned unscathed.

This was just the beginning of a good number of Nickel Raids, as they were called. On the night of 20/21 March, Flight Lieutenant Charles Tait of 103 Squadron flew the first Nickel Raid to Coblenz (in K9246) successfully.

Two nights later, 88 Squadron sent two aircraft out, but night flying was still proving a problem, especially if, as in this case, one of the Battles lost its radio.

| F/O D.L.R. Halliday | Sgt S.C. Boyton | LAC Wigglesworth | P2247 |
| F/O J.A.F. Machlachlan | Sgt A.G. Power | LAC L.V. Davies | K9321 |

David Halliday spent five hours in the air, most of it in 10/10ths cloud, and with his radio u/s they finally had to bale out. They all landed safely by parachute at Pont-sur-Yonne, just after 1 a.m., having taken off at 8.05 p.m. the previous evening.

*

As mentioned earlier, 18 Squadron was changing its Mark I Blenheims for Mark IVs at this time. On 21 March, Pilot Officer Hulton took off for England with a crew and a corporal fitter passenger in a Mark I (L1427). At the English coast they ran into fog and in trying to get in underneath it, they crashed into the top of a hill near RAF Tangmere. Hulton and his observer were killed while his gunner was slightly injured and bruised. The fitter was burnt about the face, hands and legs.

| P/O H.S.P. Hulton | Sgt O.W. Dumbreck | LAC Oultram | Cpl G.E. Lapwood |

On the 24th, 12 Squadron sent two crews out:

| F/O G.D. Clancy | Sgt K. Anderson | LAC P. Ferebee | L5249 |
| F/Lt W. Simpson | Sgt E.N. Odell | Cpl R.T. Tomlinson | L5190 |

Both dropped Nickels over Audernach and Coblenz and then carried out a recce mission, meeting some flak.

Amid these now fairly regular excursions over Germany, practice flights were maintained, especially at night, now that the Battle squadrons were flying more night operations. This, of course, increased the chances of accidents and crashes.

Above Battles of 226 Squadron.
'X' (K9180) was burned on 20 May and
'G' (K9176) shot down, on 14 May.
(*R.C. Bowyer*)

Left The Battle pilot's 'office'. (*R.D. Max*)

Below A 103 Squadron Battle taxies out
at Berry-au-Bac. (*via R.C. Bowyer*)

The first of four crashes occurred on the night of the 26th. A 105 Squadron crew crashed west of Cheniers and the crew were killed. The pilot and observer had joined the squadron in December but the gunner had been with the squadron since April 1937 and was considered to be the best WOP/AG on the unit:

| P/O A.M. Edgar | Sgt Pettitt | Cpl Jones | L4980 |

It was 103's turn the following night: the Battle crashed on take-off for a night bombing exercise. Again all three flyers died:

| P/O I.P. Hinton | Sgt D.O. Findlay | AC J.A. Sharpe | P2256 |

On the last day of the month, it was 105 Squadron again, but this time it was the squadron's experienced flight commander, an Australian (he had been with the squadron since April 1937), and his gunner that were killed. They were flying an anti-aircraft co-operation detail and crashed north of Champigneul. They did not have an observer with them:

| F/Lt C.R. Mace | Cpl Coughtrey | P2250 |

That night 150 Squadron flew some low bombing practice sorties. One of the first pilots out soon returned when a heavy ground mist was encountered. However, another crew then became overdue and at 6 a.m. the squadron received a telephone call from 71 Wing HQ that an aircraft had crashed near the bombing range. The Battle had been seen flying low on the run-up but had hit a rise in the ground, obscured by the ground mist. All three men on board were killed:

| F/O D. Devoto | Sgt C. Wall | AC1 W.F. Taylor | P2244 |

Returning from a night cross-country navigation exercise on the night of 8 April, a 142 Squadron Battle crashed five miles to the south of Neufchatel. Yet again all were killed:

| P/O Farrell | Sgt Roper | Cpl Willburn | N2088 |

*

By this time there was another Battle squadron in France, No. 98, which flew out from Finningley, to take up residence at Nantes. However, 98 Squadron acted as a reserve squadron –

in reality a pool of pilots and crews. Replacements for casualties were taken from this unit. One of the pilots was Pilot Officer Alan Frank:

> I was an ex-Oxford University Air Squadron reservist and I was initially with 98 Squadron, which I joined in February, which was the pool squadron. We went out to France in the middle of March. There was absolutely no reason why we shouldn't have done some night flying training. The weather was improving by that time but we did practically nothing. Most of the squadron pilots seemed to be my sort of standard, we were reservists. We'd done a crash FTS course, very little flying on Battles, and could have done with any flying possible.
>
> *Pilot Officer A.D. Frank, 150 Squadron*

The Battle of Blenheim squadrons were put on the alert on 11 April when the news that the Germans had invaded Denmark and Norway, two days earlier, was confirmed. Was something happening at last? Was this period, called by everyone the 'Phoney War', coming to an end? Tension was heightened at 142 Squadron's base at Berry-au-Bac, when the men watched an air battle between French fighters and enemy aircraft in which one Heinkel 111 and a Dornier 17 were shot down in the vicinity of the airfield, one crashing at Juvincourt.

What also excited 142 Squadron was the arrival that day of No. 1 Squadron with their Hawker Hurricane fighters. They had been quickly moved from their base at Bar-le-Duc so something must be going on. But within days the tension eased, and the Hurricanes returned to their usual base.

John Hobler remembers:

> Occasionally a German reconnaissance aircraft came over our area, and once one was shot down on our airfield. It was a Heinkel 111 and we all took comfort in what we saw of the aircraft. Its navigational mountings were apparently made of tin and the aircraft didn't look very strong, whereas ours, of course, would last about 1,000 years! The Germans knew they didn't need that!
>
> I was sent forward on a reconnaissance during one period, to find possible advance landing grounds up nearer the

Maginot Line, near the French frontier. These would be used for us to operate from as soon as we advanced. We really believed we would, or somebody believed it! I flew up to Metz, scoured the countryside, picked locations that would be useful to us, then flew back. At Metz the French were at a peak of optimism, who gave us a guarantee that there would never be a Hun on French soil again. They believed it – propaganda was very strong. From time to time we saw the French army moving up, marching along, singing their famous war songs, and tanks rolling along the cobbled streets. We found it very business like. One day, however, we saw some horse-drawn transport going along; this didn't seem so business like!

Squadron Leader J.F. Hobler, 142 Squadron

The weather was now improving. Snow and ice slowly disappeared leaving the countryside lush and green. A number of the Battle squadrons lost their April records in the May retreats, so full details of their pre-Blitz days have been lost. However, during the second half of April, most of the squadrons were again assigned to flying Nickel leaflet raids after which they made a reconnaissance sweep.

If I record the flights of just one squadron, it will show the sort of operations that were being flown at that time. 12 Squadron, still at Amifontaine, south of St Quintin, operated on the nights of 20/21 and 21/22 April:

F/Lt P.H.M.S. Hunt *Sgt P. Wilks* *LAC H. Cooke*	P2243 'U' Took off 8.30 p.m., landed 11.15 p.m. Nickel raid over Bonn, 10,000 ft, then recce between 3/4,000 ft from Bonn to Neuwied. Many searchlights but little flak.
F/O B.G.F. Drinkwater *Sgt A. Seymour* *Cpl J.S. Campion*	L5249 'D' Took off 9.30 p.m., landed 1.10 a.m. Nickels over Audermach, recce over the Rhine Valley. Some AA fire.
F/O D.E. Garland *Sgt J. Stewart* *LAC L.R. Reynolds*	P2204 'K' Took off 10.05 p.m., landed 0.38 a.m. Nickels over Coblenz then recce of Rhine Valley. Ground mist, some AA fire.

Sgt Parkhurst *Sgt T. Gray* *LAC J.L. Perrin*	L5227 'J' Times not recorded. Nickels over Lahnstein, recce of Rhine Valley. Some AA fire.

On the second night:

F/O E.R.D. Vaughan *Sgt C. Shelton-Jones* *AC1 J. Wright*	P2243 'U' Took off 9 p.m., landed 0.30 a.m. Nickels over Coblenz, recce Rhine Valley. Over Coblenz five Me110s seen circling. Some AA.
F/O N.M. Thomas *Sgt B.C. Long* *LAC F. Walker*	P2332 'F' Took off 9.35 p.m., landed 10.50 p.m. Op aborted due to W/T failure.
P/O A.W. Matthews *Sgt A.A. Maderson* *LAC C. Senior*	P2204 'K' Took off 9.45 p.m., landed 11.55 p.m. Raid abandoned on way to Bonn due to an oil leak developing at 11.02.

A Battle of 218 Squadron was lost on the night of 20 April. The pilot, Howard Wardle, survived as a prisoner, but his crew were reported killed:

P/O H.D. Wardle	Sgt E. Davison	AC1 A. Bailey	P2201

It was not always the flying men that made the news. 150 Squadron was also flying Nickel raids in April, and on the 22nd, a Battle aircraft was set on fire by a faulty parachute flare while being prepared for flight. The aeroplane's bomb load of four 250 lb bombs had been placed beneath the aircraft ready for loading and were thus in danger of exploding.

Sergeant William Henry Franklin, a fitter/armourer, supervised the removal of three of these bombs, but then the party was driven back by the intense heat of the burning bomber. Regardless of the danger, Sergeant Franklin returned alone and got the fourth bomb clear. We will read of Sergeant Franklin again.

On 30 April, 57 Squadron lost a Blenheim. It failed to return from a mission when it force-landed in Belgium where the crew were interned:

| Sgt A.W.S. Thomas | Sgt J.J.F. Talbot | LAC R.G. St. James- Smith | L8875 |

*

As the fateful month of May began, a fourth Air Component reconnaissance squadron became operational, No. 59, based on Poix, equipped with the Blenheim IV. On the 1st it made its first war sortie, when Flight Lieutenant Norman Hallmark carried out a successful night recce of the Ruhr. Like some other Army Co-operation squadrons of the period, Hallmark was an Army man (a lieutenant in the Cheshire Regt) with an honourary rank of flight lieutenant with the RAF while on secondment.

| F/Lt N.B. Hallmark | Sgt Barker | Sgt Dunlap |

No. 53 Squadron lost a Blenheim on the 3rd – L9329 'TE-L', when it failed to return from a reconnaissance operation.

At Amifontaine, the men of 12 Squadron were given a holiday on 8 May, no flying being ordered after the usual stint of Dawn Readiness. It was, nevertheless, a time of tension in France. With the arrival of spring and with the Germans already well on their way to subduing Norway, it was obvious to everyone that if something was going to happen it would be soon.

Meantime, France stood confident behind her massive defence system, the famed Maginot Line with its massive concrete forts and defence works, its heavy guns pointing towards Germany, the defenders deep inside its underground bunkers and command posts. For them there was to be no trench warfare that had bled their armies, and those of their allies, white during the 1914–18 War.

To the north, Belgium stood neutral, and thereby, in theory, immune from assault from possible hostile neighbours. The problem here was that she had been neutral in 1914 but that had not stopped Germany then. Would it now?

Further north still stood Holland. Since almost the beginning of May, the Dutch authorities had felt convinced that a German invasion was imminent and they had done all in their power to prepare for it. Her army stood ready, fully mobilised while the lock-gates to her famous Water Line were ready to be opened. Some areas had indeed, already been flooded, just in case. However, all her defensive activity proved too little and too late when the might of Germany's war machine rolled over her.

All that could be done was to wait and see what Germany and Hitler would do. The French hoped that if the attack came from the east, German troops and armour would smash themselves to pieces against the Maginot Line. Whatever course an invading army might take, and there were a few options, what was imperative was to crush the invading forces quickly. If it could be bloodily repulsed, then things might look very different from the enemy's standpoint, and Hitler might have to think again. After all, the Germans had failed to conquer France in four years of bloody conflict during the First World War.

As the daylight of 9 May faded, Hitler's oft threatened, long delayed, many times postponed offensive in the West was just hours away. Unknown to the men of the bomber squadrons of the Advanced Air Striking Force in France, and indeed, the bomber crews of the 2 Group squadrons in England who would support them, the time of dreary waiting was almost over.

They were all peacetime, regular, professional airmen, trained and ready. Yet in their heart of hearts they were all only too aware of the shortcomings of their equipment, especially in the Battle squadrons. Those that had met the German day fighters knew how vulnerable they were. They had been stopped from flying operational day missions since those first one-sided meetings and their job now, in the event of a German offensive, was for tactical bombing in close support of Allied ground forces. Flying at low level, perhaps they would not meet the Messerschmitts, and any German fighters in the air would be taken care of by RAF and French fighters. That was the theory. The only problem with theories was that nobody could tell if they were right until proved in actual battle.

Whatever the Battle and Blenheim squadron crews lacked, one item quickly emerged of which they suffered no shortage. Cool, grim, determined, gut-wrenching courage.

CHAPTER FIVE

The Balloon Goes Up

Dawn, Friday, 10 May 1940

At 4.35 a.m., the aerodrome at Berry-au-Bac, the home of 142 Squadron, was bombed and machine-gunned from between 600 and 1,000 feet by six Heinkel 111 bombers. The surface of the flying field was damaged, and several unexploded bombs were scattered around. Many were still a hazard six days later. One UXB went through the trailing edge and flaps on the starboard wing of a Battle, while another bomber was damaged by flying splinters of shrapnel. Both aircraft were serviceable within 48 hours. Bétheniville and 103 Squadron were bombed at dawn but sustained no damage.

Exactly one hour later, 88 Squadron was bombed at Mourmelon. The squadron had been alerted and put on four hours' Readiness notice at 4 a.m., changed at 5 a.m. to 50 per cent of aircraft at two hours' notice. At 5.30 this was changed again to 30 minutes' notice, while the rest of the squadron was to be on two hours' notice. Five minutes later the Germans struck.

Two Battle aircraft were damaged in the raid, one severely. Two soldiers were injured and some slight damage done to the oil dump.

At 6 a.m., 142's base was attacked again but by just one enemy aeroplane which did little damage. 226 Squadron was also attacked, German bombers dropping 16 high explosive and 70 incendiary bombs over the airfield but no damage to aircraft or personnel occurred. The RAF base at Rheims/ Champagne was also bombed, while some 45 French and eight Belgian air bases were also bombed at dawn or soon after.

At Amifontaine, 12 Squadron saw enemy planes at 6 a.m. No bombs fell on the airfield but the air and ground crews were quickly making their way onto the aerodrome, many of them running beneath trees in order to keep under cover as much as possible. One of the squadron WOP/AGs was Gordon Patterson, a Canadian, who records:

> While we were running we saw a Heinkel 111 diving on one of our machine gun pits, shooting first from the nose gun, then banking over to let the top and lower rear guns fire. Our gun pit was manned by one of our WW1 veterans. For armament he had four pan-fed Lewis guns, mounted on a wooden framework which in turn was mounted on a heavy post sunk into the ground. The pit he was in was well surrounded by sandbags.
>
> He fired almost steadily at the Heinkel, and as it pulled out, it appeared to slide off to one side, crashing into some trees about one-quarter mile from the gun-pit, then exploded and burned – there were no survivors. When we got to the airfield, our veteran gunner had reloaded his guns with fresh ammo pans, and was sitting down in his pit, smoking a cigarette. The sandbags around him had been well cut-up with bullets but none had hit him. We sort of looked at him, astounded, and hoped we could remain as cool under fire as he was.
>
> *Leading Aircraftman G.N. Patterson, 12 Squadron*

No. 12 Squadron was brought to 50 per cent available at 30 minutes and 50 per cent at two hours. Other squadrons received similar orders. Only the targets and take-off time were awaited. Everyone stood by. It had begun.

> When the Balloon went Up on 10 May, our first notification was bombs on the airfield. It was a shattering of the quiet enjoyment we'd had for some months. Then we saw nearby buildings burning and there was a sinister feeling in the air, for we knew finally we were in it – up to the neck!
>
> We had our Ops Room quite well set-up and the facilities for despatching information, intelligence and sorties, was well tried thanks to our training period. Battles went off in sections to attack bridges largely, and road junctions, to stop the enemy's advance; as it appeared he was moving inexorably forward, so more bridges were attacked.

Our own squadron carried on, sending out sorties when we could. Some didn't come back, others had to be repaired.
Squadron Leader J.F. Hobler, 142 Squadron

*

The German attack when it came was swift. Ignoring, sensibly, the Maginot Line, the thrust went into Holland, Luxembourg and – neutral Belgium. In the early hours, German aeroplanes crossed the Dutch frontier and struck at Amsterdam and the Hague. Shortly afterwards waves of transport planes appeared which disgorged highly trained parachute troops on key points, while bombers attacked airfields.

Soon after dawn further formations of enemy aircraft were bombing Belgian targets, including Brussels and Antwerp. Meantime, German troops and armour crossed the three frontiers. The Dutch were resisting along the Maas and Iyssel Rivers but already the fortifications at the latter had been breached with the capture of Apeldoorn. Over France, German aircraft attacked airfields of both the French and Royal Air Forces. The Hurricane squadrons of the AASF, 1 and 73, were quickly airborne and in the thick of the fighting. They would hardly stop for the next fortnight.

The only natural defences for the Allies were the rivers and canals of northern France and Belgium. These were, mainly, the Albert Canal that ran from the town of Maastricht to Antwerp, and the River Maas, that wound its way north and north-west towards Nijmegen, roughly parallel to that part of Germany's border. Further south the Maas River (Dutch spelling) became the Meuse as it entered France, which with the River Sombre, ran to the south from Maastricht through the Ardennes and on towards Verdun.

In most cases, plans had long been made for these bridges to be blown up by the defenders before they could be captured, but in the majority of cases it had not been done. Some had been over-run and captured too quickly for the demolition charges to be exploded, and in one case the officer whose duty it was to set the charges, had been killed in the dawn attack.

The actual bridges in the town centre of Maastricht had been blown up, but the three main bridges across the Albert Canal, which ran parallel to the Maas, just to the west of the town, had all been captured in the early hours by German gliderborne Fallschirmjäger troops. These were at Breigden, Veldwezelt and Vroenhoven, although Belgian troops later returned and destroyed the Breigden bridge.

With, therefore, most of the vital bridges intact, the German troops and tanks were now pouring into Belgium and Holland. Luxembourg, of course, had fallen although at its southern frontier, the French were holding. To meet the threat into southern Belgium, the British and French forces between the northern end of the now useless Maginot Line and the Channel coast were executing a movement on Mezières in order to advance through what had been neutral Belgium towards a pre-selected defence line, Meuse-Namur-the Dyle-Antwerp.

Obviously the initial picture was obscure and although the AASF bombers waited for orders, it would take time for priorities to be sorted out. In the meantime, Air Component Blenheims would have to fly recce missions to gather the necessary intelligence on which to base a reaction. Meanwhile, authority was only given for recce and fighter aircraft to overfly Belgian territory.

Although, of course, some records were lost or destroyed during the French campaign, it would seem that 53 Squadron was the first away. At 8.55 a.m. it sent the first of seven aircraft, which would fly ops this day, out towards the area of the German advance into Belgium:

| P/O D.P. Massey | Sgt Whetton | AC Vickers | L9332 |

They were hit by anti-aircraft fire but returned and landed at the advance landing ground at Vitry, at 11.40.

In England, 2 Group had been alerted and were on stand-by, but like their brothers in France, had to wait. 40 Squadron, however, was ordered to fly recce missions and sent off two Blenheims at 9.05 a.m.:

| S/L B. Paddon | Sgt Beattie | P/O Edwards | L8833 |
| F/O R.M. Burns | Sgt J.R. Brooker | Cpl G. Hurford | L8776 |

Brian Paddon headed out over Holland and was attacked by a Ju88 after crossing the Dutch coast and driven off to the south. Some time later, while circling to establish their position, they saw large numbers of enemy aircraft around the Hague, some on the ground, others in the air. He quickly headed back to England with this information. As he landed, one of his engines caught fire, but he and his crew were all right. Robert Burns and his crew, in aircraft 'K', failed to return, and were later reported as prisoners of war.

What was happening of course, was that German airborne troops had seized the aerodrome of Waalhaven, while others had struck and captured the main bridges across the Meuse, especially the important Moerdijk bridge, which was the principal transport link between Rotterdam and Antwerp. The bridge was taken before the set charges could be detonated.

Waalhaven was reported occupied by German paratroops by 10.25 and requests for air bombardment were beginning to be made, while at 12.55 Ypenburg and two other aerodromes were reported to have been captured. These airborne assaults in the heart of Holland caused the utmost confusion in the vital Hague/Rotterdam areas.

At RAF Abingdon, 15 Squadron sent out two Blenheims at 9.15 to take photographs of the destroyed bridges on the Dutch-Belgian border. They met some flak but returned with some good pictures:

F/O A.R. Oakshott	Sgt A.F. Taylor	LAC V.F.E. Treherne	P6913
F/O R.B.G.E. Clarke	Sgt B.S.J. Piff	LAC Murphy	L8847

Meanwhile, in France, 18 Squadron too sent off two Blenheims at about the same time:

P/O G.F. Harding	Sgt K.N. Shrosbee	LAC R.B. Townsend-Cole	L1405
P/O P.D. Smith	Sgt C.J. Hann	LAC Shepherd	L9185

Both were to make a recce of the vital bridges over Maas and Meuse Rivers, and of the Venlo area. Pilot Officer Harding did not return. Pilot Officer Smith nearly met a similar fate. Making a low level recce over the same area, he met intense light AA fire and was then attacked by a Me110. However, he managed to evade by flying right down on the deck although the Blenheim was hit and damaged by cannon and machine-gun fire.

A Blenheim of 59 Squadron took off at 9.15 a.m., piloted by Pilot Officer C.J.E. Chamberlain (N6173), returning to Vitry at

11.55. Orders had also been received at 8.30 for an aircraft to take off as soon as possible to take 12 photographs of the bridges and railway crossing across the Maas and the Turnhout Canal. It was away at 9.40. While making their pinpoint runs, they saw large formations of enemy fighters to the south-east and descended to 2,000 feet, turned north, then returned and took the rest of the pictures. They brought them back at 12.40.

F/O H.F. Wood	Sgt Sanderson	AC Findlayson	N6169

At 9.20 there was the second sortie by 53 Squadron which flew out to see what was happening to the enemy advance, returning without opposition at 11.45. This was followed at 10.10 by a third sortie, this time flown to the River Dyk area by Flying Officer Panton, again without hindrance.

F/O I.H. Bartlett	Sgt Aldridge	AC Sheldrick	L4848
F/O A.D. Panton DFC	Sgt Christie	AC Bence	L9459

This same squadron (53) completed the morning's recce sorties with two sorties, one to the Dyle and Dendre areas, the second to the River Dendre and eastwards, flown at 11.05 and 11.35. Both returned without trouble:

P/O P.K. Bone	Sgt W.J. Cronin DFM	LAC J. Bromley	L9399
P/O J.D. Stuart-Richardson	Sgt Cooper	AC Latham	L9330

*

On this morning, Fairey Battles of the Belgian Air Force had attacked the Albert Canal bridges. Nine aircraft, led by Captain Glorie, each with a two-man crew, had taken off from an emergency landing ground between Ghent and Bruges. They had no bomb sights and only carried light 100 lb bombs, virtually useless against concrete bridges. Of these nine only three returned, badly shot up.

Three Battles each attacked the three bridges, Vroenhoven being the target of the section headed by Captain Glorie. Two of the pilots did not drop their bombs during the first run in as they had difficulty with their bomb release gear and the bombs of the third Battle fell into the Canal. The first two Battles, by now riddled by flak fire, came round again but both were shot down. Glorie, however, before being shot down, placed his bombs right on the bridge but they only chipped the concrete from part of the parapet. Some accounts tell of Glorie then trying to crash his Battle T-70 into the bridge but missing. In the crash his observer/air gunner was thrown clear and badly injured.

Afternoon, 10 May
As far as the AASF bomber squadrons had been concerned, none had been sent out during the morning. All had been on stand-by but it wasn't until late morning that enough information was to hand from the reconnaissance aircraft to gain enough of the picture of what was happening in Belgium. Of the five AASF Bomber Wings (71, 72, 74, 75 and 76) most lost their records in the eventual retreat. Only 75 Wing managed to retain something like a full record of events, but we can assume that their orders were very similar to the other Wings.

No. 75 Wing sent out the following order to its 103 and 218 Squadrons at twenty minutes past mid-day:

Despatch two half sections each squadron to attack enemy mechanised column between AZ 42 and Dippach. Town must be avoided. Position and troops as notified but special care to be taken if target not found as indicated. Above sections may attack between AS 55 and AZ 39. Position of our most advanced troops is at a point 3½ miles south of Dippach and another lot at Mont St. Martin, 10 miles SW of Dippach.

A similar type order obviously went from 76 Wing to 142 Squadron, who had the dubious honour of being the first AASF squadron to make an attack on the enemy on this fateful day.

Apparently, Air Marshal Barratt, anticipating the orders but frustrated by the French delay at actually issuing them, sent the bombers off on his own initiative. Barratt said later that the French were extremely glad when he took the plunge for them!

No. 142 Squadron, in whatever form, received their orders late morning, for at exactly mid-day, eight Battles took off from Berry-au-Bac to attack columns of German troops advancing along the Luxembourg to Dippach road. The eight machines, flying in half sections (in pairs) each carried four 250 lb bombs:

F/O A.D.J. Martin	Sgt H.F. Trescothic	Cpl H. Todd	L5517
Sgt Heslop	Sgt Hemmings	LAC Gillam	L5880
P/O W.H. Corbett	Sgt G.B. Irvine	LAC Gaston	P2246
F/O A.D. Gosman	Sgt Pollock	LAC Cave	L5242
F/O M.H. Roth	Sgt W.F. Algie	AC H. Morris	L5231*
P/O F.S. Laws	Sgt R.F. Miller	AC L.M. Langton	L5578*
Sgt A.N. Spear	Sgt S.J. Brooks	LAC R.H. Nugent	L5238*

*The * will denote a missing aircraft on all subsequent lists.*

(The eighth Battle, K9367 flown by Pilot Officer I.C. Chalmers had to abort when he found his wheels would not retract.)

All seven Battles attacked enemy column on the assigned road but came under heavy ground fire. In addition to the three Battles which were shot down, Pilot Officer Walter Corbett was wounded in the ankle and his observer, George Irvine, a Scot, was killed. Corbett later received the DFC.

Leading Aircraftman Cave was slightly wounded in the arm, but he would return to duty before the fall of France. Later Flying Officer Michael Roth and his crew were reported prisoners of war. Frederick Laws and his crew were all killed.

Sergeant Arthur Spear, his Battle crippled by ground fire, force-landed at Colmey, north of Verdun, and he and his crew returned to the squadron the next day. Thus this historic first sortie against the invading German hordes had cost the AASF three out of seven aircraft, seven men killed or missing and two wounded. It was a portent of things to come.

*

At Ecury-sur-Coole, 150 Squadron had had five aircraft at 30 minutes' Readiness since dawn, the rest at two hours' notice. At 9.45 a.m. eight aircraft had been brought to 30 minutes, the other eight at two hours. By 1.10 p.m., the crews of four aircraft had received a preliminary briefing for an attack on a German column located between Echternach and Junglinster in Luxembourg. Meanwhile, they awaited the order to go from 71 Wing HQ.

Meanwhile, other squadrons were preparing for operations. Having received their orders, 103 and 218 Squadrons were airborne at 1.45 and 2.30 p.m. respectively; 103 Squadron sent off two pairs, Blackie Wells and Sergeant Lowne taking off first.

Above Officers of 103 Squadron, 14 April 1940. *Back row* (*l to r*): P/O Hayter (NZ), F/O T.B. Fitzgerald (NZ), F/O MacDonald (IO), F/O M.C. Wells (POW 10 May), P/O E.E. Morton (NZ) (Killed 12 May), P/O K.J. Drabble (Killed 10 May), F/O Ryce Price (Servicing Unit), F/O D.D.A. Kelly; *Middle row*: P/O T. Pugh (SA), P/O V.A. Cunningham (NZ) (Killed 13 May), F/O J.R. Havers, Doc Mahon, P/O Taylor (Equip Off), F/O A.L. Vipan, F/O J.N. Leydon (POW 26 May), F/O G.B. Morgan-Dean (Can) (Killed 12 May), *Front row*: F/O W. Rayne (Adj), F/Lt J.A. Ingram, S/L H.G. Lee AFC, W/C T.C. Dickens, F/Lt C.E.R. Tait, F/Lt Fallowfield (IO). (*via Mrs J. Tait*)

Below Battles of 226 Squadron. (*via R.C. Bowyer*)

F/Lt M.C. Wells	Sgt H.F. Bullock	LAC T.H. Bowen	K9372*
Sgt C.H. Lowne	Sgt C.J.S. Poole	LAC O.A. Hutchinson	K9270*
F/Lt J.A. Ingram and crew			
P/O K.J. Drabble	Sgt V.V. Smith	LAC P.J. Lamble	K9264*

Unfortunately, 218 Squadron was one of those units who lost its May records in the retreat and evacuation. The squadron, however, sent off four Battles in this raid. 103 Squadron also lost its records but the survivors reconstructed what they could remember, after the fall of France.

Blackie Wells led his companion into the attack area, finding the enemy column as briefed. He dived at low level and released his bombs which straddled the road although his gunner, who was spraying the column with machine gun fire, was too occupied to see what damage they had caused. The crew did, however, see the bombs of the second Battle undershoot the target.

They had been met by intense machine gun fire, and Ingram later reported that he thought that low level attacks rendered the aeroplane susceptible to this fire. Two other Battles were seen making low level attacks, three miles east of Dippach at 150 feet. The number two aircraft to Ingram was then seen to be brought down in flames in the vicinity of Petange, while Ingram's own Battle received 20-30 bullet holes in its wings and fuselage, while the port petrol tank was holed and emptied. Blackie Wells:

On the 10th May, the German Blitz started. B Flight were on stand-by, of which I was Acting Flight Commander. AASF Ops ordered two aircraft to take off at 2 p.m. to bomb the spearhead of the German convoy advancing through Luxembourg. We were told of the position of the French Army and told to fly at zero feet over their positions. The intelligence was incorrect. In fact the Germans were in the reputed French positions which we learned to our cost.

They threw everything at us. Sergeant Lowne's Battle got hit badly and burst into flames and crashed. I went on and carried out a low level attack on the main road convoy and straddled the road with four 250 lb bombs. To do this we went through a barrage of incendiary bullets and cannon shells which hit the engine and started a fire, and also burst the coolant tank which covered the cockpit with smoke and steam. As I got high as I could, telling my crew to jump but the inter-comm had gone. I held the aircraft level at 200 feet until my legs started burning and then jumped at about 150 feet. I did one swing in the parachute and landed pretty hard on the ground, adjacent to the burning aircraft.

I did not know whether Sergeant Bullock or Bowen had got out, but I got into a small wood but found I was unable to get out as it was completely surrounded by Germans, who eventually captured me. Tony Ingram and Pilot Officer Drabble took off a few moments later to bomb a similar target in which Drabble got shot down and Ingram got back with his aircraft riddled with machine gun bullets.

I had to wait two years before I managed to meet up with Bullock and Bowen at Stalag Luft 3, to learn they were still alive. They apparently jumped about four miles back and managed to walk for four days before the Germans caught them.

Flight Lieutenant M.C. Wells, 103 Squadron

After Ingram, the sole survivor, landed, he was asked for a full report and gave the following significant observations to Wing HQ.

He mentioned his feelings about the dangers of low level attacks for his impression had been that all the enemy vehicles on the ground were armed. Stationary vehicles had troops dispersed on the north side of the road and in ditches at the side. As he passed over, Ingram had fired at some with his front gun. He felt that a higher approach would eliminate the danger from the intense ground fire that had obviously accounted for all three of the following Battles, although he realised in doing so, they would risk being seen more easily and thus intercepted by roaming enemy fighters.

Of the missing aircraft, Wells and his crew were prisoners, Sergeant Lowne too was a prisoner, his crew dead, while Drabble and Lamble had been killed.

Meanwhile, the four 218 Squadron aircraft also found the enemy. The first section attacked stationary vehicles on the Dippach-Luxembourg road, carrying out a low level raid under heavy ground fire. One air gunner was killed and both Battles were severely damaged. The second section also attacked a stationary column of vehicles on the road, one mile east of Dippach and scored three direct hits. Again both aircraft of this section were damaged.

When the leader of this attack landed and reported on the raid, he, in contrast to Ingram, felt that a low level attack with a sharp turn to the starboard, followed by a low level getaway was much preferable to a higher approach followed by a shallow dive.

After these first attacks, further strikes came quickly. First, however, we shall record events in England following the return of 40 Squadron's sighting of enemy aircraft around the Hague earlier that morning.

What Brian Paddon had observed was an airborne assault on the two main airfields of the Hague where Ju52 transport aircraft had landed crack troops. BAFF (British Air Forces in France) requested Bomber Command at 12.05 p.m. to attack Waalhaven with a squadron of Blenheims. This was instead of an attack on advancing enemy columns whose exact whereabouts, in any event, were not wholly known. The Blenheims of 15 (XV) Squadron, at Wyton, were assigned the task.

However, a strike had already been prepared, not by bombers but by fighter Blenheims of 600 Squadron at RAF Manston. Six aircraft were sent as a result of a Cabinet ruling that fighters, rather than bombers, be employed in order to avoid possible casualties to Dutch soldiers or civilians! They took off at 12.30:

S/L J.M. Wells	Cpl B.A. Kidd	'R'* plus Sgt Davis, Obs
F/O J.H.C.Rowe	P/O R.W.H. Echlin	'K'*
F/O T.N. Hayes	Cpl G.H. Holmes	'O'
F/O C.R. Moore	Cpl L.D. Isaacs	'W'*
P/O M.H. Anderson	LAC H.C.W. Hawkins	'L'*
P/O R.C. Haine	P/O M. Kramer	'N'*

It was a disastrous raid. During the attack on the Ju52s on the ground, the Blenheims were set upon by a dozen Me110s and five were shot down. The Blenheim 1Fs had all been fitted with IFF (Identification Friend or Foe) but without self destructors, and some concern was felt about the possibility of the apparatus falling into German hands. The missing Blenheims were numbered L1335, L1401, L1514, L1515 and L1517, the latter crash-landing on the beach at Scheveningen.

The only 600 Squadron crew to return was Flying Officer Norman Hayes and Corporal G.H. Holmes. They had destroyed one Ju52 on the ground before the 110s attacked. As Hayes avoided the 110s, Corporal Holmes told his pilot how to avoid their attackers and finally they escaped. Later they saw a Ju52 in the air, and although their own Blenheim had been damaged by the Messerschmitts, Holmes attacked and the Junkers went down with one engine on fire. He then went on to attack three Heinkel 111s, breaking up their formation. Later both men were decorated with the DFC and DFM.

Pilot Officer Dickie Haine made a forced landing in Holland and then he and his gunner returned to England in a destroyer evacuating the Dutch Royal family. Both flyers received DFCs. Of the others, James Wells and his air gunner Corporal Kidd had been killed, and also dead were Charles Moore, Mike Anderson with their respective rear men, plus Pilot Officer Echlin; Flying Officer Rowe seems to have survived, as did Sergeant Davis.

Finally at 2.15 p.m., the nine 15 Squadron Blenheims, led by Squadron Leader Hector Lawrence, set off to attack Waalhaven aerodrome, south of Rotterdam:

S/L H.Y. Lawrence	Sgt R.G. Hopkins	LAC E.L.H. Thomas	L8849
F/Lt P.G. Chapman	Sgt W.J. Stephens	Cpl J. Sutcliffe	P6912
Sgt H.R. Hall	Sgt E.R. Perron	LAC E.J. Fagg	P6917
F/O A.E. Oakley	Sgt D.J. Avent	LAC D.V. Woods	L9030
F/O F.D. Dawson-Jones	Sgt A.J. Box	LAC C.E. Watts	L8852
F/O P.F. Webster	Sgt R.A.M. Stone	LAC R.E. Hunter	L8853
F/O P.F. Eames	Sgt Phillips	LAC Austin	L8850
Sgt F.R. Pepper	Sgt R. Booth	LAC J. Scott	N6151
F/O L.H. Trent	Sgt Prior	?	L8855

They found the aerodrome littered with tri-motored Ju52s as they swept in at 3,000 feet in shallow diving attacks. Hits were claimed on a dozen or more transport aircraft, seven of which were left blazing, hangars and AA guns that the Germans had already deployed. Several of the Blenheims were hit by return fire but all returned.

Len Trent headed down and through the flak, collecting holes in his wings as he did so. As he and the others got right down on the deck and began heading away, Trent saw six

Above 15 Squadron before the Blitz. *Back row (l to r)*: W/O-?, P/O W.H. George, F/O R.F. Eames, F/O R.B.G.E. Clark, (Killed 11 June), P/O T.G. Bassett (NZ) (KIA 12 May), F/O L.H. Trent (NZ), P/O C.R. Frankish (KIA 12 May), F/Sgt Nightingale and F/Sgt MacDonald, both groundcrew; *Front row*: F/O P.N. Douglas (KIA 12 May), F/O A.R. Oakshott, F/Lt P.G. Chapman (KIA 18 May), S/L J.G. Llewelyn (KIA as CO 40 Sqdn, 23 May), W/C J.L. Wingate, F/O P.F. Webster, F/O F.D. Douglas-Jones (KIA 18 May), F/O A.E. Oakley (KIA 12 May), P/O C.H. Robinson. (*W.H. George*)

Below Officers of 59 Squadron outside their mess at Château Courcelles, May 1940. *Front row*: F/Lt G.V. Smither, F/O M.J. Muspratt-Williams, S/L J.B. Fyfe DFC, F/O G.D. Arscott, F/O A.J. Handley, F/O H.F. Wood, F/O J.C. Millar, F/Lt A.C.G. Wimbush, F/O F.D. Bird (KIA 22 May); *Middle row*: F/O J.W. Hicks (Adj), F/Lt N.B. Hallmark, P/O C.J. Hitch (WIA 13 May), S. Morin (Interpreter); *Back row (l to r)*: P/O R.N. Chudleigh, F/O D.G. Smith (Doc), F/O G.H.D. Evans, F/O J.E. Horton (Eng Off), P/O E.F. Pippet, P/O C.J.C. Chamberlain (NZ) (WIA 13 May), P/O M.I. Murdoch (KIA 15 May). (*G.H.D. Evans*)

Me109s fly overhead, but either they didn't see the Blenheims, or they had other business to attend to. As if all this was not enough, a seagull later hit the front of Trent's Blenheim, smashing through the bombing window, covering Sergeant Prior in blood and feathers, and sending a howling gale back through the aeroplane.

Later, at 3.45, 12 Blenheims of 40 Squadron attacked the aerodrome of Ypenburg (requested by BAFF at 2.25). At 3.30 the Air Attaché at the Hague had signalled Air Ministry that the Dutch had recaptured Ypenburg but this news was not received in time to prevent the squadron from taking off, nor is it certain that the Air Attaché's information was correct.

Again they used a shallow dive attack, going in in four sections of three aircraft. A hangar was left blazing but three Blenheims were shot down:

S/L G.W.C. Gleed	Sgt Burge	LAC A.F.W. Sammells	P4927
F/O R.H. Jacoby	Sgt M.R. Chouler	AC Rodgers	L8824
Sgt D.J. Rice	Sgt R.C. Moffat	LAC D.E. Peters	P4917
F/Lt R.H. Batt	Sgt B.L. Harris	P/O Ewels	L8757
F/O G.D. Hill	Sgt Jeffery	AC A.F.H. Barber	L8836
F/O C.W. Bromley	Sgt Bloodworth	AC F.H. Jones	P4918
F/Lt H.L. Smeddle	Sgt B.C. Wooldridge	LAC G.D.P. Quinn	L8827
F/O P.J.H. Rowan	Sgt G. Beardwood	Cpl T.F.S. Clark	L8828*
Sgt I.L. Thomas	Sgt V. Spurr	LAC H. Bridson	L8831*
F/O J.C. Stevenson	Sgt Usher	LAC J. Cooney	P4908
P/O P.F.T. Wakeford	Sgt Ashplant	AC Baker	N6236
Sgt A.J. Robertson	Sgt F. Checkley	AC J.A. Webster	P6901*

Leading the third section, Flight Lieutenant Smeddle ran into a large number of Me110 fighters two miles from Ypenburg. His two wingmen were shot down and Hugh Smeddle and his observer were wounded when a cannon shell exploded in the cockpit. Shortly afterwards another exploding cannon shell wounded his gunner and knocked out the radio. His machine was damaged and its compass knocked out but he got home and was later awarded the DFC. Of the missing, only Aircraftman Webster survived, as a prisoner of war.

The last raid came at 4.50 p.m. by 12 Blenheims of 110 Squadron at RAF Wattisham, led by Squadron Leader John Sabine, which attacked German transport aircraft at Waalhaven and on the beach eight miles north of the Hague.

S/L J.S. Sabine	Sgt W. Evans	Sgt J.V. West	P4858
P/O G.R. Worboys	Sgt Cooke	LAC V.J. Swallow	L9217

Sgt A.R. Storrow	Sgt E.C. Parker	LAC Underwood	L8780
P/O P.V. Arderne	Sgt G. Robson	LAC J. Tippett	L9241
P/O E.R. Mullins	Sgt R. Lowe	AC P. Aherne	L9214
Sgt T.C. Prescott	Sgt Hodder	LAC W.W. Street	L6754
S/L G.F. Hall	Sgt K.F. Quarrington	Cpl T. Hoggard	L8749
F/O G.R. Gratton	Sgt Patterson	LAC F.J. Allam	L9175
Sgt H. Gandy	Sgt Robson	LAC B. Gray	P4860
F/O J.K. Buchanan	Sgt Lumsden	LAC Dunn	N6210
F/O P.H.A. Simmons	Sgt Friendly	LAC J. Smith	N6207
Sgt F. Lewis	Sgt H. Rhodes	LAC E.N. Edwards	P6889

The first six bombers went in at low level and attacked five Ju52s, then the second six attacked. One Ju52 was seen to be lifted right off the ground by an explosion. Six Blenheim fighters of 600 Squadron took off and flew a patrol off the Belgian coast between Zeebrugge and Flushing, but did not cross the coast.

*

While these raids on the German transport aircraft had been taking place, the AASF Battle squadrons had been active. At 3 p.m., 105 Squadron had sent out two half sections to attack German troops moving across Luxembourg on the Echternach–Luxembourg road. The four crews were:

F/O R.N. Wall	Sgt Woodhouse	Cpl Greenwood	P2190
Sgt Richardson	Sgt Donlon	LAC R.W. McCarthy	K9188
P/O D.G. O'Brien	Sgt D.F. Eastick	AC S.R. Wright	P2200*
Sgt Bowles	Sgt Radford	LAC Clegg	K9338

They found and attacked an enemy column but met intense AA and small arms fire. Apart from the Battle which failed to return, all three survivors were so badly shot about that they were beyond the ability of the squadron to repair. Two of the gunners, LACs Clegg and Robert McCarthy were wounded. McCarthy was badly wounded in both legs and in the stomach but continued to use his radio on the flight back. When his pilot landed back at Villeneuve-les-Vertus, he was extricated from his rear cockpit by the squadron MO, Flight Lieutenant J.E. Furness, whose prompt action and medical skill saved the gunner's life. McCarthy's courage was acknowledged with the award of the DFM.

Daniel O'Brien and his crew were all taken prisoner; both the crewmen had also been wounded.

The crews of 150 Squadron had been awaiting orders since dawn but it was not until 3.15 that 71 Wing HQ gave them a target. This was a German column between Echternach and Junglinster in Luxembourg. Four Battles were assigned:

F/Lt E. Parker	Sgt J. Whalley	A/Cpl R.K. Rye	K9390*
F/O A.C. Roberts	Sgt E.H. Ward	AC1 D. Mayrick	L5540*
F/O W.M. Blom	Sgt E.D. Martin	AC C. Cooper	K9369
Sgt R.A. deC. White	Sgt C.W.K. Booth	LAC R.H. Burrows	L5539*

They failed to find any sign of the reported column but did spot a column on the Luxembourg-Gevenmacher road, five miles to the west of Gevenmacher. They attacked with their 250 lb bombs and the gunners and observers also strafed the road as they flew along it at 100 feet. Flying Officer Blom's Battle was hit by ground fire and the port petrol tank holed, sending spray and fumes into the cockpit. This made it difficult for Blom to fly the aeroplane and his vision was impaired. He got it back, however, and landed safely despite having both tyres punctured. Walter Michael Blom, who was an Australian, was later awarded the DFC while both his crewmen received DFMs.

Ray White and his crew crash-landed and returned to the squadron on the 13th. Eric Parker crashed at Gosselies, near Charleroi, but was killed. His crew were taken prisoner, Corporal Rye also being wounded. Flying Officer Roberts belly-landed his crippled bomber with a wounded gunner on board, and all three men were taken into captivity.

Shortly after 3.30 p.m., 57 Squadron sent off a Blenheim to fly a recce op to Hertogenbosch:

F/Lt G.M. Wyatt DFC	Sgt W.J. Gardiner	Cpl F.T. Russell	L9246

They too met heavy ground fire near the Dutch/German border at 4.30 which hit the Blenheim and wounded Geoff Wyatt in the arm, and also wounded his observer. They later had to force-land near Brussels at 5.55. Geoff Wyatt:

Came the 10th May and a general air of flap and crisis, one Heinkel being shot down nearby. I was briefed to go off at low level up to Nijmegen to see how far the Germans had penetrated Holland. We cracked off (same old crew) across Belgium, seeing smoke from various places, but no actual air or ground activity. Into Holland, past Hertegonbosch, nothing much to see on the ground, when there was a bit of a bang, and a tug at my right arm. Wearing white overalls, I saw that the sleeve was becoming bloodstained, and things started to hurt a bit.

I decided this was no time for heroics, shoved the throttles 'through the gate' (9-lbs boost) and beat it on a reciprocal course. Bill Gardiner then did a job of cutting off overall and tunic sleeves, and tying on tight a 'First Field Dressing' stopping the flow.

Russell pushed out a signal to base explaining the situation and we made it (left handed) to Rosières – no unusual aircraft activity – Gardiner working some of the taps for landing. There was a hole in the front perpsex, a hole in my shoulder, and a hole in the top canopy, all in a line. What we'd been hit by I never knew – probably light ground stuff, as I couldn't see any other aircraft around.

The following few days were confused and uncomfortable; surgery in a Casualty Clearing Station, a very tiring period in a hospital train halted because of bombing (so we were told), two or three days in a base hospital at Dieppe, and eventual evacuation by hospital ship (SS *Worthing*) to Newhaven. As I say, all very confused and tiring, but I remember one splendid incident. Before we were carried off at Newhaven, the first visitor below decks was a Customs Officer. 'Anything to declare?' A ragged cheer went up from the wounded heroes: all hell was breaking loose behind us, but British formalities had to be observed. We were home!

Resting place for the next month or so was a large, former mental hospital at Botley's Park, Chertsey. I don't know where the previous occupants had gone, but somebody had preserved a sense of humour. The officers' ward still carried its former designation – MLG, which stood for Male Low Grade! We did our best to live up to it.

As some of the earliest casualties at Botley's Park, we were suitably 'visitable', and I remember one well-meaner remarking (again shades of the First War) that she expected that I couldn't wait to get back into the fray. Her face fell, however, when I replied that I was very grateful to be out of it for a while!

Flight Lieutenant G.M. Wyatt, 57 Squadron

Two other recce missions by 57 Squadron on the afternoon of the 10th, resulted in another loss:

| P/O Hayter | Sgt Midgely | AC Davies | |
| P/O A. Thomas | Sgt P.L. Thomas | AC1 L.F. Jordan | L9245* |

Hayter's had been a photo op to Vilno-Wesel-Hamburg-Cologne, landing back at Villeneuve. Alan Thomas was sent out over the battle zone in Belgium and did not return.

More recce sorties were called for. 18 Squadron sent out a crew at 4 p.m. to have a look at the Albert Canal at low level. They did not return and later a report came in that they had force-landed at Phaton, in Belgium. The next day a telephone message was received that they had force-landed due to lack of petrol but that the Blenheim was then destroyed by a bomb while on the ground.

| P/O L.T. Dixon | Sgt Peach | LAC Townley | L8860 |

Two 53 Squadron Blenheims went out in the late afternoon, both flying to the east of the River Dyle, and both returned, meeting no opposition.

| F/O A.D. Panton | Sgt Christie | AC Bence | L9459 |
| P/O J.D. Stuart-Richardson | Sgt McRae | AC Latham | L9330 |

Finally, at 4.25, 12 Squadron got its orders to fly. They too were to send four Battles out to attack the strong column on the Luxembourg–Junglister road. They took off in two sections around 5 p.m.:

F/Lt W. Simpson	Sgt E.N. Odell	LAC R.T. Tomlinson	L4949*
P/O A.W. Matthews	Sgt A.A. Maderson	LAC J.C. Senior	L5190*
F/Lt P.H.M.S. Hunt	Sgt P.E. Wilks	LAC H. Cooke	P2243*
P/O C.L. Hulse	Sgt A. Young	LAC J. Aitken	L5249

Although Bill Simpson was the commander of B Flight, it was Peter Hunt and his No. 2 who took off first, followed by Simpson and Al Matthews, a Canadian, fifteen minutes later. Before reaching the target, Hunt's Battle was hit and damaged by ground fire which shot away the bomb release cable. He force-landed at Piennes but later returned to the squadron. Pilot Officer Hulse went on and attacked the target at low level despite intense ground fire which wounded his observer in the shoulder. However, at least one of his bombs landed on the road on which armoured fighting vehicles (AFVs) were travelling.

Simpson and Matthews had decided to head in at low level in order to escape detection by advance German ground observers and hostile fighters. As they hedge-hopped along they spotted some small parties of motor cyclists, probably advanced scouting parties from the column they were searching for. These began firing at the Battles, Simpson replying with his front gun. Flying down a wooded valley and then coming over the rise at the far end, they caught sight of their target.

There was a moon-shaped clearing in a large wood, through which ran the road out of Germany towards Luxembourg. On the road the enemy column had halted, a whole mixture of vehicles. With bomb doors open, Simpson turned into the attack, but not before he saw Al Matthews' Battle diving down behind some trees, trailing white smoke from the engine. (He and his crew were all taken prisoner.) Matthews had been hit a glancing blow across the forehead by a shell fragment which knocked him out. Another fragment smashed the observer's elbow. The Battle, already low down, simply bellied in and slithered to a stop. Jack Senior, the gunner, was not injured. All three survived the crash landing, and from the wrecked machine, Jack Senior proceeded to shoot up the nearby German road convoy, until he was hit by an armour-piercing bullet. The three wounded airmen were then taken prisoner, the Germans treating Senior as something of a hero!

Simpson, meantime, had attacked, opening up with his gun as he did so. He released his bombs from around 30 feet, while Tomlinson was standing up in his rear cockpit, taking photographs. Then they were hit.

The cockpit filled with petrol fumes and escaping glycol sprayed onto Simpson, then he felt a thud. Flames began pouring from great jagged holes on the left side of the engine cowling while lumps of molten metal flashed past his head (he had opened the cockpit to let the fumes out). His engine still functioned and he maintained a height of around 100 feet, looking for a place to set down. Luckily he spotted a clearing on a hilltop and made a successful belly-landing on a sandy track that ran across it. As the Battle came to a halt, the flames licked back and ignited the fuel and fumes in the front cockpit in which sat Bill Simpson.

He was suddenly engulfed in flames which roared up between his legs, shooting to around 30 feet above his head. His hands, desperately trying to release his seat harness, burned and seized up, while his legs and face also caught the force of the searing heat. Unable to release himself, he waited for death, feeling his flesh burning his mind in mental torment as not for a second did he lose consciousness.

It had only taken seconds, although it seemed like hours, but then just as suddenly, Odell and Tomlinson were releasing his harness despite the red hot metal of the release catch. He heard Odell's gasp of horror as he saw the state of his pilot, then he was out and being rolled on the grass to put out the flames. They got him away from the burning Battle, as flares and ammunition began exploding, then the fuel tanks blew up.

For Bill Simpson, whose burns were among the worst any airman was to suffer, it was the start of a long period of recovery, beginning with long sojourns in French hospitals. He was eventually repatriated to England via Spain in 1941. He was awarded the DFC and Edward Odell and Robert Tomlinson received DFMs. Odell went immediately back to the squadron, but Tomlinson spent some time in hospital with burnt hands. Unfortunately he was to die in a flying accident in February 1941.

Bill Simpson related his experiences in three books; the first, *One of our Pilots is Safe*, was published in 1943. In 12 Squadron, his B Flight was taken over by Flying Officer Don Garland.

*

The last Battle sorties of the day were flown by 226 Squadron, that sent out four aircraft shortly after 5 p.m.:

F/Lt B.R. Kerridge	Sgt D.I. Anthony	Cpl G.H. Nixon	K9183*
F/O D.A. Cameron	Sgt C.S. Hart	AC G.G. Ward	L5247*
Sgt G.McLoughlin	Sgt E. Marrows	AC Russell	K9330
Sgt H.J. Barron	Sgt D.E. Bingham	Cpl L. Smith	P2180

Finding a German column of 30 to 40 vehicles south-west of Luxembourg, the Battle pilots made a dive bombing attack at 6.20. Brian Kerridge and his No. 2, Sergeant Barron, bombed in the face of intense ground fire. Hubert James Barron was hit and wounded in the left leg when a bullet passed right through it, but he managed to fly back despite his injury. As they pulled away from the attack, Barron saw Kerridge's Battle crash in flames.

The other section was also in the midst of the ground fire and again it was the leader that was shot down. However, McLoughlin survived, and his gunner blazed away with his gun as they flew over the road. Sergeant Barron was awarded the DFM later in the month.

Flying Officer Douglas Cameron died of wounds two days later, his crew being taken prisoner, Ward being wounded in the wrist. Kerridge too was killed and his crew also went 'into the bag'.

*

This ended the afternoon's bombing effort by the AASF Battle squadrons. Of the 32 sorties despatched, 13 had failed to get back, while another had force-landed, and virtually all those that had returned were damaged. It was a severe price to pay for the day's operations in the area of the Dippach–Luxembourg road, results of which were uncertain. AASF were later to list a total of 21 Battles lost on this first day, presumably adding the few destroyed in the dawn bombing raids plus damaged aircraft which were later written off owing to their battle damage (as well as a later bomb raid on 88 Squadron).

Four Air Component reconnaissance Blenheims had been lost, and Bomber Command's 2 Group had lost one Blenheim on a recce mission and three on a bombing raid: a total of 29 aircraft lost or written off, not to mention five AASF and Component Hurricanes lost, plus 600 Squadron's fighter Blenheims.

At RAF Watton, 21 Squadron had been at Readiness all day, but had not been called upon. Finally at 6.10 p.m., two aircraft were sent out on a recce mission over German roads along their invasion routes. Flight Lieutenant A.D. Watson (L8739) and Pilot Officer R.G.M. Gilmore (L8742) both returned safely at 8.15.

At 6.40 p.m., 88 Squadron's base at Mourmelon was hit again. This time four Ju88s dive-bombed the field from 6,000 feet. The armoury was left ablaze, and three Battles and a training aircraft were set on fire.

The day's final sortie was yet another recce by 59 Squadron. Flying Officer Bird flew to Vitry (in N6164) to stand by for a night mission, which was called for at 10.50. He returned at 1.55 on the morning of the 11th, then flew back to Poix. His flight ended the first day of real war on the Western Front and heralded the new day. What would the next days bring for the Battle and Blenheim pilots in France? Could it be worse than the first day?

CHAPTER SIX

The Second Day

Saturday Morning, 11 May

The second day of the German invasion of the Low Countries found them over-running indefensible frontier provinces of the north-east of Holland. They had now passed Apeldoorn and Arnhem while heading for Utrecht. Further to the west, the paratroops had more than consolidated their grip of the Rotterdam area.

In Belgium, the British and French forces had started to reach their Dyle positions although reports coming in suggested that the Belgian troops ahead of them were failing to stem the enemy's advance. Having burst through the obstacles of the Meuse and Albert Canal, near Maastricht, by 1.45 p.m. the Germans were in the position of Tongres. This forced the Belgians to fall back to make a new stand at the River Gette so as to still protect the Allied advance to the River Dyle.

South of this was rapidly developing a new threat, a thrust from the direction of Maastricht through the Belgian Ardennes. It had always been thought that this heavily forested area would be impenetrable for tanks and mechanised infantry. The Germans were about to disprove another theory.

Quite suddenly, the screening elements opposite the Ardennes, consisting of the French 9th and 2nd Armies, encountered advancing German forces of a strength that constituted a major threat.

The AASF bomber squadrons stood by, but information about where the enemy was was again the first priority. 18 Squadron sent out a Blenheim at 3.35 a.m. – to make a low level reconnaissance along the Albert Canal. This was quickly followed by a second aircraft at 4 a.m.:

| Sgt E.E.B. LeVoi | Sgt J. Sands | LAC R.D. Davies | L9255* |
| P/O M.P.C. Holmes | Sgt F. Miller DFM | LAC B.M. Harding | R3590* |

Nothing more was heard from Sergeant LeVoi although later he and his observer were reported prisoners.. Melville Percival Conrad Holmes also flew to the Albert Canal and found that the Germans had indeed succeeded in crossing this waterway. He also found they were awake. Gunfire greeted them and their Blenheim which was hit several times but they got themselves clear and made for home. As they flew away they were hit again, this time in the port engine which was put out of action, and Holmes was temporarily blinded in the left eye. Reaching French territory he found his wheels would not come down so he was forced to belly-land near Châlons – at Vaucogne, ably assisted by his observer.

Squadron Leader J.A. Roncoroni of 57 Squadron also flew out at just after 4 p.m. but he returned without hindrance.

The Battle squadrons had come to Readiness well before first light, but just as the previous day, all they could do was to wait. Not so the Luftwaffe, who once again hit the Allied air bases at dawn.

At 4.30, 88 Squadron was bombed, although there is no record of any damage. Not so at Condé, the home of 114 Squadron. The squadron had left for Perpignan on 26 April, beginning their return on 9 May. They were actually arriving back on the 10th when the Germans opened their offensive. They were left alone on the first day, but the Germans struck at 5.45 a.m. on the 11th.

It was just light when nine Dornier 17Z bombers of 4/KG2 carried out a low level attack on the aerodrome. Five minutes earlier a high flying German aircraft had been spotted, and later everyone thought it might have been a decoy, for it was then seen heading south-west being chased by a fighter. Then the Dorniers struck, but the ground defences were awake.

They had flown up the Marne River, roaring over Juvigny at low level, then passed above Vraux to make a right hand turn before coming in over B Flight's dispersal area. One of the first sticks of bombs set fire to A Flight's petrol dump which was to burn for some hours, and two nearby Blenheims.

More bombs rained down, estimated in total to about 150 of 50 kg size. Five Blenheims were destroyed and another so badly damaged it was a write-off. Having dropped their bombs the Dorniers then swept across the airfield to strafe the other aeroplanes, also hitting the Flight Office, transport and shelter trenches. One German aircraft was seen flying repeatedly to and fro during the raid, obviously coordinating the attack. It was fortunate that there were only two casualties, ground defence personnel wounded by bullets but not fatally.

The ground defence gunners put up a terrific show and several Dorniers were hit and seen to stagger away obviously in trouble. In fact, when the AOC visited the squadron on the 14th, he told the commanding officer that the gunners had probably brought down eight of the raiders. These aircraft, riddled with bullets, had been found in the vicinity and as they were unclaimed by either fighters or anti-aircraft batteries, it had to be assumed they had been hit by Condé's defences. In fact 4/KG2 suffered no fatal casualties in the raid, although at least one bomber was later damaged by ground fire on the trip home.

Two of the gallant defence gunners were later awarded Military Medals, Aircraftman Second Class F.S.G. Upton and AC1 G.G. Bonham. They had manned a gun pit that morning and despite the exploding bombs and the sweeping machine gun fire, they had maintained a continuous return fire, hitting a number of the bombers. Finally a stick of bombs fell across the area of their pit which blew the gun from its mounting. Both airmen remounted the gun and continued to engage the enemy. As well as the danger from bombs and bullets, two of the squadron's aircraft standing just 150 yards from them, blew up, showering the area with debris.

Two other members of the ground echelon were also decorated for heroism: Pilot Officer William John Hadnett and Sergeant D.R. Levinson who both received the Empire Gallantry Medal (EGM). After the bombers had gone it was quickly discovered that more than 30 unexploded bombs littered the airfield. With some courage, these two men carried out the dismantling and demolition of these bombs. They were all electrically fused and the internal mechanism and booby-traps were unknown to them. It naturally took some time to render all the UXBs safe, and the dangers were emphasised when some of the bombs were still 'live' up to a week later.

The squadron, however, was in a sorry state. All the

Blenheims were out of action, six having been totally destroyed and all the others damaged to some degree. The ground crews quickly set to work on those that were repairable, and later that morning the squadron heard that three replacement aircraft were available at the AASF stores park. Two of these were collected by mid-afternoon.

At Ecury, 150 Squadron was on the receiving end of German bombers, when at 6.10 a.m. an estimated 18 to 24 bombers hit the field from 12,000 to 15,000 feet. Again about 150 bombs fell, dropped across the south-eastern end of the base. Part of an adjacent wood, the armoury tent and pyrotechnic store was set on fire and destroyed. Battle P2334 was also set on fire and then destroyed as two of its four 250 lb bombs exploded. Battle P2335 was also damaged. There were 18 bomb craters on the aerodrome itself and five UXBs at the northern edge.

Sergeant W.H. Franklin, who, it will be recalled, helped get bombs away from a burning Battle back on 22 April, was again in evidence on this morning. When Battle P2334 exploded with two of its bombs, there were still two 250-pounders amid the flames and debris. With other Battles standing nearby, there was an obvious danger that if the bombs went off, other aircraft could be damaged. Sergeant Franklin, assisted by Flight Sergeant J.L. Price, a fitter/armourer, removed the detonators from the two bombs rendering them safe. Franklin was awarded the EGM.

*

The day's bombing effort that morning began when two half sections from both 88 and 218 Squadrons were ordered to attack German columns. 218 were away at 9.30, 88 at 9.45. 218's four crews were:

F/O A.J. Hudson	Sgt N.H. Thompson	AC1 A. Ellis	K9325*
P/O H.M. Murray	Sgt P. Stubbs	AC2 I.G. Adams	P2249*
F/O C.A.R. Crews	F/Sgt T.S. Evans	Sgt Jennings	P2326*
Sgt C.J.E. Dockrill	Sgt P.F. Dormer	AC1 K.G. Gregory	P2203*

88 Squadron:

F/Lt A.J. Madge	Sgt E.J.M. Whittle	Cpl A.C. Collyer	P2251*
P/O A.W. Mungoven	Sgt R.A.P. Kirby	AC E.W. Maltby	P2202*
P/O B.I.M. Skidmore	Sgt F. Robson	AC1 W.L. Parsons	P2261*
P/O N.C.S. Riddell	?	?	?

Top Flight Lieutenant C.A.R. Crews and Flight Lieutenant J. McM. Hughes of 218 Squadron. Both received the DFC in France; Charles Crews was taken prisoner on 11 May, John Hughes was killed on active service later in the year. (*via Mrs G. Crews*)

Above Air Marshal Arthur Barratt, AOC-in-C of the BAFF in France, and Air Vice Marshal Philip Playfair, AOC of the AASF.

Below Blenheim IV of 59 Squadron. (*MoD*)

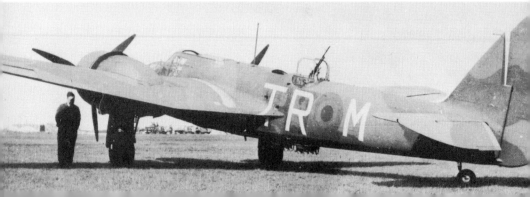

Only Pilot Officer Norman Riddell (and presumably his crew) returned, but by road as he had been forced to land at Vassincourt (the base of No. 1 Squadron) with his aircraft badly damaged. He saw Flight Lieutenant Madge land in a field between Bastogne and Neufchatel with wheels up. Riddell then took over the leadership of the formation but later lost the other two Battles near St Vith when they came under heavy ground fire. After all this, he was unable to release his bombs as his bomb gear had been damaged. On his way back he was followed by a Me109 which made no attempt to attack.

Riddell later reported that the Battles were coming under ground fire for some time despite every effort to avoid what to them, appeared to be the main ground opposition. The fire that seemed to do the damage came from two columns whose vehicles had stopped and mounted machine-guns on tripods. It also appeared that the Germans had hastily erected gun positions at all strategic points, covered with corrugated iron sheets, from which machine guns pointed. Just before his Battle was hit, Riddell saw one of the other two machines fly forward and make a steep turn right in front of him. He managed to avoid it but did not see the other Battle again.

When he was hit, his observer reported petrol in the cockpit so he quickly decided to return, and attack a concentration of vehicles he had earlier spotted in a gorge. He relocated these and made an attack but then found his bomb release gear damaged, but his gunner fired at them as they flew by.

Later, Pilot Officer Riddell gave some useful comments to 75 Wing HQ. He remarked that it was very difficult to navigate while flying at low level in the hilly countryside of the Luxembourg frontier, and he had had to make a number of very steep turns to avoid the brows of hills. He found that a formation of three was cumbersome and thought himself, that he'd prefer to carry out missions of this sort on his own.

Flight Lieutenant Madge and his gunner became prisoners, Sergeant Whittle was killed. Skidmore and his crew all died, while Mungovan and his gunner were also captured, the observer being killed.

None of the four 218 Squadron aircraft returned. Hudson and Murray, with their crews were taken prisoner. Charles Crews and his observer were also captured but his gunner was killed. Sergeant Dockrill and his crew all died.

Charles Crews and his observer had a miraculous escape. Leading his half section towards a bridge two miles north of St Vith, the two Battles headed over the wooded areas of the Ardennes, which to Allied planners had seemed too impenetrable for the Germans even to contemplate an advance through. They they began to meet German road convoys and came under heavy ground fire.

Almost at once, Crews had his instrument panel shattered in front of him by machine gun fire but pressed on towards his target. Yet at low level they were hit by all manner of ground fire which peppered the Battles. Crews ordered his No. 2 to turn for the run in to the bridge but, as he did so, his Battle was again hit badly. Flames and hot glycol came from a hole in the engine cowling while burning petrol poured along the floor of the cockpit under his seat. Crews was choking with smoke and heat from the flames which threatened to stifle him.

Below him stretched trees in all directions, no place even to contemplate a crash landing. But being so low, to bale out seemed equally impossible. But with the heat and flames, the latter choice was the only one. They were well below 100 feet now, but he ordered his crew to get out while he tried desperately to gain every inch of height. Holding the stick between his knees, he pulled back the cockpit canopy as his engine began to die. Close to the stall, but having gained a little height, Charles Crews stood up, his hand still pulling back on the control column – then it was time to go. The Battle was as high as it was going to get.

No sooner had he jumped and pulled the rip-cord than he was amongst the tree tops, his face scratched by pine needles. The parachute caught in the branches and he was jerked to a stop, dangling from the pine tree, virtually unhurt but alive. Evans too, was hanging in a tree nearby, equally alive. The two men just stared at each other, not believing they had survived. It was then they saw Jennings. He was only about 30 feet from them. His parachute had streamed but not deployed and with no saving tree beneath him, he had been killed instantly as he hit the ground.

Crews and Evans made an attempt to get back but were captured. However, Charles Crews was determined to get home and finally, after three unsuccessful escape attempts, managed to feign illness sufficiently well for the Germans to put him on a repatriation list, returning him home in September 1944. His wife, meantime, was working for a Prisoner of War aid organisation, and received a number of letters from her husband, carefully coded and full of valuable information. He later became a wing commander but died at the early age of 47.

*

Following their two losses in the early hours of the morning, 18 Squadron were requested to try again at ten o'clock, to make a recce of the Albert Canal. One crew, captained by a Canadian, Roger Whelan (a future Air Commodore CBE DSO DFC), did so but were hit by flak which damaged tail and the elevator controls, forcing them to land at Vitry:

P/O J.R. Whelan	Sgt Moncey	LAC Brown	L9192

No. 53 Squadron were also flying recce missions, again over the River Dyle area, keeping a watch on the advancing Germans and the retreating Belgians.

Afternoon, 11 May

It was obvious by this time that although difficult to secure an exact picture of the situation west of Maastricht, there was undoubtedly a serious threat and air support was urgently required. By 2.30 that afternoon, French aircraft of the 1st Army reported continuous traffic streaming from the town over an undemolished bridge at Tongres.

BAFF had already asked for a strike of Bomber Command, and 21 and 110 Squadrons, on stand-by, had been alerted and briefed. At ten minutes to three, 110 Squadron's Blenheims began to take off:

F/O P.H.A. Simmons	Sgt Friendly	LAC J. Smith	L8756
P/O G.H. Pemberton	Sgt K.F. Quarrington	LAC Dunn	N6210
Sgt Miller	Sgt Duffy	AC Greenwood	P4860
F/O G.R. Gratton	Sgt T. Patterson	LAC F.J. Allam	L9175*
F/O G.O. Lings	Sgt Martin	AC J. Bingham	N6207
P/O S.G. Rose	Sgt D.A. Ashton	LAC E.N. Edwards	P6889[1]
F/Lt H.D.H. Cooper	Sgt J.S. Robertson	LAC Simpson	L9217

[1] failed to take off due to engine trouble.

P/O E.R. Mullins	Sgt R. Lowe	AC P. Aherne	L9214
Sgt G.C. Bennett	Sgt A. Colling	AC E. Hannah	N6208*
P/O P.V. Arderne	Sgt G. Robson	LAC J. Tippett	L9241
P/O G.R. Worboys	Sgt Muirhead	LAC K. Cooper	L8751
Sgt G.W. Forster	Sgt Gainsford	AC Underwood	P4858

The squadron's objective was the bridges at Maastricht. They headed out over the North Sea, then across the Belgian countryside, flying at 3,000 feet. Before they reached Recklein flak began bursting around them. At Maastricht they came under intense AA fire and enemy fighters too were encountered; only three of the Blenheims returned entirely undamaged. Flying Officer Gordon Gratton failed to return, and only his gunner survived as a prisoner. Sergeant Bennett's machine was hit by a German fighter, although his gunner claimed one fighter shot down. Bennett brought his crippled bomber down in Belgium, but his observer was killed. Bennett and LAC Hannah were later reported to be in a French hospital. The bridge was claimed as severely damaged.

Meanwhile, 21 Squadron's twelve Blenheims had taken off at 3.10 p.m.; their target was the German armoured columns heading west from Maastricht. They were led by the CO:

W/C L.C. Bennett	Sgt E. Jones	LAC Appelby	L8732
P/O H.D.S. Dunford-Wood	Sgt Rawson	LAC D.R.C. MacLagan	L9023
Sgt J.J. Outhwaite	Sgt G. Lewis	AC J.E. Bartley	L8738
S/L G.A.M. Pryde	Sgt A. Summers	LAC O'Connor	L8746
F/O J.C.G. Sarll	Sgt Jennings	LAC L.H. Lightfoot	P6890
P/O D. Macdonald	Sgt Sidlow	AC Charlton	P6886
F/Lt L.V.E. Petley	Sgt E. Hart	LAC W. Harris	L8735
P/O W.A. Saunders	Sgt W.H. Eden	LAC C. Webb	L8745
P/O J. Harrison-Broadley	Sgt B. Williamson	LAC D.V. Cleaver	L8744
F/O S.F. Coutts-Wood	Sgt Swann	LAC Gibbs	L8743
F/O S.L. Sigurdson	Sgt Bailey	AC J. Guest	L8758
F/O F.C. Gibbs	Sgt Edwards	AC Chisholme	L9029

They found the columns at 4.30 and each Flight attacked in a shallow dive in succession. Ground fire damaged eleven of the Blenheims, and Aircraftman Charlton, in Pilot Officer Macdonald's machine, was killed. Several vehicles were hit and the road too was damaged. The bombers flew home but after landing, eight of them were deemed unserviceable following the damage they had sustained.

*

The mid-afternoon recce flights by Air Component squadrons did not fare well. 53 Squadron had one aircraft reported missing, brought down over Belgium; the pilot had been wounded and was evacuated to England. He was, however, back with the squadron in June:

| F/O A.D. Panton DFC | Sgt Christie | AC2 Bence | L9459* |

Flight Lieutenant Gerald Smither of 59 Squadron, took off from Vatry at 3.05. He spotted 16 motor vehicles travelling along the Eindhoven to Boxtel road but the Blenheim was hit in the port engine by small arms fire. Smither, however, brought the aeroplane safely back on one engine:

| F/Lt G.V. Smither | Sgt R. Tull | AC D.J. Pitcher | L4856 |

At 4.30 88 Squadron was ordered to send off three Battles to attack columns near Bouillon. No details survive but two of the three aircraft did not get home. At 5 p.m. the squadron was bombed yet again. The hangars were again hit and the receiving radio station became u/s and all telecommunications broken.

In the early evening, 53 Squadron flew another recce, while 18 Squadron ended its disastrous day by losing yet another Blenheim, sent out to fly to the Albert Canal area:

| F/O C. Bellis | Sgt H.D. Welch | LAC K. Parry | L8861* |

That evening too, 150 Squadron, following its attack soon after dawn, dispersed its B Flight to an advance landing ground (ALG) at Vatry.

*

The AASF bomber losses on the 11th, coming after those of the 10th, caused grave anxiety at BAFF HQ, about the whole future of operations by the Battle squadrons. Seven Battles had been lost, an eighth written off (and perhaps two more if the 88 Squadron note of two afternoon losses is correct) while it is recorded that 18 AASF Blenheims were lost. This latter figure seems high but obviously refers (in part) to the losses sustained by 114 Squadron, caught on the ground at Condé.

> We quickly had to change our tactics, it was hopeless bombing straight and level with the bomb aimer down in the nose, it just didn't work. Then we had to go and do a bit of

quick practice dive-bombing which was something we really hadn't done. The pilot then released the bombs from a release on the control column. We also had to change the bomb fuses. We had short delays at first which would go off on impact, but once we were going in at low level you had to be very careful and choose the 11-second delay to allow you time to get away from it before it exploded. We also found flying in formation a bit dicey. It was tricky if we were going for a bridge, you had to attack one behind the other, so they were just picking us off one after the other.

We all thought the world of the Battle; it was really a solid rugged aircraft and at one stage, before we went out to France they had a lot of trouble with the engine cutting out. We would take off and as soon as we pulled the control to change from fine to course pitch, at about 200 feet, the engine would cut. There was some carburration trouble I think, but if the engine did cut you would have to keep going straight ahead and crash land. A number of boys did crash land and it would go through trees and hedges, across fences – it really was solid. And the pilot invariably got out with no injuries at all, although the aircraft would be pretty badly damaged. Thank goodness for me, and most of us, the engine would often pick up again just before hitting the ground. However, they got all that sorted out before we went to France.

The only thing that was really vulnerable on the Battle was the cooling system. You only had to have one tiny piece of shrapnel through the glycol tank and you were in trouble. This awful steam would start fizzing out and I think this was what brought a number of Battles down. Its speed too was against it – it just didn't have any speed at all. We obviously weren't high but at 9,000 to 12,000 feet we were going through all sorts of flak which could reach us there and then there were enemy fighters too. This was why we had to change our tactics so quickly to the dive-bombing and the low level approach. At low level it was fine – apart from speed – but we all thought very highly of it and in fact we were not in a hurry to go rushing off to re-equip with Blenheims because we didn't think they were that much better. None of us had got any twin-engined experience anyway.

Flying Officer R.D. Max, 103 Squadron

On the evening of the 11th, Air Marshal Barratt telephoned the Chief of the Air Staff at Air Ministry, explaining that he had not made further attacks during the day in view of the obvious necessity of conserving his forces. It was a strange situation, that the RAF in France knew almost precisely where enemy columns could be found but was unable to afford the cost of attacking them.

However, he obviously had something in mind, for earlier that afternoon, (4.15 p.m.) 75 Wing received a message from AASF HQ that although all aircraft were to stand down, they were to be placed at three hours' notice as from 4 a.m. on the morning of the 12th.

If Sir Arthur Barratt was concerned about his losses on the 11th, his concern would increase the following day.

CHAPTER SEVEN

Into the Hell of Flak and Fighters

Sunday morning, 12 May
Conflicting reports continued to come in about what exactly was happening in Holland, although it was believed that further airborne troops had been landed in the Hague and Rotterdam areas.

In Northern Belgium the Germans were pressing towards the Turnhout Canal. In the south, the British and French were rapidly establishing themselves along their chosen positions towards which retreating Belgian troops were heading. The French General Alphonse Georges (the French Second-in-Command) issued a directive on the night of the 11th, in which he felt that the Germans would have three main lines of advance on the 12th:

(a) Maastricht to Tongres to Gembloux
(b) March to Dinant
(c) Neufchâteau to Carigan.

For delaying action from the air, he gave first priority to advance (a), in order to secure the Allied advance to their Dyle-Gembloux-Namur line. RAF effort, therefore, was directed to that area, although later in the day, attacks on (c) were made.

Also during the night, BAFF HQ received messages from Air Ministry in London, which stressed the importance the Belgians attached to securing the destruction of the bridge over the Albert Canal, three miles south-west of Maastricht. This was the bridge that had not been blown up by its defenders the first morning, as the guard commander had been decapitated by a shell as the attack opened, at which time all telephonic communication had been cut. The bridge was situated on the

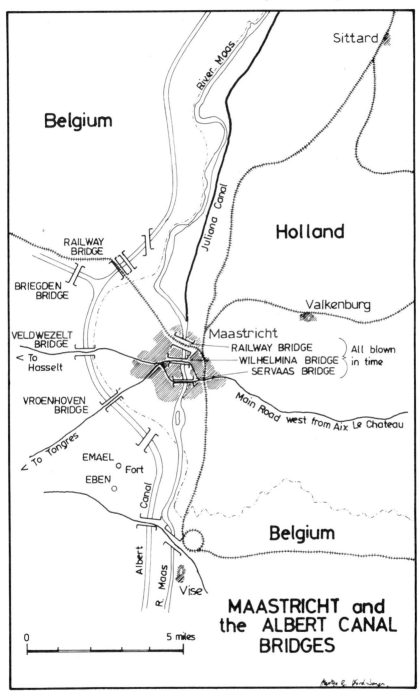

Belgium

River Maas

Sittard

Juliana Canal

Holland

RAILWAY
BRIDGE

Valkenburg

BRIEGDEN
BRIDGE

VELDWEZELT
BRIDGE

< To
Hasselt

Maastricht
RAILWAY BRIDGE
WILHELMINA BRIDGE
SERVAAS BRIDGE

} All blown
in time

VROENHOVEN
BRIDGE

Main Road west from Aix Le Chateau

< To Tongres

EMAEL   o Fort

EBEN   o

Canal

Belgium

Albert

R. Maas

Vise

MAASTRICHT and
the ALBERT CANAL
BRIDGES

0   5 miles

Maastricht–Tongres Road, near Vroenhoven, which with a similar bridge near Veldwezelt on the Maastricht-Hasselt Road, had been the subject of a request to attack them, also made on the 11th.

Therefore, whatever Barratt thought about the vulnerability of his Battles, he had little option but to commit at least a force of them to try and knock out these bridges. Yet he knew only too well what he would be asking of his aircrews. From losses already sustained over this general area during the last two days, he knew that place would be a hotbed of German AA and fighter defence. Too much time had gone by not to believe the Germans would not have brought up massive defensive fire.

Accordingly, he issued instructions that the attack should be undertaken by six volunteer crews from the squadron assigned. In this case it was to be 12 Squadron at Amifontaine, who was given the task, as they were the nearest squadron to the target. Each bridge was to be attacked by a section of three Battles at 9.15 a.m. on the morning of the 12th, while two Bomber Command Blenheim squadrons would attack crossings and columns in Maastricht itself at the same moment. The Battles would at least have the benefit of fighter escort.

However, the first attacks of the day had already been assigned to 139 Squadron, at Plivot, and 103 Squadron at Bétheniville, for first light. 103 sent out three Battles to bomb columns while 139 had also been ordered to send nine Blenheims to hit road columns, carrying a mixed bomb load of 250 and 40 lb bombs.

Sergeant James Paine, one of the squadron observers, had, along with other NCOs, been awakened at 3 a.m., when everyone had been ordered to the airfield. He was not immediately required but was later told to follow the others – driving there in the 'Blood Wagon' which did not seem too good an omen. When he arrived, he found the Blenheims, with engines ticking over. A map was thrust into his hand and he was told he was flying with the CO. Without much of a clue as to what was happening, Paine was told to navigate the squadron!

As Wing Commander L.W. Dickens AFC taxied out, he ran over a discarded metal wheel chock which damaged the rear fuselage. The squadron warrant officer immediately told the

CO that the Blenheim was u/s, but received a terse but definite answer!

Led by the CO, 139 Squadron took off at 5 a.m., with James Paine trying to map out a course and an ETA to the target. As he looked out, he could see the morning sky was clear, with patches of broken cloud.

One Blenheim failed to get away: Flying Officer Menzies was delayed by a technical fault and so took off later. This undoubtedly saved him and his crew from the disaster that was about to engulf the squadron.

W/C L.W. Dickens AFC	Sgt J.R. Paine	LAC Crowley	?
S/L W.I. Scott	Sgt T.W. Davis	LAC W.A. McFadden	N6216*
S/L T.G. Tideman	Sgt Hale	LAC Rooney	P4923*
F/Lt A.W. Lee	Sgt J.B. Keegan	LAC C.C. Child	P4826*
F/O G.E. Gray-Smith	Sgt P.C. Gray	A/Sgt C. Taylor	N6219*
F/O A. McPherson DFC	Sgt F.W. Gregory	LAC H.F. Over	N6215*
F/O N.E.W. Pepper DFC	Sgt T.E. Hyde	W/O Hill	L9416*
Sgt T.C.R. Harrison	Sgt N.S.D. Jones	LAC H.T. Garbett	N6229*
F/O Menzies	Sgt Bonney	LAC Tribbick	?

The other eight Blenheims found road targets west of Maastricht and Louis Dickens, after signalling to his squadron to form into echelon, led them in a dive-bombing approach from 6,000 to 3,000 feet. But the Luftwaffe were up early too, and almost immediately the Blenheims were set upon by Me109s and Me110s.

James Paine remembers:

A rattle of fire came from our gunner, operating his Vickers gun and having to change a drum every 100 rounds. Green tracer bullets were, meanwhile, ricocheting off the catwalks of our aircraft. The gunner then gave a terse 'I'm hit!', and then silence. I looked out of the side window and to my amazement saw an Me109 formating on us! I could see the pilot clearly. I objected to having him sit there and not being able to answer back.

I glanced at the CO, as white faced, he was flying at deck level, under electricity cables, shaving church steeples, but doing a good job of it. I reached over and pulled down the two Plus-9 boost levers, which certainly made a difference. Pulled over the rotary switch which released all four 250 pound bombs, rotated the compass 180 degrees and clamped it.

I thought I'd better go and see what had happened to the gunner. Owing to the Blenheim's main spar going through the fuselage, only a little space was available for anyone to crawl through. To get through, one had to divest oneself of the bulky parachute harness. Off it came and I was through in a couple of shakes. When I got to the turret the gunner was slumped forward, so I rotated the turret and got hold of him and dragged him to the shelf on the centre spar and leaned over him. I could see no blood but he was wearing an Irvin jacket, so couldn't tell. He had a hole in the palm of his hand, so I slapped a field dressing on it, turned and climbed into the turret.

Ammunition pans were strewn all over the floor, most of them empty, but I found a full one, slung it on the gun and started to operate the turret. On the right there was carnage going on, and on the left was our old friend the 109, now having a job to keep up with our added boost. I sprayed him with a copious burst! Heinrich must have had a shock when the turret was pointed at him and spitting lead. He did a smart break-off and disappeared. He was probably out of ammunition anyway, and waiting for us to make a boob and write ourselves off while skimming over the terrain at deck level. Another look round and the assorted Messerschmitts were falling back. I gave them a good squirt at maximum deflection as a farewell present.

I plugged in the intercom and told the CO, 'It's all right, they have broken off; the gunner is wounded.' All I got was a laconic, 'Come back here, you bugger!'

Sergeant J.R. Paine, 139 Squadron

Seven of the Blenheims were hacked from the sky, two falling in flames. Tom Tideman crash-landed, but he and his observer survived their ordeal. The Blenheim crashed in flames; LAC Rooney was killed instantly. Tideman and Hale scrambled clear and managed to reach a Belgian fort, where the occupants were very reluctant to let their guests leave because of the danger. However, they grabbed a couple of bikes, cycled away and later commandeered a car – which had been left by some earlier

Above Blenheim IVs of 139 Squadron.
(*IWM*)

Below Sergeant J.R. Paine of 139
Squadron won the DFM on 12 May 1940.
(*J.R. Paine*)

Right Flying Officer Andrew McPherson
of 139 Squadron on the day he received
his DFC. He was the first RAF pilot to fly
over Germany, but was killed over
Maastricht on 12 May 1940.
(*R.C. Bowyer*)

German holidaymakers! In this they joined the mass of refugees on clogged roads, being bombed and machine-gunned on several occasions. They finally arrived at base, complete with the 'liberated' car.

Flying Officer Pepper also survived, baling out into Allied lines and returning in a French armoured car. Only Menzies was unscathed. Having followed the others, after eventually taking off, they found the sky clear of fighters, bombed the target and returned.

Andrew McPherson had been killed. It will be remembered he had flown the first RAF aeroplane to cross the German frontier back on 3 September 1939, and had received the first DFC. Now he was gone. He had even been flying the very same Blenheim – N6215. Everyone else, with the exception of Flying Officer Gray-Smith, who was taken prisoner, was killed.

Louis Dickens later received the DFC, while James Paine, who had taken off his parachute harness in order to go to the gunner's aid, and then engaged the Messerschmitts, received the DFM. By his actions he had also saved the wounded gunner's life, for he had been hit in the body as well as the hand. James Paine had been in the RAF since 1931, and with 139 since 1937. He was later commissioned and flew a tour with Coastal Command.

News of the disaster must have just been coming in to BAFF HQ when the orders to 12 Squadron were going on. It could not have given Barratt any comfort to know that he had had one of his two Blenheim squadrons almost knocked out of the ground the previous day, and now the second had been severely mauled in the air. The only good news was that all three of 103 Squadron had returned. Nevertheless, AASF HQ sent its orders to 12 Squadron at Amifontaine.

Operations Order to 67 Wing, 75 Wing, repeated to 71, 75 Wings and North Eagle. From Panther:
Operation Order 617 dated 12.5.40, timed 0815:
Confirming telephone instructions, two sections of Battles of 12 Squadron are to attack Bridges 190 degrees AM30, 2 miles and 180 degrees AM30, 4 miles. Time over target 0915 hours. One section against each bridge. Aim of attack is to destroy or damage bridges. Ten fighter aircraft No. 1

Squadron are to provide support for Battles during execution of this mission. Officer Commanding bomber and fighter formations should concert method of co-operation. German ground and anti-aircraft defences are likely to be strong in the neighbourhood of target. Bomber Command aircraft will be operating against targets in same area at about the same time. Two squadrons of Air Component aircraft will also be operating over the same area simultaneously.

(North EAGLE was the code name for HQ BAAF North, PANTHER was BAAF HQ.)

At Amifontaine, the squadron, as previously instructed, had been at Readiness since 4 a.m. At seven o'clock came the telephoned orders of which the above was the formal orders. It was a grim-faced CO who called his pilots together, told them of the task and then requested volunteers. There were no illusions. No one hesitated; all volunteered.

When the request was made for volunteers, I think every man on the squadron had his hand up. It was then pointed out that in A Flight (mine) our crews were due for the next mission. The same response came from B Flight, so the two flights of three were selected – all volunteers. Our squadron commander told the two flight leaders, Flying Officer Thomas from A Flight and Flying Officer Garland from B Flight, that they could decide how they would carry out the attack. Thomas opted for dive-bombing, and Garland preferred a low-level attack. As the weather was good, with a broken cloud layer at 9,000 feet, Thomas decided our attack would be made from that altitude. My pilot was Pilot Officer Davy and my observer was Sergeant Mansell. Our third aircraft was to be flown by Flying Officer Brereton. As soon as all the details were worked out between the two flight leaders, and the rest of us briefed, we all got aboard our aircraft, ready to go.

I don't remember having any premonitions, but I recalled later that I did a couple of things I had never done before:

(i) I raised my machine gun up to its operating position, and put a loaded ammo pan on it although I did not 'cock' the gun ready to fire before we started to taxi. This was still a major offence had it been a more peaceful situation.

(ii) I wore my parachute, a chest pack, the entire trip. Maybe I thought it would stop bullets. In addition, I opened the canvas covering over the rip-cord, cut the two strings that normally are broken when the rip-cord is pulled, and inched the metal tongues that are the actual rip-cord, as far as they could go without opening the 'chute – equivalent to putting a hair-trigger on a gun. My gas mask kit and steel helmet were put down into the camera well, their usual stowage position – the one area on the floor by my feet that was not protected by armour plate. Even today, I do not know why I did all this.

LAC G.N. Patterson, 12 Squadron

F/O N.M. Thomas	Sgt B.T.P. Carey	Cpl. J.S. Campion	P2332*
P/O T.D.H. Davy	Sgt G.D. Mansell	LAC G.N. Patterson	L5241*
F/O T.F.S. Brereton	Sgt P.J. Boddington	LAC J. Aitken	?
F/O D.E. Garland	Sgt T. Gray	LAC L.R. Reynolds	P2204*
P/O I.A. McIntosh	Sgt N.T.W. Harper	LAC R.P. McNaughton	L5439*
Sgt F. Marland	Sgt K.D. Footner	LAC J.L. Perrin	L5227*

Engines were started but just as they were about to taxi out, Tom Brereton's WOP/AG reported their radio was not working. They quickly switched to the spare Battle only to find the hydraulic gear on the bomb rack was not working properly. By now it was too late to prepare another machine, for to be on target at 9.15 a.m., they had to go. The five Battles took off in sections, the first at 8.18, the second at 8.22.

Thomas and Davy took off and started circling, hoping that Brereton would soon follow but after several minutes it was obvious he was not able to get away, so the two crews set off. They climbed to 9,000 feet, Gordon Patterson keeping his eyes peeled for enemy fighters.

In Battles 'F' and 'G', Thomas and Davy constituted the first section and their target was the concrete bridge at Vroenhoven, while Battles 'K', 'N' and 'J' would go for the metal bridge at Veldwezelt. The two section leaders, having decided upon their method of approach, headed for the target.

Seven of 1 Squadron's Hurricanes, led by Squadron Leader P.J.H. 'Bull' Halahan, went ahead (as was the policy at that time) with the intention of clearing any enemy fighters over the target area while three more flew with the low level Battles. Halahan and his pilots were promptly swamped by a large bunch of Me109s from JG27 and were therefore helpless to protect the incoming bombers.

When still some miles from the target, the bombers saw more 109s, and the three Hurricanes with them were quickly engaged. Then the target was ahead. The sky became black with exploding AA fire as the town came into view, while seemingly all around flew Me109s – scores of them!

Gordon Patterson noticed a number of abandoned gliders on the ground. Later he was told these were the gliders used by German troops when they flew behind the Dutch lines during the night of 9/10 May, to capture the bridges. Then he looked up and saw three fighters. At first he thought they were their promised fighter escort, of which these two Battles had seen nothing. However, as the fighters closed in behind, Patterson gave them a warning burst, then, as the fighters began firing too, he recognised them as Me109s:

My first reaction to the firing was to dive under the armour plating. I had just bent down when I felt a terrific blow on the left side of my head. I put my hand up there, thinking my ear was shot off. It was only the earpiece of my headset, mounted in my leather flying helmet. While I know it sounds stupid finding I was not wounded was such a relief, I sighted my machine gun on the leading fighter, aiming for the cockpit and fired a continuous burst about ten to fifteen rounds. The fighter immediately caught fire and slanted down into a vertical dive. The other two fighters had broken off to come in again. I had been continually advising Davy where the fighters were and what they were doing.

The second fighter came in nearly level. I had had a chance to reload before his attack. Again I fired directly at the cockpit. This aircraft banked slightly then fell into a dive. I never saw anyone bale out.

The last aircraft came in and I had only fired one short burst when my gun seized up. I recocked the handle, but the gun wouldn't fire. With the VGO there was only one stoppage – a defective bullet locking itself in the pan. I pulled the gun down under the armour-plating, removed the defective ammunition pan, and put a new one on, cocking the gun ready to fire. When I came up ready to fire, the fighter was only about 100 feet away, but not firing. I think to this day, that the fighter pilot felt he had finished me as he must have seen me going down into my cockpit, and he was coming in for a close shot to finish us off. I shot first – I have never missed at 100 feet – and saw my bullets push his goggles off his head. It was a scene that haunted me for a long, long while. His plane was still coming in toward us, on a collision course. I practically screamed at my pilot who, looking back, turned and climbed the plane so that the Me109 passed directly under us, probably not more than ten feet away. The fight was over.

It was then I saw the damage to our aircraft. I had indirectly heard the bullets striking into the fuselage. I had been hit myself three times plus the smash on the ear, but the perspex canopy was broken in pieces and the wings were full of holes, leaking fuel like it was vapour trails. On reporting all this, the pilot ordered the observer and myself to bale out. He probably thought the aircraft could catch fire at any instant and, as we were over Belgium, friendly territory, his order was fully justified. I tried to climb over the side but was unable to as I had no protection from the slipstream due to the shattered canopy. I pulled up my seat, stood on it but bending down, and, with my hand tightly holding the D-ring of the rip-chord, I threw myself sideways, over the side. Here, hindsight must be called in as I do not know exactly what happened. However, my flying suit must have caught on the small, retractable step on the fuselage side, and prevented a clean fall. In any case, I was dragged back into the tail assembly. Considerable damage was done to the tail – the leading edge of the empennage was dented in, as was the rudder post. Somehow my parachute opened, and I floated down, unconscious, onto a cement-surface courtyard between two wings of the Hospital des Anglais in Liège, Belgium, breaking the arch-bone of my left foot. I recovered consciousness in a hospital bed, about four hours after baling out.

LAC G.N. Patterson, 12 Squadron

Norman Thomas's Battle was quickly shot down and he and his

crew were captured. Tom Davy, with his machine streaming smoke and flame, headed down, and ordered his crew to bale out. Davy then managed to nurse his aircraft back, but finally had to crash-land at St Germaincourt. Mansell came down safely and got back on a bicycle but Gordon Patterson was later taken prisoner.

Meanwhile, Don Garland, known inevitably as 'Judy', was heading in at low level. But this didn't fool the defenders. They knew how important the bridges were and it was ringed by anything up to 300 light guns of all calibres which could put up a wall of iron. Ian McIntosh had his petrol tank holed and the Battle caught fire. He jettisoned his bombs, crash-landed and was taken prisoner. Fred Marland dived into the flak, released his bombs but was then hit. His Battle pulled up, winged over and dived into the ground. Garland too was down. He headed in, his Battle surrounded by exploding gunfire. The German gunners blazed away, hitting the aircraft repeatedly, but the bombs went down, then the Battle dived into the ground, smashed by a veritable curtain of steel. (Another version is that Garland's Battle plunged into the bridge and blew up.)

What damage had been done was not clear at the time. Later, damage appeared to have been inflicted to the Veldwezelt bridge. When he finally got back to base – by road, courtesy of the French – Tom Davy reported he thought his bridge to be already damaged. When his observer, Sergeant Mansell, got back he said he'd looked down and saw their bridge matched the other for damage. Some of the Hurricane pilots reported seeing bombs bursting on or near the target.

Whatever doubts there might be about the amount of damage to the bridges, what was not in doubt was the degree of heroism it had taken for the attack. All five Battles had been shot down although one had managed to fly some distance before it had come down. Two crews had been captured, two lost and one was safe, though minus a gunner.

Davy was later awarded the DFC. His gunner, LAC Gordon Patterson, who had been captured, had shot down one or two 109s before his bale out, and received the DFM. He was the first Canadian to receive a DFM in World War Two.

For the leader of the attack, Donald Garland, and his observer, Sergeant Tom Gray, who both died, went Britain's highest awards for gallantry, the Victoria Cross. By one of those strange quirks of fate, the gunner in Garland's aircraft, LAC Lawrence Royston Reynolds, received no posthumous award.

It was an ill-conceived attack. As a German officer said to one of the captured airmen, why did the RAF wait so long before attacking? The bridge was captured on Friday and it was not until Sunday morning that the attack came. In the meantime, the Germans had been pouring across the river and brought up and placed its anti-aircraft defences. When the Battles arrived, the Germans were waiting for them. It was too easy for them. It was like 'shooting fish in a barrel'.

And why should Lawrence Reynolds receive no award? That omission has never been satisfactorily explained. He could only have received the Victoria Cross that his fellow crewmen were to receive. To ignore his part in the attack is almost to deny he was there. As the Victoria Cross was given to Tom Gray, one should also have gone to Reynolds.

Meanwhile, two Blenheim squadrons of 2 Group were over Maastricht. 107 and 15 Squadrons, of 2 Group, each sent 12 Blenheims, led by Wing Commander B.E. Embry DSO and bar, AFC.

W/C B.E. Embry DSO AFC	P/O T.A. Whiting	Cpl G.E. Lang	L8777
F/O J.W. Stephens	Sgt W.J. Barrett	LAC E.C. White	N6190
F/O R.C. Rotheram	Sgt R. Brown	LAC E.C. Coote	L8748*
F/O G.T.B. Clayton DFC	Sgt M. Innes-Jones	Cpl L. Yeomans DFM	N6228
P/O W. Carter	Sgt R.D. Cook	AC2 H.T. Dennison	P4925
P/O K.D. Taute	Sgt L.S. Fearnley	LAC J.R. Waterhouse	N6191
P/O G.B. Murray	Sgt G.A. Wilson	LAC A. Moses	L9323
P/O O.H. Keedwell	Sgt J.L. Merritt	AC2 L.A. Berridge	P4914*
F/O W.H. Edwards DFC	Sgt V.G.L. Luter	LAC W.E. Palmer	P4905*
F/O D.J.A. Rose	Sgt D. Haige	LAC W.R. Stokell	L9306
F/Sgt H.J. Ratcliffe	Sgt P.J. Crowley	LAC D.S. Harrison	P4857
P/O S.G. Thornton	Sgt L.K. Mellorship	AC2 J.R. Mayor DFM	L8733*

The squadron had recently been in receipt of several awards for their activities over Norway. Embry had received a bar to his DSO. Flying Officer Gareth Clayton the DFC, his gunner, Len Yeomans, the DFM. DFMs had also gone to Sergeant Dick Gunning, and another air gunner, AC2 John Mayor. A DFC had also been awarded to Flying Officer William H. Edwards, a New Zealander. (Sergeant Brinn, who was born in Cardiff, and

Above Battle L5540 flown by F/O A.C. Roberts of 150 Squadron, shot down 10 May. He and his crew were taken into captivity. (*Bundesarchiv*)

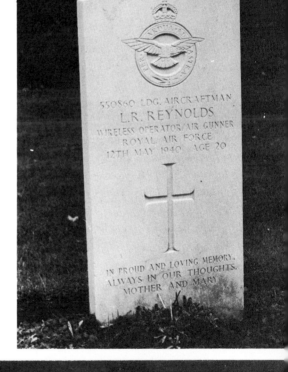

Right The final resting place of LAC Lawrence Reynolds, aged 20. 'In Proud and Loving Memory. Always in our Thoughts. Mother and Mary.' (*J. De Vos*)

Below The graves of Garland, Grey and Reynolds of 12 Squadron, Haverlee Cemetery, Belgium. (*J. De Vos*)

had joined the RAF as an apprentice in 1929, age 16, was soon to receive the DFM too. He was usually Dick Gunning's observer.)

Leading the second box on this day was Flying Officer Gareth Clayton who records:

Twelve aircraft from the squadron were detailed for the job and we were to fly in formation, in two boxes of six aircraft, one box behind the other. Once airborne, we circled the airfield a few times to allow the last aircraft off, time to take up their places. That done, the 'Boss' set course due east in a steady climb to our cruise altitude. The day was beautiful, without a single cloud in the sky.

Soon we were passing over Ipswich and almost dead above the small terraced house in which my wife Marian and I had rooms. As we flew on I wondered if she, and our two-month-old daughter, would be watching as we flew overhead.

Within minutes Felixstowe was beneath us, then the placid and empty North Sea was stretched out ahead, shimmering in the sunlight. We had climbed to 6,000 feet, our best altitude for accurate bombing. No need today to fly higher to help navigation as the journey to Maastricht was a comparatively short one. Then we were crossing the coast of Holland.

'Ten minutes to run to the target, Skipper,' said my New Zealand navigator, Sergeant Innes-Jones, over the intercom, then turning in his seat, busied himself with the bombsight and fusing switches. A single Hurricane fighter approached us and I wondered if this was a straggler from our promised escort. But the pilot took one look at us and flew off. That was all we saw of friendly fighters.

'Maastricht dead ahead,' called Innes-Jones. Leading the second six I closed in hard behind and just below Embry's leading box, making it a tight formation of twelve, flying in on the bomb run, but this did not last for long. Ahead of us I could see exploding AA fire – as well as being a good bombing height, six thousand feet was also perfect for the German's excellent 88 mm gun.

Flying Officer G.T.B. Clayton, 107 Squadron

Fifteen miles from Maastricht, 107 Squadron came under heavy ground fire which gradually increased as they approached the target area. Eleven of the Blenheims were hit on the way in and Pilot Officer Stan Thornton was shot down while Flying Officer Ronald Rotheram's machine was badly damaged, forcing him to leave the formation just after he bombed. Thornton and his crew were all killed.

Observer to Pilot Officer Keith Taute, a Rhodesian, was Sergeant Leonard Fearnley, who together had flown several ops during the Norwegian campaign. He remembers:

> At Maastricht we did a high level attack and we got loads of flak. My log book entry reads: 'Formation attack on bridges at Maastricht on German frontier. Three 250 lb and 18 × 40 lb bombs. Heavy AA fire – and how – and attacked by fighters. Four machines shot down. Photos obtained.'
>
> There was an observer called Ginger Mellorship in Thornton's crew. Ginger was a marvellous chap of Scottish ancestry, red hair, large handlebar moustache, and about 6 ft 3 in tall. How he ever got into the Blenheim's glasshouse I never understood. He must have been completely hunched up. The area in the front of the Blenheim was very tiny and when not lying to look through the front bombing panel, we sat sideways-on to do our nav work.
>
> I saw their Blenheim hit by flak and they went straight down and straight in. The flak was terrific, real black stuff. I remember we skedaddled pretty quickly. Embry was pretty good at getting us away from it all. Tight turns you'd never expect from Blenheims, but we did them.
>
> *Sergeant L.S. Fearnley, 107 Squadron*

On the way to the target, Len Fearnley had been busy taking recce photos, especially of the bridges across the Albert Canal in order to give Headquarters some idea of the damage 12 Squadron had inflicted earlier.

Gareth Clayton continues:

> As we ran in, Innes-Jones suddenly exclaimed, 'My God, all the bridges are down; somebody's been doing good work. They've put a pontoon bridge across, looks like we'll have to bomb that.'

Above Left Flying Officer Gareth Clayton DFC, 107 Squadron. Behind him is Pilot Officer Keith Taute. Both were over Maastricht on 12 May. (*G.T.B. Clayton*)

Above Right Sergeant Len Fearnley was Keith Taute's observer in 1940. He too was on the Maastricht raid and photographed the Albert Canal bridges during the mission. (*L.S. Fearnley*)

Below The bridges at Maastricht, photographed on 12 May. Note railway bridge to the north and nearby, a pontoon bridge already across the Maas.

Anti-aircraft fire began to explode around us. I breathed a sigh of relief as our bombs finally went down. Ahead, Embry's six began to turn. As I banked over to follow, there was an almighty crash and we were blown almost upside down. As soon as I'd sorted that out I looked ahead but could only see one Blenheim, so made for that, at which time my Geordie gunner called, 'Fighters astern, Skipper!'

Meanwhile, the rest of the squadron had reached the bridges and bombed but the intensity of the ground fire made it necessary for the formation to open out. Before they could close up again, German fighters took the opportunity to engage. Edwards and Keedwell were both picked off, but the rest managed to reform and fought off the 109s for the next 20 minutes, during which time, the gunners claimed one 109 destroyed and another as probably so. Edwards and his observer became prisoners; his gunner and Keedwell and crew were all killed.

Gareth Clayton:

As I reached the other Blenheim I saw another coming in from the port beam so we would not be entirely alone. Looking about me I began to take in the damage we'd sustained. Holes were all over what I could see of the port wing, others in the cockpit canopy, with another through the top cylinder of the port engine from which I could see a two foot jet of blue flame. From somewhere behind the instrument panel a small jet of liquid sprayed itself towards me.

I was relieved to see the aircraft ahead of me was the CO's and I tucked myself tightly behind his starboard wing. As I did so, two other Blenheims joined us, and together the five of us made some sort of opposition to the 109s which were now attacking us. It was then that I realised my navigator wasn't in his usual place. Looking down I found him sitting on the cabin floor, his intercom disconnected and he seemed busily engaged scratching the inside of the leg of his flying suit. I reached out and grabbed the lead and plugged him in. From what he said I quickly gathered he'd been hit and wounded. Calling my gunner, he said the 109s had pushed off and that his turret had jammed anyway. So I told him to come forward and see to Innes-Jones. It was not easy for Corporal Yeomans to do this as he had to clamber through a narrow space between the main spar and the top of the fuselage, but he was soon helping the nav, and giving him a shot of morphia.

Innes-Jones had been caught by a piece of shrapnel which had come up through his seat – I could see a jagged hole in the seat, about three inches across. He was asking me to land and get him to a doctor, but below, all I could see was the ground littered with parachutes. We were obviously right over a battle ground and no place to deposit my damaged aircraft and crew. I flew up to Embry and because we had been told to maintain strict radio silence, gesticulated to him to 'step on the gas'. Yeomans now had cut open the nav's flying suit to find a bloody mess. It looked as if he'd been hit in the middle of the crutch, just behind his testicles. It was impossible to bandage, so Yeomans made a ball of a bandage and jammed it over the injury as best he could. He was obviously in pain so we decided to give him the second morphia syringe.

We were now over the North Sea. With my wounded navigator and badly shot-up Blenheim, the next twenty minutes seemed very long. However, we made Wattisham, only to discover my wheels and flaps were not working. I brought the aircraft in on a long flat glide, turning off the fuel and engines shortly before we reached the boundary fence. After a bit of a float we made a surprisingly soft belly landing, skating to a halt after some two hundred yards.

Emergency vehicles were round us, and crews from other aircraft soon appeared and a debate began as to how best to get Innes-Jones out. Amid this, a huge aircrew sergeant, a former policeman, decided it would be quicker to carve off the nose of the Blenheim with one of the axes we carried for just this sort of emergency. He made two or three mighty strokes with the axe before it slipped out of his hand, flashed across my navigator's face and buried itself in the base of the pilot's seat, just six inches away. Innes-Jones passed out, and so we then bundled him out unceremoniously through the roof hatch. A waiting ambulance drove him off to a hospital in Ipswich where he made a full recovery.

That evening I was invited for drinks with some friends. It was a peculiar feeling standing with a drink in my hand, surrounded by the inconsequential chatter of a cocktail party, when only a few hours before, I had been over Holland having the hell shot out of me!

Flying Officer G.T.B. Clayton, 107 Squadron

Ronny Rotheram recalls this raid:

We took off early on 12 May from RAF Wattisham in a formation of 12 Blenheims. The weather was fine and as we approached our target the bridges at Maastricht, I could see intense flak as another formation attacked the bridges ahead of us. We were about 6,000 feet on our bombing run when we were subjected to very heavy flak. My aircraft was hit repeatedly and Sergeant Brown was wounded in his arm. As we turned away from the target, after dropping our bombs, I found that the controls to my port engine were severed and the starboard engine was damaged and I started to drop out of formation.

At that moment, I saw Me109s coming down on us, they looked just like a swarm of bees; I went into a steep dive with two 109s on my tail. Before they could further damage me, I was lucky to enter a small patch of cloud; I promptly did a 180 degree turn and saw no more of the 109s. They should have got us, for there was not much cloud about but we got away. Shortly afterwards, the port propeller and reduction gear blew off with a loud bang and I had no alternative but to land as soon as possible. I crash landed across three small fields and stopped about 50 feet from a row of trees.

Shortly after the crash, a crowd of people started to gather in a rather menacing manner and I had to explain to them in my best school-boy French, that I was an English aviator (I opened the dinghy pack to get at the survival rations which contained a small jar of rum!).

I tried to keep the crowd away from the aircraft as much as possible as the area was becoming flooded with petrol from the damaged tanks. I tried to get someone to attend to Sergeant Brown and LAC Coote, who had damaged his legs in the rather violent crash.

Eventually someone in authority arrived and Sergeant

Brown and I were taken by car to a fort where I was brought in front of King Leopold, who was anxious to find out whether we had destroyed the bridges. I was also cross-examined by Sir Roger Keyes.[1] (I have a photograph in my log book which shows that the bridges were already down at the time of the attack and that traffic was pouring over two pontoon bridges upstream and downstream of the main bridges!).

At this point I was separated from Sergeant Brown and I was driven to Brussels and thence to Rheine and flown back to England. On the roads we passed the advancing British Army but we were extremely lucky not to be attacked by German aircraft, who had been very active against road traffic the day before. My fellow passenger was a Flying Officer Pepper [139 Squadron] another downed Blenheim pilot.

Flying Officer R.C. Rotheram, 107 Squadron

Close on the heels of Embry's formation were 15 Squadron, led by John Glen, OC A Flight:

S/L J.G. Glen	Sgt Colbourn	P/O Gordon	P6917
F/O L.H. Trent	Sgt W.J. Stephens	Cpl J. Sutcliffe	L8855
Sgt H.R. Hall	Sgt E.R. Perron	LAC P.J. McDonnell	P6914*
F/O A.E. Oakley	Sgt D.J. Avent	LAC D.V. Woods	P6911*
P/O C.H. Robinson	Sgt S.C. Readhead	LAC Horton	L8800
P/O C.R. Frankish	Sgt E.G. Roberts	LAC E.W.L. Cooper	P6912*
S/L H.Y. Lawrence	Sgt Hopkins	LAC Thomas	L9024
F/O P.F. Eames	Sgt Phillips	LAC Austin	L8850
Sgt F.R. Pepper	Sgt R. Booth	LAC J. Scott	N6151*
F/O P.F. Webster	Sgt R.A.M. Stone	LAC R.E. Hunter	L8851
F/O T.G. Bassett	Sgt N.G. Middlemass	LAC W.T. Cavanagh	L8847*
F/O P.N. Douglass	Sgt W.O. Shortland	Sgt W.E.M. Davies	L8849*

They too met massive ground fire and fighters, although they had been promised fighter cover over the target, but 1 Squadron themselves were still fighting for their lives. Bombs rained down from a diving attack despite the ground fire.

The Blenheims came out at low level – their usual tactic – and began hedgehopping away. Len Trent saw a line of German soldiers appear ahead of him and he began firing with his front gun. As he did so he suddenly became aware of a line of poplar

---

[1] Churchill's personal emissary to King Leopold of Belgium.

Above Flying Officer Ronnie Rotheram crash-landed in Belgium after the Maastricht attack but got back and received the DFC. (*R.C. Rotheram*)

Below A well known wartime photograph, it is actually Ronnie Rotheram's Blenheim going down, with a Me109 nearby.

Bottom Two Sergeant Observers of 107 Squadron, Syd Clayton (left) and Robert Cook. Both flew missions during the French campaign. Clayton went on to win the DSO, DFC and DFM and complete 146 missions, the last 46 as a pilot. (*L.S. Fearnley*)

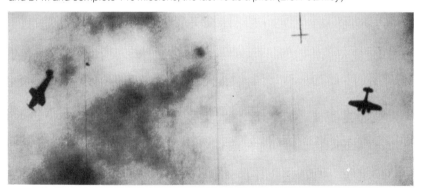

trees in front of him. He hauled desperately on the control column, clipped the uppermost leaves, then with a sigh of relief, dropped back down to the deck. Soon afterwards they flew past a burning Belgian airfield, hangars and aircraft ablaze. Anyone was game on this day, and the Blenheim collected ground fire from the Belgian ground gunners as it flashed by.

It was another massacre. Six of the Blenheims were shot down and the rest damaged, and had wounded aboard. Three and a half hours after take off, six badly shot-up Blenheims returned to RAF Wyton.

Flight Lieutenant Peter Webster had superficial bullet wounds to his foot. Pilot Officer Robinson had had his hydraulics system shot out by fire from a 109 and with no flaps, trim tabs or undercarriage, had to make a belly landing. Flying Officer Percy 'Red' Eames landed safely but had been wounded. He was taken to hospital with bad flesh wounds to his knee and wrist. An explosive shell had smashed into his cockpit between seat and rudder bar.

The crews of Sergeant Hall, Flying Officer Bert Oakley, Pilot Officer Frankish and Flying Officer Bassett had all been killed. Sergeant Pepper and his crew had been taken prisoner. Flying Officer Douglass was missing, his gunner dead, his observer in captivity. At the end of the raid, 15 Squadron had just two of the 12 Blenheims serviceable.

The morning's effort by AASF and 2 Group, therefore, had thus far cost them five Battles and 16 Blenheims. As an indication of recent casualties, 71 Wing reported the following aircraft states for its squadrons, as at 12 noon:

    105 Squadron – 13 aircraft, 16 crews
    150 Squadron – 10 aircraft, 15 crews
    114 Squadron – 0 aircraft, 18 crews
    139 Squadron – 4 aircraft, 6 crews

*

As well as Luftwaffe fighters, its bombers had also been active this Sunday morning. 226 Squadron were bombed by more than a dozen Heinkels at 7 a.m. that came in bombing and strafing at low level, while 218 Squadron also received the enemy's attention a half hour later. 142 were also attacked and an A Flight Battle (K9259) received a direct hit and was destroyed.

At Bétheniville, 103 were bombed, but two He111s were shot down by the aerodrome defence gunners. One of these was also claimed by the local village Gendarme who had been blazing away with a rifle – using, it was said, his entire ammunition allowance for 20 years! As the bombers were flying at around 20,000 feet, the RAF were not over enthusiastic about the Frenchman's claim.

Air Component Blenheims had been out since first light, Flying Officer J.R. Grant of 57 Squadron making a recce at dawn, while 59 Squadron had provided an aircraft for another dawn recce. Flying Officer G.H.D. Evans had also flown out before first light, and carried out a recce from Vitry. He returned to Poix at 9.35 with his machine slightly damaged after an encounter with an He111. His L4859 was serviceable again that evening.

| F/O G.H.D. Evans | Sgt Barry | AC2 C.C. Cleland | L4859 |

David Evans recalls:

On 11 May I flew up to Vitry-en-Artois for standby and the following morning I took off before dawn and carried out what was inaccurately called a strategic reconnaissance of Belgium and Holland. I have my old maps and I see that we went up the Maas Canal to Roermond and then back down the River Maas to Hesselt, Telmond and then skirted Brussels and then back to, I presume, somewhere near Lille. My chief recollection of that particular trip is that we saw quite a number of aeroplanes, one of which my air gunner, (AC Charles Cleland, a Canadian) shot down and was rewarded, as an AC2, with a DFM for doing so. My log-book records that we were chased by a single-engined fighter, an Me110 (twin-engined fighter) and an He111 (twin-engined bomber) at various times. I gather that the latter scored a hit on our aircraft but have no record or recollection of this.

We took off just before dawn and flew east. At this time we had been briefed to fly at 50 feet, or even lower if we could, and taking off before dawn, my windscreen had been covered with dew. Blenheim IV aircraft had long perspex noses which were liable at night to reflect light, so the nose had been covered overnight by a camouflage canvas apparatus tied with strings round it. The groundcrew had taken this off, seen the dew and wiped my windscreen with a dirty or oily rag, so that forward visibility could have been better once we got airborne. Having taken off in the dark and flying towards the rising sun at 50 feet, it wasn't very comfortable not being able to see where we were going. However, I don't think we can have seen many enemy troops, one or two perhaps. I think I recall seeing a motorcycle detachment, but I don't remember seeing any lorries or armoured fighting vehicles or anything similar. Although we were flashing past and looking through trees – poplars I suppose – on the roads up which we were flying; if we had seen anything we would almost certainly have been shot down. Some days later a great friend of mine (Flying Officer F.D. Bird), with whom I'd shared a billet in Poix and who had been through Cranwell with me and we had stuck together for a number of years, was killed on his second trip. Apparently because he had run slap-bang into a divisional headquarters which, of course, was surrounded by flak. After that our instructions were to fly between 4,000 and 6,000 feet, which was a relic of the First War, when the theory was that you were out of the range of .303 and below predicted heavy AA fire. From then on we stuck to that height. Within a week or so of operations, we'd lost most of our aircraft.

Flying Officer G.H.D. Evans, 59 Squadron

Afternoon, 12 May
The afternoon bombing effort was directed to the increasing threat of advancing German forces through the Ardennes. The French 2nd Army urgently requested air support and a section of Battles of 103 Squadron was sent to attack a pontoon bridge across the River Semois, near Bouillon.

Led by Pilot Officer T.B. Fitzgerald, they took off at 12.57, flying in close vic formation at first then changed to echelon starboard. An item of interest is that the squadron diary records that the squadron stopped carrying observers when engaged on low flying dive-bombing raids, as the pilots released the bombs, not the observer, when dive-bombing.

Over Sedan, at 4,000 feet, the Battles were chased by enemy fighters but they dived to ground level and lost them. Heading on, they then found the village of Bouillon and struck the river about a mile to the east of it. They spotted an old concrete bridge which had already been destroyed, but beside it was a pontoon bridge under construction by the Germans. No other bridges could be seen, so the Battles attacked.

Tom Fitzgerald dropped his bombs on top of the works, and although the second pilot failed to see the target, the third did, and also saw his leader's bombs hit a pile of timber on the north bank and then bounce against an old building close by. He then let go his bombs at 20 feet. When on their return flight, they saw a cloud of smoke rising from the locality of their attack.

They then saw a red flag on which was a black swastika, on the road at the entrance to Bouillon village. On the French side of the river there was also a column of large tanks, although their nationality was in doubt. The three Battles returned at 1.42.

No 71 Wing's two Battle squadrons were sent out at 2.30/45 p.m., 105 Squadron briefed to attack columns reported on the St Hubert-Paliseul Road, 150 to go for a mechanised column between Neufchâteau and Bertrik.

105 Squadron:

F/Lt H.C. Samuels	Sgt F.B. Abbott	LAC R.D. Hughes	P2176
P/O D.C.F. Murray	Sgt Hemmingway	AC Hill	L5523
P/O T. Hurst	Sgt W.J. Anning	LAC C.R. Wells	K9485*

150 Squadron:

F/Lt R.A. Weeks	Sgt W.D.P. Pittar	LAC L.O. Grant	P2262
P/O I. Campbell-Irons	Sgt T.R. Barker	LAC R.H. Hinder	P2336*
Sgt S.E. Andrews	Sgt N.J. Ingram	LAC H.R. Figg	P2184

Both squadrons met the now familiar hail of ground fire. The two survivors from 105 Squadron who landed at 3.50 found their aircraft beyond repair, they were so badly shot about. They had, however, bombed a bridge and a village near Bouillon, packed with German troops.

The three crews of 150 had seen that a bridge across the Meuse near their target area had been destroyed, then they came under heavy ground fire from the cross-roads one mile east of Neufchâteau. A direct hit was scored on Ian Campbell-Irons' Battle, whereupon it exploded and crashed in flames. The other two bombed the column they had been seeking, dropping eight 250 lb bombs (with the usual 11 second delay fuses) from 100 feet.

Later in the afternoon further sorties were sent out: 103 Squadron made another foray, with 218 Squadron. 103 took off at 4.30 with two men aboard each aeroplane:

F/O G.B. Morgan-Dean	AC H.B. Sewell	K5512*
P/O V.A. Cunningham	AC J. Johnson	?
P/O E.E. Morton	AC A.S. Ross	P2693*

Only one, Pilot Officer Cunningham, returned. The target was again enemy columns near Bouillon but Cunningham didn't get that far. He saw some tanks moving towards the French frontier about 1½ miles south of Bouillon, on the Bouillon-Sedan road at a point where the road turns to the south west from the river. Believing that this was the head of the column, Cunningham dive-bombed them, releasing his bombs from 1,000 feet. Heavy rifle and machine gun fire accompanied him and he failed to see where his bombs exploded but he saw soldiers dispersing into woods west of the road. His two companions were not seen again.

The section from 218 approached Bouillon at 1,000 feet:

Sgt J.B. Horner	Sgt L.C. Flisher	LAC L.D. Davies	K9353*
P/O Anstey	?	?	?
P/O F.S. Bazalgette	Sgt W.H. Harris	LAC H.B. Jones	P2183*

Collecting gun fire from the wood immediately to the west, the leading Battle was hit and crashed, exploding in flames as it hit the ground. Flying Officer F.S. Bazalgette in the third Battle, bombed targets in Bouillon, seen by the second aircraft to hit the road in the town, but that was the last Pilot Officer Anstey (in the number two aircraft) saw of his surviving comrade.

Anstey himself then bombed Bouillon from 1,000 feet but could not make out any results. 14 to 20 armoured cars, light tanks and lorries could be seen stationary in the woods to the west as he turned over it. Surrounded by fire from these woods as Cunningham had been earlier, Anstey dived to low level and cleared the area.

Freddie Bazalgette crash-landed his Battle in front of the Allied lines but on the enemy's side of the river. He was badly hurt and although his crewmen made a valiant effort to save him, while being fired on by German machine gunners and shell fire, he died. Harris and Jones, destroyed their downed bomber and then made their way back through the lines and home. They both received Military Medals for their escape and evasion.

Sergeant Horner and his two crew were also later reported killed.

*

Afternoon recce missions had been flown by 59 Squadron. Pilot Officer J.S. Booth landed from his mission at 4.35, having been wounded in the leg, but still carried out an excellent reconnaissance. He had been hit by Belgian AA fire while flying at 1,500 feet near Renaix, flying N6169.

The Blenheims of 2 Group completed the afternoon bombing raids with 21 and 82 Squadrons. Nine aircraft of 82 Squadron bombed the road bridge over the Albert Canal north of Hasselt without loss. 21 Squadron went for German troops seen in the defile of the town of Tongres:

S/L G.A.M. Pryde	Sgt A. Summers	LAC O'Connor	L8746
P/O H.D.S. Dunford-Wood	Sgt Rawson	LAC D.R.C. MacLagan	L9023
F/O J.C.G. Sarll	Sgt Jennings	LAC L.H. Lightfoot	P6890
F/Lt A.D. Watson	Sgt A.L. Webb	LAC A.C.B. Burgess	L8739*
P/O R.G.M. Gilmore	Sgt Pearce	LAC Wilson	P6886
Sgt Rowson	Sgt Keates	LAC Bartley	L8732
S/L R.D.C. Gibson	Sgt Barns	Cpl Horton	P6954
Sgt Wilton-Jones	Sgt Smeurin	LAC Lang	L8737
Sgt Bailes	Sgt Twamley	AC Thompson	L8872

As they approached the target, enemy aircraft appeared. The formation closed right up but then came under intense AA fire from Tongres. Avoiding action was taken but it was extremely difficult. Spread out and the fighters would pick them off. Stay bunched up and the ground gunners had a better target. In any event several were hit, but the Blenheim flown by Flight Lieutenant Arthur Watson, leading the second section, was hit, blasting away the rear half of the fuselage, then the front section smashed into the ground. The rest bombed the target, then headed out of the flak and away, landing at 10.30 p.m.

It had been another costly day for the RAF. The AASF had

lost seven Blenheims and five crews. Eleven Battles had been shot down plus others written off or severely damaged. 2 Group had lost 11 Blenheims with others damaged or written off. BAFF also noted the loss of ten Hurricanes.

That evening it was the turn of the Chief of Air Staff to contact Arthur Barratt. The CAS's message (in part) read:

> I am concerned at the heavy losses incurred by the medium bombers. I must impress on you that we cannot continue indefinitely at this rate of intensity. If we expend all our effort in the early stage of the battle we shall not be able to operate effectively when the really critical phase comes.

In modern parlance this message would seem to be 'a blinding flash of the obvious' as far as Barratt was concerned. He was more than aware of his casualties but equally aware that he had to do something to try and stem the alarming speed of the enemy's advance movements. His French Allies had been asking for help and support for three days. Their own airforce, although large in number, was, in reality of modern front line aircraft, almost no larger than his BAFF force.

The CAS's message smacks of a senior officer covering himself just in case things go wrong. After all, when was the critical phase? Things in France and Belgium looked pretty critical already. Should, in the light of this message, Barratt ease off and wait until an even more critical time arrived? And how would he know then if that was 'the' critical time? It was not an enviable situation.

It is difficult to see what else Barratt could have done. He was handicapped with a relatively small force, harassed by bombing from the air, stretched to comply with constant requests for support on two parts of the front – Maastricht and now Sedan – labouring with inadequate aircraft, a poor fighter escort policy, and outdated bombing tactics which he had no time to improve. Due to his small force, he had to send out aircraft in 'penny packages', which were vulnerable to enemy fighters and ground fire.

If he could have afforded to send out larger raiding forces it might at least have divided the enemy's ground fire, giving more bombers the chance to attack and survive. He could, in hindsight, have had his fighters fly ground strafing missions against these columns as the bombers made their approach – it would certainly have kept the German gunners' heads down – but fighters were few, and their role was still air fighting. Fighters as ground attack aircraft, was, as a concept, still in the future. Few even contemplated, certainly not at this early stage, the use of fighters for ground support. It was simply not considered.

Knowing very well what his force had gone through over the past three days, Arthur Barratt sent his own message, to his wings, which read (in part):

> I am full of admiration for the magnificent courage showed by your bomber squadrons, who have cheerfully accepted any tasks in spite of casualties that have occurred. Message received from C.N.G. Land Armies, who wish to express their appreciation of the tasks carried out by the Battle squadrons in the Bouillon-Neufchâteau-St Hubert area which they considered had checked the German advance and saved a serious situation.

He would have more serious situations shortly.

CHAPTER EIGHT

All the Brave Young Men

Monday, 13 May

This day, the fourth since the German offensive began, was to see less air activity for the AASF, and a respite for Sir Arthur Barratt, although in reality, he had, as directed, decided to limit bomber operations. The weather too was with him for it was not very good this day.

The situation on the ground was that the French 7th Army had taken a bad knock in the north and that the Belgian army was now moving back to take up positions between Louvain and Antwerp were they would come between the French 7th Army to their left and the BEF on their right.

So far the BEF had not yet been engaged to any great extent but to the front of their Wavre–Louvain line, the German pressure was increasing, especially where the Belgians were retreating, and to the south-west where the 7th Army were falling back.

The French were retreating towards Bergen-op-Zoom and urgently requested air support when it became clear that a German tank force was in danger of cutting off some of its forces. The tanks were moving south from Breda towards Antwerp. Seven Battles, therefore, were ordered to attack.

Up till then it had been a quiet morning. The Battle squadrons had been placed on Readiness alert at dawn as usual but no orders were issued to them. Another dawn raid by the Luftwaffe had taken place in the vicinity of Bétheniville where 103 Squadron's base had been reinforced with four Bofors AA guns the previous day. A large force of enemy bombers passed over and three were shot down. One German airman's parachute failed to open and the luckless man's body was collected and buried. At 8.15 the local village was bombed with many casualties amongst civilians. There was no French organisation, so the squadron's medical personnel attended the injured and the squadron helped to bury 12 of the dead.

While 226 Squadron had been preparing for their raid, a large force of enemy bombers flew over the vicinity but the base was not attacked. Then at 10.20, the seven Battles began to take off:

F/Lt R.G. Hurst	Sgt B.G. Evans	Sgt Allen	P2180
P/O D.A.C. Crooks	Sgt T.C. Davies	LAC W.R.J. Green	P2267
Sgt G.G. Martin	Sgt N. Anderson	AC H.K. Wyatt	L5418
F/O R.W. Bungay	Sgt D.E. Bingham	Cpl L.H.W. Smith	L5438
Sgt Groves	Sgt Nixon	LAC H.E. White	K9343
P/O D. Salway	Sgt Thompson	LAC D. Palmer	K9176
P/O W.M. Waddington	Sgt G. Stephenson	LAC J. Hope	P2353*

The pilots had been briefed on the importance of stopping or at least delaying the tank column and the road junctions at Boeimeer, just south-west of Breda and at Rijsbergen, were thought to be the best places.

On the flight out the Battles were engaged by ground fire when two miles north-west of Antwerp and from woods to the south west of Wuestwezel. To the north of Antwerp could be seen a number of Dorniers, presumably bombing the city.

Initially the crews could see no sign of troops on the road, therefore bombed a factory building at Boeimeer, bringing it down across the adjacent road junction. Flight Lieutenant Hurst led the bombing, 12 bombs going into the building at 11.40. Sergeant Martin hit a high-tension cable on his run but he returned safely. Only one Battle was lost, Pilot Officer Waddington's machine being hit on the way out, wounding the pilot slightly, but he force-landed near Brussels without further injury. The success of the raid brought forth messages of congratulations from Barratt and the Chief of the Air Staff.

A Blenheim of 59 Squadron was reported lost at about this time, although the exact details are obscure. Pilot Officer C.J.E. Chamberlain (RNZAF) was the pilot, but he later turned up in Luxembourg, although he'd been wounded. His was the first squadron loss (N6173).

As an indication of the problems facing some of the units in France, details of a damaged 59 Squadron Blenheim are worth relating. Blenheim L4856, which had been damaged on a sortie on the 11th, when Flight Lieutenant Smither had returned to Vitry on one engine, was in need of repair away from the squadron's main base at Poix. The Engineering Officer, Flying Officer J.E. Horton, therefore, had to go to Vitry which he did in the late afternoon of the 12th, taking Sergeant Baird and four airmen with him.

Baird and the airmen travelled by lorry, collecting a new engine from No. 1 Repair and Service Unit at Glisy, on the way, arriving at about dawn on the 13th. After inspecting the damaged aircraft, the team found great difficulty in off loading the engine from the back of the lorry as no lifting equipment was available at Vitry. Ever inventive, the team took the lorry and engine to a nearby cement works where they were able to unload it onto a ramp and then manhandle it onto a low trolley. They then towed the trolley back to the airfield.

They were equally unable to lift the damaged engine from the aeroplane, but by using shear legs together with brute strength they eventually removed the engine and installed the new one, although it was a long and tedious job. However, they did it, and L4856 was ready for further repairs.

The afternoon of the 13th was quiet on the RAF front. The only major operations were recce missions by the Component Blenheim squadrons. These led to a loss by 57 Squadron in the early evening:

| P/O C.R.K. Drimmie | Sgt G.F. Couzens | AC R. Shuttleworth | P6930* |

No. 18 Squadron sent out an aircraft at 6.15 to recce the Albert Canal, which was carried out at between 3,000 and 4,000 feet. They encountered the usual enemy flak and the Blenheim was damaged but they returned safely:

| S/L D.D. Rogers | Sgt A.J. Gulliver | LAC D.C. Moore | L8866 |

If the 13th proved comparatively quiet, the next day was to witness the biggest bombing effort by the AASF and 2 Group's squadrons – and their greatest loss since the beginning of the war.

Tuesday, 14 May
The Germans were no fools. Whatever turmoil had resulted following the non-destruction of the various bridges at

Maastricht or later in the Sedan region, the Germans had to have anticipated the strong possibility that the bridges would be blown by the defenders. That they captured several intact was a bonus and resulted from good planning and surprise. Nevertheless, they had to face the probability that they might not secure them, or that the Allied air forces might bomb them, and had thus brought pontoon bridges with them for just this eventuality.

A serious situation had developed on the evening of the 13th, when the French had informed their British Allies that the Germans had begun crossing the upper Meuse. This not only threatened the front but also the whole area around Rheims where the AASF squadrons had their airfields and bases.

Shortly before midnight on the 13th, the AASF was ordered to prepare to attack, at first light the next morning, three pontoon bridges in the Sedan sector and two pontoon bridges reported in the Dinant area. Both targets were to have equal priority, and had to be destroyed.

However, during the night, word was received that the French had successfully attacked and destroyed the Dinant bridges, and they had also attacked German convoys on the Cenay-Dinant road and other movements on the roads leading into Sedan from the north and east. Therefore, the bombers would only have the pontoons at Sedan to worry about. The following order was issued to the wings:

Operation Order No. 664 to 75 & 67 Wings, repeated 71 & 76 Wings & N Eagle. From Panther. 14.5.40.
Cancel my Ops No. 662, 13.5.40. Confirming telephone conversations at 0100 hrs and 0110 hrs with Group Captain A.H. Wann. Requirement is now to attack three pontoon bridges which enemy are reported to have built between 153 degrees AR4 30 miles and 140 degrees AR4 37 miles (ie in the Sedan section between Vrigne and Douzy). Strength of attack four half sections. Aim of attack, to destroy bridges. Tactics left to discretion of formation leaders but attack should be made as early as light permits. One flight of fighters to be detailed by OC 67 Wing to operate in support of bombers. Method of co-operation to be concerted between numbers 75 & 67 Wings. Enemy opposition expected to be

strong in neighbourhood of target. timed at 0145. Immediate.

This message was followed by others during the early hours of the 14th. The first was timed at 2.20, confirming a telephone call reducing the number of half sections to three. Operation Order No. 668 followed, which informed the wings that the French territory on the left bank of the Meuse was now in German hands, and gave the map references to the specific area.

At Bétheniville, 103 Squadron were on stand-by at 3.30, and eight Battles began to take off at 5.05, led away by Flying Officer J.R. Havers. These flew to the target area and found four bridges over the Meuse and one across the River Cheres within a radius of six miles of Sedan.

Attacking these bridges, one hit was claimed on one bridge a mile north of Villers but although the others were bombed, no more than near misses could be claimed. Hurricanes were above, but no enemy fighters were in evidence, and all eight Battles returned, although ground fire did hit one Battle. This was crewed by Sergeant C.D. Parry and AC A.R. Layfield (possibly Battle P2191.) Charles Parry was severely wounded in the thigh and stomach but brought his machine back to the vicinity of the aerodrome before having to force-land when he felt he was about to pass out. He was later awarded the DFM.

An early recce mission by 57 Squadron met with mixed fortunes:

P/O W.G. Spencer	Sgt R. Pike	AC O. Beaumont	L9180

Taking off at 5.37 a.m., they ran into a Dornier 17 over Belgium, possibly on a similar mission to themselves. They had what was described as a successful fight with this German aircraft, but they were forced down near Tirlemont, with the observer wounded and the gunner dead. Getting clear of the aeroplane, Spencer and Pike went searching for petrol so they could fly back to Poix but during their absence someone set fire to the Blenheim and it was destroyed.

No 59 Squadron also sent out a recce aircraft, piloted by Peter Hawks, an Army officer (The King's Regiment) seconded to the RAF. He and his crew failed to return and all were reported killed:

| F/O P.A. Hawks | Sgt F.J.T. Evans | AC1 C.G. Shaw | P6926* |

Meanwhile, a further order was sent out from AASF HQ at 6.50 a.m.:

Operation Order 669, 14.5.40. One half section to attack solid looking pontoon bridge reported one mile north-west of Remilly–Allincourt. If possible, pilots to report whether any damage observed on bridges nearby, previously attacked. Fighter protection will be provided. Immediate.

At Ecury, 150 Squadron had been ready since dawn following a call from Group Captain Field to have two half sections on stand-by. At 6.30 a call came from Wing that a target had been found, and at 7.35, two Battles took off:

| P/O A.R. Gulley | Sgt Berry | LAC D. Phillips | L5524 |
| P/O S.R. Peacock-Edwards | Sgt Scott | LAC Dearnley | P2179 |

These two attacked two pontoons across the Meuse, 1½ miles south of Sedan. Considerable light flak came at them, especially from the east of the town. The Battles dive bombed the targets from 4,000 feet at ten minutes to eight (ie: just 15 minutes away from their base) and although several hits were observed, results were again uncertain.

Already a second half section was airborne:

| Sgt R.G. Beale | Sgt Tutt | Cpl Carter | L5457 |
| P/O D.G. Long | Sgt Minchin | LAC Davies | K9483 |

These two located the pontoons, west of Douzy, and dive bombed with exactly the same results as their companions. Amid much light flak the two Battles jinked away and got home at 8.37, landing within minutes of the first two aircraft.

Shortly after these raids, 114 Squadron were requested to despatch a single Blenheim on a recce of the Sedan-Givonne-Bouillon areas and report on enemy troop movements. Bombs were to be carried and dropped if a suitable target presented itself. Fighter cover was promised for the general area. The Blenheim took off at 8.55:

| P/O N. Tasker | Sgt Summers | LAC Levack | R3703 |

The weather was hazy with visibility down to about a mile but Tasker reached the area and saw heavy troop movements in and around woods through which ran the Sedan-Bouillon road, although the road seemed blocked at Givonne, but some Germans appeared to be beyond this point. Columns were also moving down all roads from Bouillon and Sugny and converging on Sedan. Machine-gun nests could be seen beside the roads and the Blenheim was fired on by light and small calibre gun and cannon. The aircraft was hit by a bullet through the port rear spar and by a cannon hit in the starboard engine nacelle. Finally, when a column of lorries and motor cycle troops were seen on the road leading through Bosseval, Tasker put the Blenheim into a shallow dive from 1,500 feet, and dropped his load of two 250 lb, six 40 lb and twelve 20 lb bombs but he did not hang around to see the results.

Meanwhile, the Luftwaffe had been active. At 8.30, 88 Squadron were bombed (they would be bombed twice more this day, at 1 pm and 5 pm) and at ten minutes past ten, 218 were bombed and their telephone communication broken.

In England, 2 Group squadrons had been on alert since dawn, but it was 82 Squadron which received the first support request. They too went to the northern sector in support of the French 7th Army, to bomb the cross-roads east of Breda. They took off at 11.21, led by Squadron Leader M.V. Delap DFC[1] in Blenheim P4852 'O'. They made a converging shallow dive-bombing attack, obtaining hits on roads on the eastern outskirts of Breda and on the Tilburg-Breda railway line. Heavy AA fire was met but all the aircraft returned.

Afternoon, 14 May
Pressure was still on in the Sedan sector and BAFF were planning a major effort against the enemy advance in this

---

[1] Squadron Leader Miles Delap had successfully bombed and sunk a German U-Boat on 11 March 1940, the first sunk by an RAF aircraft in WW2 (*U-31*).

region. It was now imperative to try and stop the Germans at Sedan. Perhaps this was the moment – the 'really critical phase'. At any rate, it was sufficiently critical for Barratt to bring every available bomber aircraft to Readiness, planning to hurl them all against the German thrust.

At 2.05 he sent a message to the Chief of Air Staff, informing him of the grave deterioration of the situation at Sedan, as the French had been strongly atacked before they had been able to mount their own counter attacks. If something wasn't done quickly, all would be lost and the French would be pushed back and the Rheims area would be threatened.

Having got across the Meuse, the Germans had a 14-mile front with Sedan at its centre which was being enlarged hourly. It now stretched from Vrigne-sur-Meuse to Mouzon, and in depth, about ten miles to the south-west of Sedan, French Generals Gamelin and Georges had requested maximum assistance from Air Marshal Barratt.

Barratt in turn, requested a combined effort with the French Air Force, which was agreed. Together they planned to send in four waves of bombers at approximately three hourly intervals, two by each air force. During these raids, Barratt would send two-thirds of his force against bridges, one-third against enemy columns. It was a bold plan but difficult to co-ordinate fully due to the numbers and the time involved. The French also wanted further support in the Dinant area but Barratt considered the Sedan front to be the major objective.

The first wave was mounted by the French, who were to send 40 bombers into the attack area at about 12.30, supported by fighters. While this was in progress, AASF HQ ordered attacks on the five major bridges across the Meuse:

Bridge No. 1 S of Sedan	4 a/c 3 p.m.	3 a/c 3.20/30 p.m.	4 a/c 3.35/45 p.m.
Bridge No. 2 Romilly	4 a/c 2.10 p.m.	4 a/c 3.20/30 p.m.	4 a/c 3.35/45 p.m.
Bridge No. 3 Douzy	4 a/c 3 p.m.	4 a/c 3.20/30 p.m.	3 a/c 3.35/45 p.m.
Bridge No. 4 Mouzon	4 a/c 3 p.m.	–	4 a/c 3.35/45 p.m.
Bridge No. 5 Mouzon	4 a/c 3 p.m.	4 a/c 3.20/30 p.m.	4 a/c 3.35/45 p.m.

These attacks, together with bombing of columns from Bouillon, through Givonne to Sedan at the same time, by formations of five, eight and ten aircraft respectively, totalled 77 bombers, although probably only 71 actually took part.

The following list shows how the breakdown of aircraft to

targets was achieved and the subsequent losses:

76 Wing. 1st Attack force

12 Sqdn	5 Battles against columns	4 failed to return
142 Sqdn	8 Battles against bridges	4 failed to return
226 Sqdn	6 Battles against bridges	3 failed to return

71 Wing. 2nd Attack force

105 Sqdn	11 Battles against bridges	6 failed to return
150 Sqdn	4 Battles against bridges	4 failed to return
114 Sqdn	2 Blenheims against columns	1 failed to return
139 Sqdn	6 Blenheims against columns	4 failed to return

75 Wing. 3rd Attack force

88 Sqdn	4 Battles against columns ⎫	
88 Sqdn	6 Battles against bridges ⎭	1 failed to return
103 Sqdn	8 Battles against bridges	3 failed to return
218 Sqdn	7 Battles against columns ⎧	10 failed to return
218 Sqdn	4 Battles against bridges ⎩	in total.

Totals:	71	40

Where records survive, we shall take the raids, by squadron, as they appear in this list, beginning with 76 Wing, 12 Squadron.

Ironically, as it was to turn out, 12 Squadron had just received a forwarded message from Sir Cyril Newall, the Chief of the Air Staff, a former commanding officer of the squadron, shortly before take-off time. It read:

> I send my warmest congratulations on the brilliant attack voluntarily carried out by the pilots and crews of 12 Squadron at Maastricht yesterday [sic]. As the first CO, I am proud to see the gallant and courageous spirit which exists, and which I know will continue to bring further honour and credit to the Squadron.

(As a matter of interest, the French General Georges had also sent a message dated 13 May, but it was delayed and not received for more than a week. However, it relates to the AASF's attacks of 10-12 May:

> I address my congratulations and thanks for the wonderful effort sustained through three days by the British Air Force in low flying and bombing attacks. The French Army salutes the memory of the British airmen who have sacrificed their lives for our two Countries.)

No. 12 Squadron, still reeling from its losses on the 10th and 12th, had assigned five Battles and crews to the day's mission. They began to leave the ground at 3.30, already behind the schedule:

A/F/Lt G.D. Clancy	Sgt K. Alderson	AC R.T. Ainsworth	L4952*
F/O E.R.D. Vaughan	Sgt C. Shelton-Jones	AC J.W. Wright	L4950*
P/O J.J. McElligott	Sgt B.C. Long	LAC T.O. Burgess	L5538
Sgt H.R.W. Winkler	Sgt M.D. Smalley	AC L.R. Clarke	L5188*
Sgt A.G. Johnson	Sgt E.F. White	AC F.T. Spencer	L5186*

Their target was columns along the road leading from Sedan to Givonne – someone had obviously thought the squadron had had enough of bridges! It was not going to help stop casualties.

At Amifontaine, the ground crews awaited anxiously for their return. They also had orders to rearm and refuel the returning bombers as soon as they landed, so as to be ready for possible further attacks. In the event, only one solitary Battle came limping back, that flown by Jim McElligott.

He had dive-bombed the road in the village of Givonne as no traffic had been seen. The Battles had been met by intense AA and machine-gun fire, as well as Me109s, and although he had seen Eric Vaughan bomb the same target, all had been shot down. Vaughan was dead but his crew survived as prisoners. Gordon Clancy was also a prisoner, his crew killed. Sergeant Winkler and his crew were also captured, and so was Sergeant Johnson's gunner, but Johnson and Sergeant White were both dead.

The eight Battles of 142 Squadron had taken off earlier than the other squadrons, with orders to attack the bridges between Sedan and Mouzon.

S/L J.F. Hobler	Sgt R.V.T. Kitto	Cpl. D.J. Barbrooke	P2246*
Sgt A.N. Spear	Sgt S.J. Brooks	LAC R.H. Nugent	P2333*
F/L K.R. Rogers	Sgt H.F. Trescothic	Cpl H. Todd	L5517*
P/O H.L. Oakley	Sgt Martin	AC Presto	K9333*
F/L W.B. Wight	Sgt Rudd	Sgt B.J. Rowe	L5227
P/O I.C. Chalmers	Sgt Howard	AC Pearce	K7596
F/O J. Read	Sgt D.A. Whiting	AC T. Greenall	K7700
P/O W.D.K. Franklin	Sgt Hurrel	LAC Pounds	K9386

They too met heavy ground fire and Me109s, as John Hobler recalls:

As we approached the target our section of two was attacked by five Me109s, coming along in line astern, to get some practice in on us. I had Sergeant Kitto as my observer and Corporal Barbrooke as gunner. We had worked out that we would use the upside-down VGO gun if possible, so Kitto got down on the floor, telling me where the enemy were coming from. I would have liked to have turned into them and used my front gun but these two VGO guns were very fast firing and we really thought we could do something with them.

As the 109s came in and attacked us, I was weaving away and could feel bullets striking our aircraft and felt glad that armour plate had been fitted to our positions, because this plate must have stopped a lot of projectiles from getting at us. It added to the weight of the Battle but we survived.

Kitto shouted that he'd got one of the b— Huns and I'm not sure we didn't damage another one. I'm sure we did and I know we got one. The 109s kept up their attack and shot us to pieces. I could feel the controls begin to go limp and all I could do was to try and hold the aircraft up, for we were so low there didn't seem much point in trying to get out by parachute at that stage.

Down below us were the German infantry advancing in personnel carriers, and as we got nearer to the ground, we could feel ground fire attacking us. Our glycol tank was blowing hot glycol all over me and I couldn't see a hell of a lot but I could see what I wanted to do. I was hoping to guide the aircraft between a couple of trees, so that we would more or less land evenly. But while doing this, I was aware that fire from the ground – very quick firing guns – were slowly cutting my instrument panel away before my very eyes. In other words, they were keeping pace with the aircraft as we glided down out of control and just cutting away the entire instrument panel. It was a most weird feeling, extraordinary experience. A couple of inches back and they would have been into me, but they were just cutting away at the panel. Really quite remarkable.

This went on as we came down towards the two trees and I managed somehow to put the nose of the aircraft somewhere in the middle of them. As we hit, the trees folded the wings back, stopping our descent and averting what would have been a bald, flat-out crash. So we slithered onto the ground in that manner, very undignified, with the Germans not very far

away and heading towards us like mad.
Squadron Leader J.F. Hobler, 142 Squadron

Sergeant Arthur 'Dagger' Spear bombed the target but he too was then attacked by a 109 and most of the Battle's tail was shot away. He ordered his crew to jump and was himself thrown out as the aircraft broke up. He landed in enemy-held territory but he got hold of a horse and rode back, also swimming a canal. He too received a DFM, but unhappily both his crew were unable to get clear before the Battle disintegrated and both were killed.

Flight Lieutenant Ken Russell and his crew were all killed while Pilot Officer Oakley, a New Zealander, had to force-land at Eely near Rethel. He was slightly injured but got back to the squadron and he and his crew were flying again the next day. His Battle was a write-off.

The other Battles all bombed the target, and Aircraftman Greenall, Flying Officer Read's gunner, claimed a 109 shot down.

Squadron Leader Charles Lockett led 226 Squadron's six Battles off at 3.25:

S/L C.E.S. Lockett	Sgt F.J. Percival	Cpl R.S. Clark	P2267*
Sgt Annan	Sgt A. Livingston	AC2 Jonas	P2254
F/Lt V.S. Butler	Sgt Forsyth	LAC J.P. Sullivan	K9345
Sgt E.E. Hopkins	Sgt J. Callaghan	AC D. Barber	K9383
Sgt H. Moseley	Sgt S.D. Hibberd	Cpl H.F. Little	K9343*
F/Sgt W.A. Dunn	Sgt A.F. Sedgwick	AC2 M.B. Millar	L5438*

The first two Battles had No. 2 Bridge – Douzy – as their target and both met withering ground fire on the way in. Lockett's staggered and fell crashing to the ground. Only one occupant was seen to get out and later the squadron leader was confirmed as a prisoner.

Sergeant Annan's machine was also hit by ground fire which shot away the port aileron and part of the tailplane. He was still some way away from the bridge when he found his bomb gear smashed, forcing him to abort. As he turned away he could see German troops crossing the canal south of Sedan in rubber boats.

The second section both bombed No. 4 Bridge – Mouzon – and Flight Lieutenant Vernon Butler saw two of his bombs go

Above Battle of 226 Squadron. Note single machine gun protruding from starboard wing. (*R.C. Bowyer*)

Below Pilots of 226 Squadron checking their aircraft recognition. Left is Squadron Leader C.E.S. Lockett, taken prisoner on 14 May, and third from left is Flight Lieutenant Brian Kerridge, who was killed on 10 May.

Bottom Bomb trolley – 142 Squadron, Berry au Bac. (*J.F. Hobler*)

into the river but another hit the bridge. Intense tracer fire caught his aircraft but he got away, although he thought some of the fire was from French positions. Sergeant Hopkins also bombed but was too busy escaping the deadly tracer to see what happened. His machine was also damaged, petrol tanks holed and his gunner injured in the right ankle.

The last two also went for the Mouzon Bridge but neither managed to get home. All six men were killed. Dunn had only been promoted to flight sergeant the previous day.

The first squadron of 71 Wing, 105, began taking off at 3.40:

F/Lt H.C. Samuels	Sgt F.B. Abbott	LAC R.D. Hughes	L5523*
P/O D.C.F. Murray	Sgt Hemingway	AC Hill	L5250*
Sgt A.J.C. Eagles	Sgt John	AC E.S. Rock	P2248
F/O R.N. Wall	Sgt A.C. Morgan	LAC H. Hatton	L5585*
F/O P.D.E. Pitcairn	Sgt Banks	AC Patterson	P2177
Sgt L. Wilson	Sgt Hancock	AC Williams	K9186
P/O F.A.G. Lascelles	Sgt Ordway	AC Weir	K9342*
P/O H.E. White	Sgt G.A. Cartwright	AC J. Potter	L5230*
Sgt K. Lord	Sgt Bundock	AC Dunbar	L5200
F/O C.F. Gibson	Sgt A.W.H. Hadley	AC W. Draper	K9181*
P/O F.H. Ridley	Sgt G. Atkinson	AC J.S. Thompson	L5238*

Just four Battles got home, landing around 5.15. Of these, one was so badly damaged as to be beyond the capabilities of the squadron to attempt to repair it. The other three were bombed up and made ready for another mission. The Battle flown by Pilot Officer Murray was also damaged and had to be force-landed at Suippes, the crew returning by road. Of the missing, the two flight commanders, Samuels and Wall, and their crews, were all killed. Pilot Officer Hugh White and his crew also died, and Pilot Officer Frederick Ridley also died with his gunner, but the observer survived as a prisoner. Chris Gibson crash-landed inside the German lines and he and his crew were captured. However, Gibson escaped.

While waiting for a car to take him and his men away, both of whom were suffering from concussion, Gibson managed to slip away and made for a nearby wood. He was spotted and fired at, being wounded in the hand. For four days he walked westwards, keeping to the woods and hedgerows, managing to survive on nothing more than grass, stinging nettles and stream water. Then he swam the Meuse River and eventually reached the French lines.

Almost within reach of safety, he was seen and fired on by the French, being hit and wounded in the thigh. Not being able to move he had to await the arrival of French troops, although he did not know for sure what nationality they were until they discovered him. They took him to hospital where a portion of an injured finger was amputated and the bullet taken from his thigh. Unfortunately, although news of his safety was received by the squadron on 21 May, Gibson was still in the French hospital when the French capitulated and was thus unable to leave and eventually was taken into captivity. For his determination to get back, he received the Military Cross from the British, while the French awarded him the Croix de Guerre for his efforts and for information he brought back with him which he gave to the French authorities.

After this raid, 105 Squadron did not operate again in France.

The four Fairey Battles of 150 Squadron took off around 3.20 and headed for Sedan:

F/O J. Ing	Sgt J.D. Turner	AC W.J. Nolan	L4946*
P/O J. Boon	Sgt T. Fortune	AC S. Martin	P2182*
P/O A.F. Posselt	Sgt D.J. Bowen	AC N.V. Vano	K9483
Sgt G.T. Barker	Sgt J.D.F. Williams	AC A.K. Summerson	P5232*

Little is known of their mission for all four were shot down, pounced upon by Messerschmitts, which by this stage of the proceedings were filling the sky above Sedan just waiting for fresh targets to appear. Only one man survived, Alan Summerson, from Lincolnshire.

Summerson blazed away with his rear gun and claimed later to have hit two. Behind him Sergeant Williams was killed, and then their Battle was hit, Summerson being wounded in the leg. Moments later they hit the ground. He was thrown clear and picking himself up found he was unhurt apart from the gunshot wound to his leg. The shattered Battle lay nearby, burning, the pilot still in his cockpit. He climbed onto the wing and despite the flames, got the pilot out and dragged him clear. However, his pilot was already dead.

Badly burned about the face, hands and arms, Summerson set off for some woods, determined to get back. His leg wound was bleeding while burnt skin hung down in shreds from his face and hands. He hid in the woods and then began his trek back to the French lines which was to take him two days and two nights. He hid in deserted houses and cafés, once hiding under a bed while German soldiers liberated and drank wine in the café below. His injuries caused him immense pain and discomfort and the only food he had was dried cereals and stale bread which he soaked in wine. With the burnt flesh around his eyes puffed up, he could hardly see where he was going but on the third night he stumbled into a French patrol, who quickly got him to a hospital. Later he met up with Bill Simpson who had been shot down and burnt on 10 May. For his gallant actions, the French later awarded Alan Summerson the Medaille Militaire and the Croix de Guerre.

The two AASF Blenheim squadrons were part of the second attack wave. At 114 Squadron, orders had been received in the morning for six crews to report to Plivot, as their aircraft had mostly been destroyed on the ground on the 11th. If required, they would fly with 139 Squadron, using their aircraft. 139 Squadron still had aircraft, it was crews they had lost. The two squadrons put up eight Blenheims, six from Plivot, two from Vraux:

F/O R.H. de Montmorency	Sgt H.B. Wallis	LAC V.S.G. Barrow	L9179*
Sgt Brady	Sgt Willsher	LAC S.A. Maddox	P4827*
F/O J.H. Newberry	Sgt Kendrick	LAC Baker	N6230*
P/O J.O'B. Power	Sgt P.T. Stuart-Harris	AC1 W. Parker	P6902*
P/O J.M. Hogston	Sgt Roy	AC McDougall	L8760
Sgt Roberts	Sgt McKim	AC Lyle	N6227
P/O C.B. Jordan	Sgt P.M. Southwood	AC T.W. Brown	L9464
Sgt Potter	Sgt Mulford	AC Longhorn	L9466

Sergeant Brady, No. 2 in the leading section, later reported that as they reached south-west of Sedan, flying at 5,500 feet, they saw 12 Me109s sweeping round in a wide circle in order to attack the Blenheims from behind. Ahead was some cloud and the Blenheim pilots opened their throttles in an endeavour to reach it before the fighters got to them. They failed.

While still some distance from the clouds, Brady's machine was hit; incendiary shells set it on fire, and his ailerons were shot away. The bomber began to go down in a half spiral. The front escape hatch seemed to be jammed, but it was kicked out and Brady and his observer baled out. In the rear of the aircraft, LAC Maddox failed to get clear.

On landing, Brady was later picked up by French soldiers and passed to the French air base at Souville. He was told by them that they had watched the air battle and seen six Blenheims shot down, one of which appeared to collide head-on with a 109.

Following the first section were John Newberry and James Power. They too were hacked down by the Messerschmitts, and Newberry crash-landed five miles west of Sedan. He and his observer got clear with burns, but the gunner died in the burning aircraft. There was no news of the second Blenheim, thought to be the one seen colliding with the German fighter. James Power, Douglas Stuart-Harris and Walter Parker were all killed.

The third section had proceeded independently as the No. 2 aircraft had burst its tail wheel tyre just before take-off which had delayed them slightly. Hogston and Roberts had climbed to 8,000 feet, somewhat higher than the four Blenheims ahead of them. As they approached Sedan, they could see fighter aircraft ahead, but too far away to identify who or what. The other two sections could be seen way ahead, against a layer of white cumulus cloud. As they watched, black bursts of smoke were seen and from one a long plume of fire fell away.

Reaching the target, the two Blenheims went into a shallow dive to 4,000 feet. Villages around Sedan could be seen burning although Sedan itself seemed intact. The roads seemed full of German troops and lorries, and the two pilots put their bombs along one of them, while their gunners sprayed them with their guns. Then they headed for home, pursued by bursting AA fire.

The two aircraft from Vraux made a low level approach, then climbed to 5,000 feet as the target area came up. A 109 attacked the second machine, and in evading it, Sergeant Potter became separated, and, heading once more for the target, he was attacked by another fighter. The Blenheim was badly shot up and Potter was forced to jettison his bombs to escape. Pilot Officer Jordan in the lead aircraft, failed to return, and he and his crew were reported missing, believed killed, although some reports suggest they were all taken prisoner.

The final wave was put up by 75 Wing. 88 Squadron mustered a total of ten Battles, four to attack the bridges, six to go for the roads. The bridge they attacked was located one mile north of Villers, while the others bombed a column on the Bouillon-Givonne road. Squadron records do not show who flew these missions, only the missing crew:

Sgt W.G. Ross	Sgt F.E. Beames	AC J.H.K. Gegg	L5190*

It is not known if this crew attacked the bridge or the column but all three men were subsequently reported to have been killed. (Strangely there is evidence that the squadron had Battles L5422 and L5581 reported missing on this date.)

Poor surviving records of 103 Squadron only note the three missing aircraft and crews from its raid on bridges at Sedan. The attack was made from low level and it met a wall of flak and light ground fire in addition to Me109s. The three missing were:

P/O V.A. Cunningham	AC J. Johnson	K5516*
F/O T.B. Fitzgerald	Cpl Madkins	?
Sgt G. Beardsley	LAC G.F. Lewis	?

The squadron was still flying just two man crews on all low level operations. Pilot Officer Cunningham, who had survived the 12 May raid, was seen to collect a direct hit from an AA shell and his aircraft exploded in the air. He and his gunner died instantly. Tom Fitzgerald, from New Zealand, was also brought down but not before pressing home his attack despite being wounded. He succeeded in making a successful forced landing. He and his gunner survived and returned the next day. Fitzgerald was later awarded the DFC.

Beardsley and Lewis were shot down by a 109 and crash-landed, returning on the 17th, having walked 15 miles through the forward battle area before being picked up by the French. George Lewis was later awarded the DFM.

Flying Officer Havers recalls:

I do remember that after I'd dropped my bombs in the target area – we had dive-bombed it – I was being shot at very hard but I managed to find a cloud, just one in an otherwise blue sky. I got into it and flew away and it seemed to me to take a very long time to find my way back.

Flying Officer J.R. Havers, 103 Squadron

The final squadron was 218, which sent seven Battles against columns, four to the bridges. Only one was to return. Once again, lost records do not let us know who took part, but among the missing were:

P/O A.M. Imrie	LAC A.J. Taylor		L5235*
F/O J.F.R. Crane	T/W/O T.W. Holloway		L5422*
F/O D.A.J. Foster	AC1 T.J. Bryan		P2324*
P/O R.T.L. Buttery	AC2 W.C. Waterston		L2360
P/O W.A.R. Harris	Sgt N.B. Herriot	AC1 W. Robinson	L5232*

Pilot Officer Bill Harris returned, although he was wounded. Pilot Officer Arthur Imrie, Flying Officer Foster and his gunner, and Warrant Officer Holloway were prisoners. The rest of those listed above were all killed.

Meanwhile, in the battle area, John Hobler was on the ground, having crashed during the first wave attack, after being shot down by 109s, and hit by ground fire. Both wings had been ripped off as he went between two trees: He recalls:

This is where my crew, Kitto and Barbrooke, were so good. I was burnt, glycol burns all over me, my face and hands were raw and they helped me out. We set fire to what was already a wreck and helped by them, I decided we should make for the trees of a nearby wood, with the Germans in hot pursuit. We ran and got into the trees and felt ourselves reasonably safe for a while. We ploughed on, knowing exactly where the French and Germans were by the velocity of their guns. On our left the German guns were clattering away at a rate of knots, while on the other side the French guns were just going, pop-pop-pop.

I was greatly helped by my two airmen; they were the finest kind of chaps, really reliable and responsible. I owe them a lot. We made good progress through the wood and eventually came out of it, with no sign of Germans around. However, soon we saw some grey figures advancing towards us and they began to shout and we then realised we were being faced by French troops. They very obviously mistook our blue uniforms for German, after all, we had on what looked like field boots and probably not having seen an RAF uniform before, they were going to shoot us, right or wrong.

However, we managed to explain as best we could who we were, put our hands high in the air and made no mistakes. They could then see I was fairly burnt – skin was peeling off now – so they gave us some 'Eau de Vie' and wished us luck, passing us back to their HQ. It turned out to be the HQ of General Georges, whom I met when we arrived and who was much encouraged that this was an historic day which I ought to put in my diary, for this was the day he was going to mount the offensive that would end the war!

Whilst I was there he was very kind, sending me off to his medical officer, who was busy taking a leg off a wounded soldier, in his mobile sick quarters. This French doctor immediately fixed my face up with some kind of mixture, bandaged it all over and I was told subsequently that this immediate act saved my face from being very much damaged, so I am very grateful to him for his prompt actions.

At this stage I lost track of Kitto and Barbrooke. I found out later they had been put on transport and taken back to our own area. I was given transport and joined a queue going back. This was a remarkable sight because we were in the midst of a mass of refugees, carrying all their worldly goods on their trucks, bicycles, old cars – any sort of contrivance that would move.

Stuka dive bombers periodically dropped their bombs at crossroads and they also front-gunned some of these masses, struggling to escape. There was one similarity to our earlier days in France, when French reinforcements, which were coming up and causing additional confusion, were in horse drawn waggons – Boer War sort of things. In them were grim-faced Frenchmen, wondering what the devil they would do once they reached wherever they were going to. It didn't really give one a great deal of confidence.

I was back at our HQ by nightfall, and was immediately pushed onto the medical network, and was then on my way to the coast, where I was evacuated to England and into hospital where my burns were further attended to.

Squadron Leader J.F. Hobler, 142 Squadron

*

It had been another disaster. 71 vulnerable bombers had been flung into a modern day 'breach' and although filled 'with our English dead' it failed to stop this twentieth-century enemy.

As the planned schedule could not be adhered to, it is difficult to know which waves may have suffered more, but it seems likely that every unit had its share of flak and fighters. There was little to help them. If they flew in low they were at the mercy of every German with a gun. If they went in with some height they were picked off by the Messerschmitts. Of the 45 aircraft sent against the bridges, 25 were lost and of the 26 attacking road columns, 15 were lost. The whole force suffered an incredible 56 per cent casualty rate. The Royal Air Force was never again to suffer such a high percentage loss in proportion to the numbers involved.

And what had been achieved? Once again it has been difficult to ascertain results of this gallant effort. A BAFF Communiqué recorded that at least two permanent and three pontoon bridges had been destroyed, while after the fall of France, BAFF and AASF reports mention 'two bridges' and 'two pontoon bridges and one permanent bridge destroyed, one pontoon and one permanent bridge damaged.' Certainly the bridges at Sedan, just south of Sedan and at Mouzon had been hit, and almost certainly the Mouzon bridge had been destroyed. As for road targets, well, no amount of damage or casualties inflicted was going to stop the Germans. They were advancing and were pushing all before them. Any casualties sustained were nothing more than a minor irritation, a momentary inconvenience. Paris, France, the War, were their goals. And they were winning!

CHAPTER NINE

Stand By to Evacuate

Late afternoon, 14 May
As the AASF squadrons were licking their wounds and both BAFF and AASF HQs were beginning to realise the dreadful extent of their losses, the third bombing wave by the French was postponed. Possibly the RAF had warned them of the severe mauling they were taking over Sedan, but in any event they promised to make a further assault the next day.

Clearly too, the proposed fourth raid by the AASF was now impossible due to the losses of the afternoon. However, raids by 2 Group Blenheims, projected for some time later, were now brought forward.

Here again we see the dilemma facing the RAF commanders. On the one hand the urge to stem the Germans' advance, and that advance's route over the River Meuse and through Sedan, but on the other, the certainty that they would be throwing more bombers into an already untenable and costly situation.

The bomber crews of 2 Group had been standing-by all day, and at last they received orders to go. 21, 107 and 110 Squadrons were to put up 30 Blenheims to bomb targets at Sedan. 107 and 110, at RAF Wattisham, sent six and twelve bombers respectively. 107's aircraft, bombed up with two 250 lb and twelve 40 lb bombs, took off at 4.50 to attack columns:

W/C B.E. Embry DSO, AFC	P/O T.A. Whiting	Cpl L. Yeomans DFM	L8777
F/Lt H.P. Pleasance	Sgt R.D. Cook	LAC P.E.F. Adams	N6194
P/O J.A. Miller	Sgt R.J. Saunders	LAC W. Stokell	P4925
S/L P.B. Meagher	Sgt H. Simpson	LAC. D.S. Barnes	L9323
Sgt R.S. Gunning DFM	Sgt W.G. Brinn DFM	LAC J. Bartley	P4919
Sgt H. Warman	Sgt W.C.H. Paish	LAC J. Mahoney	N6191

The Blenheims of 110 Squadron took off at approximately the same time:

S/L G.F. Hall	Sgt D. Pennington	Cpl T. Hoggard	L8761
P/O S.G. Rose	Sgt D.A. Ashton	LAC E.N. Edwards	N6210*
Sgt H. Gandy	Sgt G. Robson	LAC B. Gray	P4860
F/O J.K. Buchanan	Sgt Lumsden	LAC Dunn	L8736
Sgt Cater	Sgt Crossland	AC Jones	P6889*
Sgt F. Lewis	Sgt H. Rhodes	AC Greenwood	L8749†
S/L J.S. Sabine	Sgt W. Evans	Sgt J.V. West	P4858
P/O G.R. Worboys	Sgt Muirhead	LAC K. Cooper	L8780
Sgt A.R. Storrow	Sgt E.C. Parker	LAC Rowlands	L9241*
F/O G.O.M. Wright	Sgt J. Fancy	LAC W.W. Street	L9214*
Sgt T.C. Prescott	Sgt Hodder	LAC V.J. Swallow	L8754
P/O E.R. Mullins	Sgt R. Lowe	AC P. Aherne	L9217*

With the exception of Sergeant Lewis (†) who had to turn back with engine trouble, the Wattisham 'wing' of 17 Blenheims headed out over the sea towards France and the waiting guns and fighters. At 5.50, 21 Squadron took off. They were supposed to number 12 but only 11 crews are listed in the squadron's records. If indeed only 11 took part, this would agree with a total of 28 sorties recorded as flown by 2 Group this afternoon.

Basil Embry, the fiery CO of 107 Squadron (and later Air Chief Marshal who was to end the war with the DSO and three bars, the DFC and AFC) recorded in his autobiography (*Mission Completed*, Methuen, 1957), that for the first time the Blenheims had a strong fighter escort on this mission, which helped keep the 109s away. This may well have helped 107 Squadron, who all bombed columns despite being subjected to moderate AA fire. This damaged five of the six Blenheims, but they all got back safely.

Me109s were in evidence, however, despite both RAF and French fighters giving cover. 110 Squadron met them in addition to ground fire, losing five Blenheims. LAC Gray claimed one attacking Messerschmitt shot down. Of those lost, Pilot Officer Stephen Rose and his crew were all killed, Flying Officer Gordon Wright and his crew were taken prisoner as was Pilot Officer Ernest Mullins and his observer although his gunner died.

Sergeant Cater was attacked by two Me109s and a cannon shell took off the Blenheim's escape hatch. His gunner was wounded, while the aircraft's hydraulics, intercom and trim controls were all damaged and the elevators became jammed.

They then ran into heavy AA fire when down to 5,000 feet. Still being chased out of control, Cater was forced to crash-land near Attigny, where his crew were taken off to hospital.

At the same time, Sergeant Storrow was also in difficulties. He had made a low level bomb run on columns moving along the Givonne road, putting 40 lb bombs down in pairs at intervals as he flew along the highway. The bombs were seen to fall among the vehicles, and then he dropped his two 250-pounders into the village of Bouillon. He then flew south to take photos of Sedan but was then set upon by three 109s.

His machine was shot about so he set a westerly course towards the coast. He got as far as Launois before he discovered the oil pressure of his starboard engine had gone, forcing him to shut down the motor and carry on on one engine. Near Lille, and down to 2,000 feet, the crew began to smell burning and then saw the cockpit begin to fill with smoke, making it highly desirable to land at once. With flaps and trim not working and the smoke thickening, he made a wheels-up landing four miles from Orchies. No. 223 Company of the Royal Engineers took charge of the Blenheim after Storrow had blown up the IFF and taken the camera and ammunition. These he handed over to the RAF at Glisy where they managed to get a flight back to Hendon.

Meanwhile, 21 Squadron, now using Bodney as well as Watton, took off from the former base at 5.50 and headed for France:

S/L G.A.M. Pryde	Sgt A. Summers	LAC O'Connor	L8746
F/O J.C.G. Sarll	Sgt Jennings	LAC L.H. Lightfoot	P6890
P/O R.G.M. Gilmore	Sgt T.R.A.D. Pearce	LAC A.G. Wilson	L8742*
F/O S.F. Coutts-Wood	Sgt Swan	LAC Gibbs	L8872
P/O H.D.S. Dunford-Wood	Sgt Rawson	LAC D.R.C. MacLagan	L9023
Sgt J.J. Outhwaite	Sgt E. Broadland	AC J.E. Bradley	L8738*
F/Lt L.V.E. Petley	Sgt Hart	LAC Harris	L8735
P/O W.A. Saunders	Sgt W.H. Eden	LAC C. Webb	L8743
P/O J. Harrison-Broadley	Sgt Williamson	LAC Cleaver	L8744
F/O F.C. Gibbs	Sgt Edwards	AC Chisholme	L8745
P/O Rogers	Sgt Huckins	AC J. Guest	L8758

They were given a variety of targets or alternative targets, among which were columns between Bouillon and Givonne, road bridges across the river at Sedan or troops in a wood, a quarter of a mile west of Givonne. All attacked targets amid ground fire and attacking 109s, two Blenheims going down. LAC Lionel Lightfoot engaged the attacking 109s after his aircraft had bombed, and he was wounded in the shoulder and his turret was damaged but he continued to engage the enemy and claimed one Messerschmitt shot down. Flying Officer 'Peter' Sarll got their shot-up Blenheim back to England but with hydraulics u/s he had to make a belly landing, which he achieved successfully. LAC Lightfoot later received the DFM, Sarll the DFC.

LAC Jack Guest also shot down a 109. This fighter flew parallel with the Blenheim and apparently did not even see it.

Pilot Officer Robert 'Gilly' Gilmore failed to make it, and he and his crew were all later reportd killed in action. Sergeant Outhwaite and his crew survived in France, although his gunner was wounded and taken to hospital. Outhwaite and his observer soon returned to the squadron.

De-briefing reports indicated that 19 Blenheims had bombed troops and vehicles, while six had attacked bridges and woods. This ended the day's effort. In total, the RAF had flown 109 bombing sorties against the Sedan breakthrough area, made up as follows:

Aircraft despatched	*Losses*		
	lost	F/L†	Dam'd
Appx 5.00 a.m. – 6 AASF Battles	–	1	–
Appx 8.30 a.m. – 4 AASF Battles	–	–	2
Appx 3.45 a.m. – 71 AASF Battles & Blenheims	40	1	8*
Appx 6.00 a.m. – 28 2 Group Blenheims	5	2	5*

† force/crash landed.
* at least.

Thus of the 109 sorties, 45 bombers had been lost, three others had crash-landed (two in France and one in England) while at least 15 others had varying degrees of damage: a loss rate on that day of 41 per cent, or 44 per cent if the three crash-landed machines were written off. With all known categories of casualties taken into account, they totalled 58.7 per cent of sorties flown.

The French Armée de L'Air had made attacks at 9 a.m., 12.30 p.m. and later a night raid. The AASF too mounted night raids – just two sorties, flown by 226 Squadron:

| P/O F.O. Barrett | Sgt H. Asker | LAC P. Kirk | P2254 |
| Sgt N.N. Hoyle | Sgt Maguire | AC Lewis | K9176 |

Both took off into a darkening sky at 8.50 p.m. Barrett dropped four bombs onto a road in the Sedan area. Even at this early stage, the Germans had brought up searchlights, which Fred Barrett saw in the night sky just to the north of the town. He landed back five minutes after midnight without encountering any opposition. Sergeant Hoyle saw movement along the Ecly-Serincourt road and dived. As he came down he opened up with his front wing gun, for already ground fire was searching for him. He dropped his bombs onto a column of lorries about a mile north of Ecly, one being seen to burst right next to some vehicles. A light AA gun ceased firing after Aircraftman Lewis emptied two pans of ammo from his Vickers gun. Hoyle landed back at 11.35, his Battle damaged and with leaking fuel tanks.

*

Whatever material damage was or was not inflicted on the German thrust, many of the ordinary German foot soldiers were only too aware of the British and French air efforts. Later evidence of German prisoners testified to the fatigue and nervousness that these repeated attacks had on them. What isn't recorded was the undoubted jubilation by these same troops at seeing so many of their antagonists being shot down.

While these afternoon raids had been carried out, the French 2nd Army had staged a counter attack on the Sedan front, and the enemy's advance had been halted. The French began to think that the situation had been saved, so much so, that General Georges believed that the 'centre of interest' would now switch back to the Dinant front. He also informed Air Marshal Barratt that the air actions had so successfully restricted re-inforcements to the advancing enemy that it had enabled their counter attack to succeed.

The German advance indeed, seemed to have faltered for several hours, but to check it fully would have needed a much greater effort by the land forces, not only at Sedan but along the whole Meuse front. Barratt also knew that he would be unable to repeat his air effort. A couple of days more of these horrendous casualty rates and his force would be totally spent.

Since 10 May, approximately 50 per cent of AASF Battles had been lost, while the two AASF Blenheim units had almost ceased to exist. 48 per cent of their air sorties had failed to return, while other machines had been destroyed on the ground. Even 2 Group had lost around 17 Blenheims with many others damaged. It could not go on.

Without doubt a major problem was the policy of the time not to give bombers close supporting fighter aircraft. As mentioned in an earlier chapter, the thinking had, for some time, been that bombers would be able to look after themselves by flying a tight defensive formation. As we have already seen, this was wishful thinking. They were vulnerable to German fighter attack, and by the very nature of their small, fleeting ground targets, the Battles and Blenheims had to fly low to see and bomb them. This in turn led them to be in lethal range of all types of anti-aircraft and general small arms fire.

The tactics had been, rather than direct escort, to send fighters to the general target area to either clear any fighters found there, or to be ready to take them on if they arrived when the bombers came to make their attacks. As these targets at the beginning of the campaign had been for the most part east and along the line of the Maas/Meuse River, this cover had to be provided by the AASF fighter squadrons, just three in number at that time (1, 73 and 501 Squadrons), or by French fighter Escadrilles. For their part, the few fighters of both the AASF and the Air Component (initially just 85 and 87 Squadrons) were fighting for their lives. Without doubt the fighter pilots of these few squadrons fought long and hard during the French campaign – their victories and losses testify to the intensity of their commitment. The plain fact was that there were just too few fighters to combat the numerically superior Luftwaffe and thus not enough to provide close fighter escort, even if the doctrine was changed.

However, the totally unacceptable bomber losses over the first few days following 10 May made the air commanders quickly re-think their fighter tactics. This was made easier by the fact that as the Allied armies retreated from the Meuse, they came within range of RAF fighter aeroplanes based in southern England. Things, therefore, were about to change, but not just yet. The major change, following the disastrous 14 May, came from Arthur Barratt.

Wednesday, 15 May

Air Marshal Arthur Barratt issued orders on this day to the effect that he no longer proposed to use Battle squadrons on daylight operations unless it became a necessity.

This was undoubtedly welcome news to the Battle crews, all of whom had lost friends and companions over the last few days. Most had been colleagues for months if not years. Some of the senior squadron pilots had been with their units since 1937. They had flown, trained, played and lived together for long periods of time. They had, like all peacetime formations, been as a family, sharing all the joys and the fun as well as the serious side of Air Force life. They had flown to France at the beginning of war, keen to join in the 'great adventure', been forced to endure a long, hard winter and now within a matter of days, almost half of them were no longer around.

The guns and fighters were no respecter of persons, flight commanders and section leaders were as likely to fall as the newest member on the squadron. The mere fact that so many of these senior officers and NCOs had been shot down could easily shake the newer elements, who had looked to them and relied on their seeming invulnerability.

There is nothing so poignant as the empty chair in the mess, the empty bed, the untidy pile of personal belongings, still lying about where the owner had left them, shortly before hurrying to his aircraft. And now they were gone.

Among the replacements to 150 Squadron was Alan Frank, who arrived from the 98 Squadron pool, together with his crew, Sergeant Jock Wilson and LAC Bill Bailey.

> I joined 150 Squadron in the first wave of replacements on 14 May. It was an inauspicious evening to arrive since the Squadron had lost all the four aircraft which it had despatched to Sedan that afternoon. Since the squadron had already lost heavily in low level raids on German columns it was then decided to switch some operations to night work.
>
> *Pilot Officer A.D. Frank, 150 Squadron*

Frank's first job was to be flown to the depot at Rheims by Wally Blom, to pick up a new Battle and fly it back. This he did, but there was some delay and it was nearly dusk when the two Battles finally took off. Frank, of course, was on his own – no crew – and had to keep hard on Blom's wing for fear of losing him for in the darkening sky, he had no idea where he was and would be lucky to find the aerodrome. But he made it and landed L5583 safely.

If the Battle squadrons seemed, even temporarily, off the hook, they had other problems. Despite the French confidence that the situation was improving, the immediate threat was to the AASF's bases themselves. Already plans had been made for a possible move back, and now the word went out to the squadrons that a move was not only likely but imminent.

At Amifontaine, they received the news of Barratt's new orders, but were also told to pack up and move to Echemines, which it did over the next two days. These moves brought further 'losses' when damaged and unserviceable aircraft had to be abandoned and destroyed. 12 Squadron destroyed one Battle.

At Ecury, 150 Squadron began to pack. At 8 a.m. the nearby town of Châlons-sur-Marne was heavily bombed by Luftwaffe aircraft. An hour and a half later, the squadron's road party began to move off, followed by nine Battles – destination, Povan, near Arcis-sur-Aube.

The Luftwaffe were also active in other parts of the area. 218 Squadron were bombed and had one of its Battles destroyed when its bomb load exploded. Between 7 and 7.30, 88 and 103 Squadrons were bombed. A Dornier was shot down by a fighter and one of the German crew landed near 103's airfield with shrapnel wounds to his back, and was taken prisoner. 103 were to see further raids during the 15th, as they too received orders to move, which began in the early hours of the next morning. At first light on the 16th, all Battles and the Hurricanes of 501 Squadron, took off for Rheges. One Battle crashed on take-off and this plus another u/s Battle were abandoned (L5234 and K9404).

The squadron was short of lorries so some of the personnel had to leave on foot across country, especially the 501 Squadron people. One bright spot was the ample supplies of pork and chickens, due to the numerous animals that had been turned loose by French farmers, which were found wandering around village streets as well as the countryside.

Roy Max remembers that when some Hurricanes were

ferried in for 501 Squadron and then flown off again one had been left behind. When its ferry pilot had revved it up it had not given full power, so it was left. When the 103 boys looked at it they realised the ferry pilot had not put it into the correct pitch for take-off! The pilots flew it on raids for a few days as their own personal escort, until 501 Squadron unhappily got to know of it and quickly claimed it back.

At Condé, 114 Squadron was told to move to Crécy, near Abbeville, while at Rheims 226 Squadron was told to get ready. The 'go' came the next morning. Squadron stores, seven Battles and two spare engines were destroyed (including L5418, K9383, P2180 and P2255), before they moved off and the last two flyable aircraft left for Faux Villecerf, south of Epernay. 88 Squadron began packing, was bombed again at 12.30 p.m., but by late evening, the first part of the road convoy was ready. The next day all available aircraft were flown to Grandes Chappelles.

*

The Component recce squadrons were active on the 15th, trying to keep an eye on the enemy's progress, perhaps in the hope that the French optimism might prove well founded.

It did not start well. At 7.45 a.m., 53 Squadron sent out a Blenheim which returned just over an hour later. Over Tournai, however, at nine o'clock, it was attacked and shot down by a RAF Hurricane. Its shooting was good and the Blenheim fell in flames. All three men aboard were killed, including the veteran Sergeant Cronin:

| P/O P.K. Bone | Sgt W.J. Cronin DFM | LAC J. Bromley | L9399* |

Pilot Officer A.B. Goldie of 57 Squadron carried out a successful recce during the morning but 59 Squadron were not so fortunate. Two Blenheims were flown to Vitry. Later, one was sent off to fly a recce mission, piloted by Flying Officer M.I. Murdoch (L4859). He failed to return.

Meanwhile, 2 Group was called upon to make a raid. 15 Squadron, who only had two aircraft serviceable after their raid on 12 May, now had three. These joined nine Blenheims of 40 Squadron to bomb exit points from Sedan. The CO of 40 Squadron led the attack, heading for the Dinant-Celles road,

Above Battle profile – an 88 Squadron bomber. (*MoD*)

Below Three New Zealand friends get their 'Wings'. Jack Edwards, Len Trent and Roy Max. Trent went on to fly with 15 Squadron, Max with 103. Jack Edwards went to 40 Squadron and was killed in action 15 May 1940. (*via R.C. Bowyer*)

Bottom Squadron Leader John Sabine of 110 Squadron relaxes between raids. (*R.C. Rotheram*)

the plan being to block the road in the middle of Dinant which led to the bridge:

W/C E.C. Barlow	Sgt E. Clark	LAC A.E. Millard	N6217*
F/O J.E. Edwards	Sgt C.T. White	LAC S. Johnson	P4913*
Sgt Higgins	Sgt P. Cody	LAC W. Furby	P4909
S/L G.W.C. Gleed	Sgt Burge	LAC A.F.W. Sammels	P4927
P/O F.R. McAuliffe	Sgt A. Spencer	AC E.G. Neville	L8834
F/O R.H. Jacoby	Sgt R.C. Moffatt	LAC D.E. Peters	P4917
F/Lt R.H. Batt	Sgt B.L. Harris	P/O Ewels	L8757
F/O G.D. Hill	Sgt Jeffery	AC A.F.H. Barber	L8838
F/O C.W. Bromley	Sgt M.R. Chouler	AC F.H. Jones	P4818
F/Lt P.G. Chapman	Sgt A.F. Taylor	LAC E.J. Fagg	L8855
P/O D.S.R. Harriman	Sgt J.R. Stanford	LAC Moorhouse	L8856*
F/O A.R. Oakshott	Sgt P. Bloomer	LAC Treherne	P6917

These aircraft met the usual heavy defensive fire, which brought down the two leading machines. Wing Commander Ernest Barlow, who had commanded 40 Squadron since April 1939, Flying Officer John 'Jack' Edwards, a New Zealander (who had trained with Roy Max and Len Trent), and their crews, all died. So fierce was the flak that many of the bombs fell up to half a mile away from the target, but some houses near the Dinant bridge were set on fire. Some of the Blenheims bombed from 10,000 feet, while others went in from a shallow dive approach from 5,000 feet in the hope that the gunners on the ground would be confused.

The three 15 Squadron aircraft also bombed the target, but Pilot Officer Douglas Harriman's Blenheim was damaged. He remained with the others till they were approaching the coast, when his propeller suddenly flew off his port engine, forcing him to make a crash landing in Holland, about seven miles from the Belgian frontier. His observer was slightly injured and had to be taken to a Belgian hospital, but Harriman and his air gunner returned to the squadron the next day. Unknown to him until after he'd landed, was that his accumulator leads had been shot away in the run up to the target, and his bombs had failed to release!

With 40 Squadron's CO lost, Squadron Leader Brian Paddon took over temporary command. A new CO, Wing Commander J.G. Llewellyn, arrived from 75 Squadron on 20 May.

Afternoon, 15 May

A lull followed from late morning till the early afternoon, but 82 Squadron, at RAF Horsham St Faith, were preparing for a raid. They began to take off at 1.30 p.m. led by Wing Commander The Earl of Bandon (P4828 'K'), their target being enemy troop concentrations at Montherme, to the east of the Meuse. They were given the benefit of fighter cover, provided by French Hawk 75s.

The squadron tried a variation in tactics in order not to present too good a target for the Germans. As they reached Montherme, the squadron split up into sections which then went into line astern before making a converging dive bombing attack.

Anti-aircraft fire was quite accurate, but with the gunners unable to concentrate on any one bomber, only two were hit and these were only slightly damaged. One crew saw their bombs fall in the town square which was full of vehicles with yellow bonnets. Houses were hit as well as the road leading to the river, which was blocked with rubble. Some German aircraft were seen. A Henschel 126 observation machine was attacked by two Blenheims but without success, while a 109 that attacked the Blenheim flown by Flight Lieutenant Charlie Breese was hit in the wing by his gunner, Corporal I.T. Harris.

On this day a message was received and distributed to all 2 Group squadrons, which read:

> *Following for AOC from CAS begins*: Please convey to the pilots and crews of No. 2 Group, my congratulations and admiration on the manner in which they have carried out the tasks allotted to them in the present operations. The determination and success of their attacks have earned unstinted praise from our Allies, and reflect the greatest credit on all concerned.

Other Blenheims in the air this afternoon were from 18 Squadron. 52 Wing asked for two crews at Vitry to fly recce missions which they did with some success, although one aircraft, piloted by Sergeant Holland, was damaged by ground fire when flying at 30 feet!

Sgt A. Thomas	Sgt J. Talbot	LAC St James-Smith	L8863
Sgt R.N. Holland	Sgt J. Chatterton	LAC F.E.A. Greaney	L6340

Shortly after 82 Squadron had flown away, 139 Squadron sent four Blenheims to Montherme, making a low level attack from 50 feet, dropping eight 250 lb bombs on a German convoy. They were met by both ground fire and German fighters, which damaged three aircraft and shot down one, in which all the crew died:

P/O K.M.A. deSouza   Sgt E.W. Touch   AC2 W.J. McCarthy   L9411*

The squadron was also ordered to move to Lannoy, near Abbeville.

Free for the moment from daylight ops, the Battle squadron, despite being in the middle of aerodrome moves, were assigned to night bombing sorties. Not that it was always easy. 142 Squadron's base was bombed in the late afternoon, and made unserviceable for night flying. However, four Battles were flown to Champagne aerodrome and that night they attacked and bombed woods in the Montherme area.

Both 12 and 88 Squadrons mounted night raids. 12 Squadron sent six machines to 226 Squadron's base and around midnight, five of these bombed enemy columns on the north bank of the Meuse at Montherme. They did not find it easy due to the darkness of the night and lack of moon. One Battle failed to start, and the section had been led off by Squadron Leader B.E. Lowe in P6597 'V'. 88 Squadron flew eight night sorties, bombing a wood to the north of Sedan although no results were observed. 226 Squadron sent two Battles to the same target. All these night sorties returned.

Thursday, 16 May
The Battle squadrons were now all on the move. Those that hadn't left their old bases on the 15th, were certainly on the roads and in the air on the 16th. Several abandoned u/s aeroplanes, as already mentioned. In addition, 142, who went to Faux Villecerf, left L5440, L5880 and L5242. At Ecury, 105 Squadron's move started to become something of a farce.

Already ordered to move to Echimines, they were delayed by the arrival of 73 and 501 Hurricane Squadrons. Then at 8.30, Ludlow-Hewitt himself arrived and told them that the move was probably unnecessary. Two hours later, 71 Wing ordered the move of all non-operational personnel. There was much confusion, Wing saying move while the AOC was surprised it was required. Added to this, some of the airmen had already left and couldn't be contacted. The discussions continued into the next day, Wing still wanted the move, Ludlow-Hewitt did not. In the event it was not until the 18th, that 105 finally got away.

Soon after dawn on the 16th, 88 Squadron received its, by now, almost daily ritual bombing, but at least the second road convoy got away.

Elsewhere, the first operations of the day were flown. 139 Squadron put up two Blenheims at first light. They were to bomb Montherme again but they were unable to locate a target so returned with their bombs. Sergeant James Paine was one of the observers:

> I was roused at 4 a.m. and detailed to fly with a pilot who had not flown operationally before. Another aircraft accompanied us, and we took off at 4.30. When we reached Charleville the other aircraft broke off to attack another target. We flew at deck level to Montherme and arrived just after dawn. I identified the bridge we were to attack, and floating over it was a queer looking aircraft known as a Fieseler Storch. I yelled to the gunner, 'That's a Storch, shoot it down,' but the pilot turned off and did all sorts of low level manoeuvres. After a while we passed up a valley, and the now familiar aircraft with black crosses on them came round. More low level flying. After having shaken them off, I wanted to go back to the target and complete our unfinished business, but no joy. I asked for a W/T bearing and was told that a bullet had mucked up the set!
>
> *Sergeant J.R. Paine, 139 Squadron*

The other recce units were also active. 59 Squadron's Flight Lieutenant Smither went off at 5 a.m. (N6168), but was attacked by a Hurricane pilot. The Blenheim's oil and petrol tanks and the hydraulics were damaged, and Aircraftman Pitcher was injured by flying perspex. However, Smither got the plane down at Vitry with wheels-up; the Blenheim was a write-off.

Two Blenheims of 53 Squadron had recce details assigned

them. One went off at 5.05 a.m., the second at 9.05. The first crew crashed near Cambrai, while Pilot Officer Robert MacPherson and his crew, flying to the Mezières area, failed to return and he and his crew were later reported prisoners.

P/O Lovell	Sgt McLeod	AC Kenneth	L4860*
P/O R.I.C. MacPherson	Sgt A.T. Morland	AC S. Robinson	L4843*

Another recognition disaster occurred during the day when a 53 Squadron Blenheim was shot down over Glisy aerodrome, the crew being seriously injured by burns:

F/Lt B.B. St G. Daly	Sgt W.R.B. Currie	AC P.J. Blandford	L4852*

At 8 a.m., 114 Squadron, which had all but ceased to exist, put up a recce Blenheim, to fly to the Montcornet-Rumigny-Dubigny areas to the north and then down to Rethel and the River Aisne in the south. When circling over Montcornet, the crew spotted three German Hs126 observation aircraft and they attacked one. Flight Lieutenant Simon Maude, who was to command 25 Squadron (night fighters) later in the war, dived on them firing with his front gun. One was seen to fall and crash and possibly a second was brought down:

F/Lt S.N.L. Maude	Sgt Hawkins	Cpl Appelbee	P6920

In the late morning, with the possible need to supplement the meagre bomber force in France, 59 Squadron was ordered to prepare their Blenheims for bombing operations, and later 53 and 57 Squadrons received similar instructions. All three squadrons prepared five or six machines, but although they stood-by, they were not called upon until the 17th.

During the day, 18 Squadron sent out Sergeant Thomas again, who had made a successful recce for 52 Wing the previous day. With his same crew and same Blenheim (L8863), they were hit by ground fire. Thomas was hit in the neck by a bullet which passed out through his jaw on the other side. In spite of his injury, he got the aircraft back to Vitry and landed, where he and his observer, Sergeant Talbot, who had been wounded in the arm, were sent to a casualty clearing station. Sadly Thomas died, due not only to the wound, which was serious, but which was not helped by the enforced move of the CCS because of the enemy's advance.

The afternoon of the 16th was very quiet from the flying point of view. Four Blenheims of 82 Squadron were assigned to lead/navigate RAF fighters to aerodromes in France from RAF Manston, which they did successfully. Squadron Leader Sutcliffe led them over. Six Hurricanes of 601 Squadron and six of 213 went into Merville.

Then 88 Squadron was bombed yet again during its move, while the last Blenheim op was flown by 139 Squadron. Sergeant James Paine was once again the observer on this sortie, with another fresh pilot who had yet to see action. His orders were simple – 'Find the German Army.' It was 7.30 in the evening, night fast approaching. When finally they did sight some enemy columns it was at a point about an inch off his map! Paine was keen to bomb them but his pilot, worried about landing back in the dark, having no night flying experience, decided to fly home, much to his observer's utter disgust! In the event they landed at another airfield, where Paine noticed with some amazement that its name was picked out in concrete in a circle for all to see – especially the Luftwaffe. The French airfield defence gunners fired as they came in, but a quick 'colours of the day' stopped that. Paine went off to try and telephone the enemy's position back to HQ with poor communications it took most of the night. The squadron thought they were missing.

At 7.40 that evening, Pilot Officer T.R. Turnbull flew a recce sortie over the Fournies Canal at Chemery, encountering light AA and machine gun fire at Plomion. He landed at Romilly due to the darkness, while at his home base, the squadron air party left for Lannoy.

Even the Wing HQs were on the move. 75 Wing, for example, left St Hilaire-le-Grand and moved to a château at Mery-sur-Seine. The next day, 71 Wing began to move towards Nantes. It was about to be disbanded. Its 105 Squadron would be going to 76 Wing, 150 Squadron to 75 Wing. 114 and 139 Squadrons would be returning to England, hence the orders for the Air Component's recce squadrons to prepare for bombing ops. These would now be the only Blenheim units left in France.

Things were beginning to break up. The cracks were starting to show.

CHAPTER TEN

Dawn Massacre

Friday, 17 May
It had now been exactly one week since the German invasion. Few would have predicted how fast the advance would move or how quickly the Germans would establish themselves across the Meuse. Certainly few would have wanted even to contemplate that in just one week the Advanced Air Striking Force bombers would have suffered around 50 per cent casualties in just seven days of an attack being launched.

The Battle squadrons were still in the middle of their various moves but AASF HQ recorded the following aircraft state as at mid-day:

75 Wing: 150 Squadron – 7 Battles bombed up
88 Squadron – 9 Battles half bombed up ⎫ none
103 Squadron – 6 Battles half bombed up ⎬ refuelled
218 Squadron – 3 Battles not bombed up ⎭

76 Wing: 12 Squadron – 5 Battles ⎫ either bombed up
142 Squadron – 3 Battles ⎬ or
226 Squadron – 3 Battles ⎭ not refuelled

Twenty minutes later, the following aircraft were waiting at Glisy for instructions:

Totals: 12 Hurricanes, 9 Battles, 6 Blenheims:

103 Squadron – 3 Battles
218 Squadron – 6 Battles
114 Squadron – 4 Blenheims
139 Squadron – 2 Blenheims
  73 Squadron – 6 Hurricanes
  1 Squadron – 6 Hurricanes

However, the Battles would not be called on; indeed, 12 Squadron noted that all flying was suspended. Obviously the situation was not serious enough for Arthur Barratt to change his non-daylight sorties policy. Instead, he had requested 2 Group to mount a dawn raid on German armoured fighting vehicles reported near Gembloux. 82 Squadron at Watton was given the task. The Earl of Bandon assigned 12 Blenheims, ten from B Flight, two from A, to be led by Miles Delap. They took off at 4.45 a.m.

S/L M.V. Delap DFC	Sgt R.F. Wyness DFM	P/O Jackson	P4852*
F/O R.J. McConnell	Sgt S.H. Fulbrook	AC H. Humphreys	P8830*
Sgt L.H. Wrightson	Sgt I.J. Beaumont	AC K.A. Thomas	P4903*
F/O A.M. Gofton	Sgt F.S. Miller	Cpl T.H. Cummins	P4838*
P/O S. Christensen	Sgt A.N. Phillips	LAC P.R.V. Ettersbank	P4898*
P/O K.S. Toft	Sgt A.G.B. Crouch	AC R. Morris	P4854*
F/L G.W.C. Watson	Sgt F.C. Wootten	AC A.G. Sims	P9213*
Sgt J.J. Grierson	Sgt J.W. Paul	AC J.H. Patterson	P9210*
Sgt T. Morrison	Sgt Carbutt	AC M.C. Cleary	P8858
F/O D.A. Fordham	Sgt F. Fearnley	Cpl A.G. Richards DFM	P4851*
Sgt R.E. Newbatt	Sgt J.K. Crawley	Sgt A.V. Knowles	P4893*
Sgt T.J. Watkins	Sgt D.J. Lees	AC K.G. Reed	P4904*

The exact target was a cross-roads at the village of Gembloux, and the route out was Felixstowe–Fleures–Gembloux. The flight out was good – no flak or fighters seen until the formation reached Nivelles, when some AA fire was seen about two miles to the left, but low down.

Then, just after six o'clock, AA fire began exploding at their level (7,500 feet). It was very accurate; in fact the first shell hit the No. 2 Blenheim in the leading section, flown by Robert McConnell. His Blenheim fell away in a dive. Although injured, he and his observer were later reported safe, although the gunner was taken prisoner. Sergeant Fulbrook later reported:

A shell hit our aircraft bomb well on the small bomb containers. Flying Officer McConnell ordered me to jump and I went out of the front gun hatch. My last sight of the pilot was him attempting to open the top hatch of the aircraft. My parachute took a long time to open and I landed in some woods about 12 km east of Cauvin.

We shall pick up his story later. Meanwhile, the other 11 Bombers commenced to take evasive action, opening out their formation to reach four or five span intervals between each Blenheim. Climbing too, they reached 9,000 feet, while making a gentle 90 degree turn to starboard. Then the gunfire stopped – fighters!

Almost immediately about 15 Messerschmitt 109s fell upon them. They were seen about a mile to port, turning into the sun so as to attack from behind. Delap quickly ordered the formation to close up again, but this had not been achieved by the time the 109s hit them. They appeared to come in in sections, in line astern, each section selecting one bomber in turn.

In the first attack, LAC Cleary, in Sergeant Morrison's aircraft, saw three or four Blenheims go down in flames, while Morrison himself saw Sergeant Grierson's aircraft, which was No. 3 in the third formation (Morrison was No. 2) fall away. From what they could see, the 109s attacked the rear sections from the port quarter, flew on up and around, then attacked the leading sections from the starboard quarter.

One by one the Blenheims were hacked down. Morrison's Blenheim was also hit, as he later testified:

LAC Cleary, my Air Gunner, saw three of our aircraft go down burning and then the 109s attacked our formation (section) from the starboard quarter. On this attack a petrol feed pipe to my starboard motor was severed and my engine lost revs immediately, which threw me out of formation. As I went I saw Sergeant Grierson's aircraft burst into flames on the port side. None of my crew were hit and it was impossible to regain formation.

I dived steeply, taking evasive action on the way down. To see what had happened I turned the petrol cock on the starboard motor from outer to inner tank and the motor caught almost immediately. On levelling out at 6-7,000 feet, there was a loud explosion beneath us and on checking the bomb racks, found that the two 250 pound bombs had fallen off in spite of all switches being 'Off'. Neither my observer or myself were certain where we were then but almost certain bombs fell in wooded area south-west of Givelt. This made me afraid of the small bomb containers, so taking another heavily wooded area I dropped the 40 pound bombs too, so that if necessary we could force land with some degree of safety. We then set off on the outward track home from target.

Sergeant Wyness, 'Paddy' Delap's observer, who had been with him when they sank the German U-boat earlier in the war (his DFM was just about to be announced), also made a report on his experiences:

After the first fighter attacked, Pilot Officer Jackson, our Air Gunner, told us he'd been hit badly. Squadron Leader Delap ordered 'Stand by!' and I put on my parachute, by which time the 109s were on their second attack. In a matter of seconds our machine was ablaze and my pilot opened the top hatch and signalled me to bale out which I promptly did. On the parachute opening I saw others very near the ground and saw them land but could not see who they were before I landed myself. On the way (down) a fighter approached from behind and fired a few rounds at me but missed.

With the exception of Sergeant Morrison, every Blenheim was shot down by the 109s, after the first had been brought down by AA fire. Morrison was now heading for home, his report continuing:

We were out in our calculations as we took a very long time to cross the Channel. I asked LAC Cleary to 'home' on Watton, which he did, getting his first bearing very quickly and then he supplied them regularly. This brought us over our base after steering an average course of 30 degrees for over 30 minutes.

As we landed at 8.20, the starboard engine petered out due to the lack of petrol, having lost a goodly amount through the various leaks in the system and having had air-lock problems. The aircraft had to be written off, principally as the centre section spar had some bullet holes in it.

The enormity of the catastrophe only began to dawn on those at Watton as Sergeant Morrison and his crew climbed down from their bullet ridden bomber and began to describe what they had seen of the fight. Paddy Bandon was on the airfield awaiting his squadron's return. He had watched the badly damaged Blenheim wobble in to land, then coast along until the engines died and the propellers jerked to a halt. As the shattered pilot got out, the Earl asked, 'Where's everybody else, Morrison?'

Many eyes looked to the south-east, at first expecting, then merely hoping that some of the others might yet make it home. When the sky remained empty, the chill of reality came home to them. Eleven aircraft. Thirty-three men – all gone. What was going wrong? How could this be? Only two days earlier the Earl had led 12 aircraft into the Sedan area and returned with just two damaged. Now about two-thirds of the squadron had simply been wiped out.

But some of the men survived. Paddy Delap was in a French hospital; Sergeant Wrightson and his crew too were safe and on their way back. Fordham and Sergeant Watkins were both safe, but their crews had died. Watkins got back on 1 June. He had just passed a cigarette to his observer when the 109s hit them. With his Blenheim blazing, Watkins ordered his crew to jump, seeing Lees dive through the nose hatch, but his gunner had been shot dead. Then, as he discovered the top hatch jammed, the Blenheim exploded and he found himself in space. The burning wreckage of his machine fell past him and after pulling the rip-cord, he landed amidst the pieces. Back in England, Watkins' first daughter was born at just about this time; his wife received the telegram reporting him missing just two hours after the birth.

Ken Toft and his observer were prisoners, his gunner dead, and so were the total crews of Alex Gofton, George Watson, the B Flight Commander, Pilot Officer Christensen and Sergeant Newbatt. Twenty men dead, three prisoners, others injured. The luckless Blenheims had fallen between the two stools, being hit by the 109s just as they had been forced to open out their close formation when fired at by German gunners. It had been a tragic piece of luck but whether the outcome would have been very much different had they still been in their more defensive formation is open to debate. What had been needed, of course, was close fighter escort.

On the ground, two of those who had successfully parachuted to safety, were about to begin their separate adventures to get back. Sergeant Fulbrook continues in his report:

On my way down I was shot at by some French soldiers who took me for a Hun parachutist. Upon landing I left my parachute, harness, etc, and headed west, circling around behind these troops who had fired at me, and confirmed they were French. On hearing noise of motor transport, I headed towards the nearest road, saw several light tanks and lorries with roundels painted on the front, so I came out of hiding and stopped one of them which had a parachute in the back. One of the crew informed me that my Air Gunner was OK and I asked if I could go to him in the village. I had his wounds dressed as far as was possible and saw that he had an injection before removal to hospital at Massigny. Then I returned to the woods and continued on a motor cycle, searching for McConnell until 8.30.

After this I met an English-speaking Frenchman – an officer in one of the regiments – and went with him to La Chappelle then whence to St Quentin by car, being strafed by three Me110s on the way. On arrival at St Quentin, at 1.30 p.m., no transport was available so we made for Péronne, as a train was leaving there for Paris at three o'clock.

At about five kilometres west of this town and at a cross-roads, there was a traffic jam and some Hun aircraft bombed the cross-roads, dropping 70 bombs. Immediately the bombing ceased the road was shelled for 30 minutes. The car was blown up and the French officer and his staff had vanished. So I started walking back to St Quentin. 'After about three hours I was picked up by a motor-bus which dropped me in the square. Tried to find an officer but could not find one to take any interest at all and a section of French troops treated me as a spy and wanted to shoot me on the spot! However, an English-speaking Frenchman came to my rescue and I stayed with him, helping him to build a barricade on the bridge over the River Somme.

We evacuated St Quentin at about 7.30 p.m., going to Amiens via Péronne. At Amiens I reported to the aerodrome at about 11 p.m. and asked for a signal to be sent to base. On the following morning I was unable to obtain any assistance from anyone so I picked a lift to Tangmere in an Anson which was taking some ferry pilots back, arriving at 11.53 a.m.

Sergeant Frankie Wyness, also continued his report:

I landed in a small clearing in a wood, releasing my parachute and stuck it in a tree as a marker for my return, before going in the direction of other parachutists, to render assistance. On the detour, after 1½ hours walking, I saw between 15 and 20 Hun troops apparently searching for someone or something, probably myself.

I jumped into a stream and followed a north-west heading under cover of some overhanging trees. After some time, I ran into a column of retreating Frenchmen who had seen my parachute in the tree and were searching for me. They were retreating fast so I joined them until we reached Braye-en-Laonnis on the Aisne. There we retired to some woods south-east of Soissons but could not reach Soissons because of the bombardment of the town.

The French left me in charge of a nurse, Madame Sorlin, who was with some Belgian refugees. The road column moved to the village of Villiers-Cotterets, and proceeded to Compiègne where we were bombed by Hun aircraft. After lying under cover for three hours we carried on along the railway line to a point where trains were running and finally I reached Paris at 6 a.m. on the 19th. There I reported to the Air Attaché who sent me to the MO for examination. I emplaned at Le Bourget in a Lockheed Electra bound for Hendon, arriving at 3.50 p.m.

During his trek to safety, Sergeant Wyness, on the road to Paris, had walked a total of 60 miles, carrying his parachute the whole way!

Squadron Leader W.P. Sutcliffe DFC with three other pilots and their crews returned from their flight to France the previous day when they had escorted/navigated fighters to

France. Charlie Breese, Attie Atkinson, Joe Hunt and Philip Sutcliffe stood before Paddy Bandon as he said, 'We're now 82 Squadron. Yes, just us.' Philip Sutcliffe recalls:

> When I returned to our base airfield, I was sent for by the Squadron Commander, Wing Commander the Earl of Bandon, who told me that of the twelve Blenheims of B Flight led by Miles Delap, no fewer than eleven had been shot down by AA and fighters over Belgium. Only one returned to Watton, and it was very badly shot up. Squadron Leader Delap survived and I received a letter from him whilst he was in a Belgium hospital. The squadron commander had the squadron up to full strength in aircraft and crews within the next three days.
>
> *Squadron Leader W.P. Sutcliffe, 82 Squadron*

Before mid-day, a message arrived from Group to the effect that 82 Squadron was to be disbanded. Paddy Bandon fought that decision. He won the day and was soon rebuilding the squadron. It says much for his determination, that 82 Squadron was ready for operations again by 20 May.

*

The rest of the morning, indeed the afternoon too, was taken up with operations by the Air Component Blenheims. The one exception was a recce flown by 114 Squadron while 82 Squadron were heading for disaster.

A report had been received during the night that enemy forces were now in Vouziers, so Wing HQ ordered a Blenheim to have a look-see along the Rheims-Rethel and Rethel Vouziers roads, and then along the Suippes road, north to Attigny. The mission was accomplished by Flying Officer Melville Kennedy but found no sign of the enemy having got this far. They landed at 8.15 after one hour 25 minutes:

| F/O M.N. McF. Kennedy | Sgt Lutwyche | AC White | L4966 |

While he had been on this operation, the Hurricanes on 1 Squadron arrived at the aerodrome.

It was to be a trying day for the recce squadrons. 53

Squadron flew three recce sorties on the 17th, two failing to
return. The first of the three went off at 8.10 a.m.

F/O I.H. Bartlett	Sgt Aldridge	AC Sheldrick	R9460
P/O P.G. Royle	Sgt E.F. Woods	AC A.H. Malkin	L4861*
P/O L.J. Huggett	Sgt A.C. Gothard	AC W.A. Christie	L4841*

Bartlett was spotted and attacked by enemy fighters but he
escaped by flying at low level, although his machine was then
damaged by ground fire. Paul Royle and his observer were
later reported as prisoners, but their air gunner was later
reported to be injured but safe, in Evesham hospital, at the end
of the month. Pilot Officer Huggett was thrown in at the deep
end, having only arrived on the squadron the previous day. He
and his crew were all killed in action.

Another recce op was flown by 57 Squadron this morning,
operating from Vitry. They ran into 15 Me109s, the observer
was wounded and the pilot was forced to land at Lequesnil in
order to get medical help for him. While on the ground the
aircraft was made unserviceable, although 70 Wing noted the
machine as destroyed:

P/O Ritchie	Sgt R.M. Wells	LAC G.C.P. Haines	?*

The threatened use of recce Blenheims as bombers was carried
out on this day. 18 Squadron sent out seven aircraft
independently – this seemed to be the best tactic, after all these
pilots were used to flying alone, and it did spread the chances
of finding targets. They went off at two minute intervals from
11 o'clock:

F/Lt R.G. Wheldon	Sgt A. Craig	Sgt F. Hawkins DFM	L8863
P/O P.D. Smith	Sgt Hann	LAC Shepherd	L9325
F/O A.J. Stuart	Sgt D. Borthwick	LAC H.O. James	?*
P/O J.R. Whelan	Sgt Moncey	LAC Brown	?*
P/O Hughes	Sgt J.H. Strong	Cpl Hutchinson	L9185*
P/O D.S. Dickens	Sgt A. Crouch	?	?
Sgt Holland	Sgt J. Chatterton	LAC Maydon	?

Richard Wheldon found and bombed armoured columns on
the Le Cateau to Cambrai road and was back at noon; Pilot
Officer Smith bombed the same convoy. The next two were
unlucky. They ran into eight Me 110 fighters in the area of the
target. Flying Officer Stuart, who seems to have been a Reserve

of Air Force Officers pilot, commissioned back in 1930, failed to return. He and his crew all died.

Whelan had his observer killed almost immediately the 110s attacked, hit by a cannon shell. Then the Blenheim's port engine was set on fire. As he tried to gain some height so that his gunner could get out, he lost control of the crippled aircraft but regained sufficient control to enable him to make a crash landing. He was badly burned and broke an arm but his gunner was unhurt. LAC Brown reported seeing another Blenheim going down in flames nearby, which must have been Stuart.

The other three all attacked columns and returned safely. The squadron had been ordered to Goyencourt, near Poix, having to leave two damaged aircraft behind, both of which had been rendered useless.

At the same hour before noon, 57 Squadron sent off three bombed-up Blenheims:

F/Lt J. Foulsham	Sgt J.D. Bates	LAC D.F. Pickerill	?
P/O W. Hutchings	Sgt Whitlam	CplA. Daley	?
P/O J.R. Grant	Sgt D.R. Simmons	AC Gray	?

All three found and bombed armoured columns. These were followed by 59 Squadron. They had made five aircraft available and the crews had been standing by all the morning. They finally got the order to take off just on 11.30 a.m. In the event, only one took off, as at the last moment, the raid was cancelled but not before the first had gone. One wonders if the order to cancel came following the news that the 110s over the area had just shot down two of 18 Squadron's machines. In the event, the lone crew was back on the ground an hour later having dropped their two 250, six 40 and nine 20 lb bombs on a column on the Cambrai-Le Cateau road:

P/O R.W. Ayres	Sgt Roper	AC Webb	N6169

This same squadron also flew a recce op in the early afternoon, which operated from BAFF HQ at Coulommières – Pilot Officer C.M.M. Grece in L9463.

The afternoon ended with a second raid by 57 Squadron who sent out seven Blenheims at 5 p.m. on an armed recce and bombing mission. One aircraft had to jettison its load when found to be overloaded, another had to get rid of its bombs when attacked and damaged by an Me109, and one aircraft failed to find a target.

Also on this day, 52 Wing (Recce) decided to abandon survey flights for the present time due to the high casualties. During this first week, the photo survey aeroplanes had flown a total of 95½ operational hours, and made 4,968 photographic exposures. Another reason for this decision was the recent failure of friendly aircraft to recognise the Blenheims, even after these had fired off recognition signals.

In fact all types of reconnaissance missions had become expensive. On this day of a total of nine flown, three Blenheims had been lost.

Saturday, 18 May

Poix aerodrome was bombed by 18 Heinkel 111 bombers. Advance warning came for the unit there, 59 Squadron, to prepare to move. In the meantime, one Blenheim took off on a recce mission over the front at dawn, having flown to Vitry first. It did not return, the squadron's fifth loss – Pilot Officer Durie and his observer were killed but the gunner returned safely later:

| P/O R.A. Durie | Sgt R. Burns | AC1 W.G. Murdock | R3702* |

One of 53 Squadron's Blenheims at Soissons overnight (L9616) was bombed on the ground and destroyed, while a second machine was also destroyed by enemy action following a sortie, when it landed at Vitry.

Meantime, 57 Squadron received some reinforcements, when 139 Squadron delivered its last remaining Blenheims to the squadron before it began their final move on their journey back to England.

The air commanders were faced with yet another dilemma on this day. The ground situation was becoming increasingly serious, with the Germans now literally pouring through the Gembloux gap from Sedan. Barratt was still loath to send out his Battles and 2 Group were still reeling from the loss of 82 Squadron the previous day.

The AASF's aircraft state as at 9 a.m. this day was not encouraging:

Battles:

12 Squadron –	4 aircraft, 9 crews
88 Squadron –	7 aircraft, 12 crews
103 Squadron –	4 aircraft, 11 crews
105 Squadron –	2 aircraft, 10 crews
142 Squadron –	6 aircraft, 14 crews
150 Squadron –	7 aircraft, 15 crews
218 Squadron –	2 aircraft, 8 crews
226 Squadron –	1 aircraft, 12 crews

Total   33 aircraft, 91 crews

Hurricanes:

1 Squadron –	11 aircraft, 14 pilots
73 Squadron –	9 aircraft, 16 pilots
501 Squadron –	6 aircraft, 15 pilots

Total   26 aircraft, 45 pilots

Nevertheless, the situation could not just be ignored, as it wasn't going to go away. There was no question about it, 2 Group would have to go.

One of the immediate reactions to the previous day's casualties was that the Blenheims should resort to night attacks only, even if results would only prove slight. The difficulty was, how would one know, and how could results be achieved in any event, if the crews couldn't see what they were bombing. Alternatively, Air Vice Marshal James Robb DSO DFC, a First World War fighter pilot, AOC of 2 Group, felt day raids should only be carried out if cloud cover was available or a strong fighter escort provided. The former, of course, couldn't be ordered up, the second could be, but it was difficult to achieve with so many calls on an already stretched fighter force.

Three 2 Group squadrons were put on the line: 21, 15 and 40. 21 Squadron were promised a fighter escort which they would pick up in France. They were briefed to fly to Poix, which they did, led by Squadron Leader Pryde. Rendezvous was to be made over Douai, but after half an hour of waiting, no fighters turned up so George 'Scottie' Pryde (an experienced, sensible Scot from Aberdeen) flew back to England.

15 Squadron, with no serviceable aircraft left at Alconbury, began to operate once more from Wyton, but could only put up six Blenheims:

Above Blenheim L9191 of 18 Squadron, crashed at Crécy 18 May 1940. (*R.C. Bowyer*)

Below Group of 82 Squadron, (*l to r*): S/L W.P. Sutcliffe DFC, W/C The Earl of Bandon, F/Lt R.J. McConnell and F/O D.A. Fordham (both KIA 17 May), and F/Lt G.F. Hall who by May 1940 was a Squadron Leader with 110 Squadron but was killed on the 22nd. (*via W.P. Sutcliffe*)

Bottom Some of 15 Squadron (*l to r*): Red Eames, Jess Oakshott, S/L H.Y. Lawrence, Pete Webster, Bert Oakley and P.N. Douglas. Lawrence led the squadron on the attack on Waalhaven on 10 May but was shot down and killed on 18 May. Oakley and Douglas were killed on 12 May. (*W.H. George*)

F/Lt P.G. Chapman	Sgt C.E. Colbourne	LAC E.J. Fagg	P6917*
F/O L.H. Trent	Sgt W.J. Stephens	Cpl J. Sutcliffe	P6913
P/O C.H. Robinson	Sgt S.C. Readhead	LAC Horton	L9030
S/L H.Y. Lawrence	Sgt R.G. Hopkins	LAC E.L.H. Thomas	L8853*
F/O F.D. Dawson-Jones	Sgt W. Baxter	LAC C.G. Watts	L8852*
F/O W.H. George	Sgt A.J. Box	LAC C.A. O'Donnell	L8848

No. 40 Squadron put up seven Blenheims, led by Squadron Leader Brian Paddon. Both squadrons took off at 12.30 and headed for France. 40 Squadron went for troops and transport at Le Cateau and were all back by 2.20 although Paddon put down at Poix. They had met fighters and one Blenheim was attacked by two Messerschmitts, they were driven off. 15 Squadron fared less well.

They went for mechanised transport and AFVs approaching the bridge, near Landrecies, over the canal at Le Cateau. The two sections of three were led by Lawrence, OC B Flight, and Paul Chapman, OC A Flight.

Flying Officer William 'Hugh' George, was in Lawrence's section and, in the number six position, was the last in the formation:

> The plan was that we should rendezvous with French fighter squadrons over Douai and that they would give us top cover. However, they did not show up and we went in without them. We met murderous AA, of an intensity that I never again saw equalled. The tracer coming up was so thick it didn't seem possible to fly through it, so I decided to use emergency boost. I went down at a fair old lick and I remember dive-bombing very quick and very low and releasing the bombs with a delay action fuse, and as we pulled up from the dive we were jumped by Me109s.
>
> Three of our aircraft were shot down (the two flight commanders and Dawson-Jones); all were killed except for one air gunner, Sergeant Thomas, who was later reported a PoW. Of the remaining three aircraft, Robbie Robinson force landed and had to abandon his aircraft which was a write-off. Trent force landed at Poix with a badly damaged aircraft which an Engineering Officer promptly declared u/s, threatening Trent with a court martial if he attempted to take off again.
>
> I also landed at Poix, out of fuel after a running scrap with

a pair of 109s. One of these 109s got on my tail and chased me over a hill, on the other side of which was a village. The main street was ahead of me so I flew straight down it with the 109 still on my tail. The next report I got from my gunner was that it was no longer there.

At Poix I managed to get filled up and tagged on to the remnants of 40 Squadron for the return to base. Landrecies had cost us four aircraft destroyed and two badly damaged, eight aircrew killed and one prisoner.

Flying Officer W.H. George, 15 Squadron

Like 15 and 21 Squadrons, 40 were the first to make rendezvous with fighters, so were scheduled to land at Abbeville, where they too were told to meet fighters above Douai and after the raid they were to land at Poix, refuel and rearm before being given a further target.

Over Douai they found the sky empty, and made the decision to attack without one. It proved a fatal error. The six Blenheims met exceptionally heavy AA fire and fighters which shot down three of the Blenheims and damaged the rest. These staggered back to Poix as ordered, but the engineering officer of 59 Squadron, upon inspecting the damage, immediately grounded Leonard Trent's and C.H. Robinson's machines. Robinson flew back in Paddon's repaired machine, as Trent was told his would be fit to fly by the next day. However, as Poix was ordered to be abandoned that evening, Len Trent's first job was to locate his crew, who, having been released for the evening, had, with others, gone into the local town. When they were located they were quite 'merry'. His observer was in no real state to navigate them back, but luckily Trent could recall most of the courses. He took off and flew his damaged bomber back to England, although he was subjected to flak and searchlights, supposedly 'friendly'. He landed at RAF Mildenhall at 8.30 p.m.[1]

That afternoon, 18 Squadron, now at Goyencourt, sent out six bombed-up Blenheims to bomb columns near Cambrai, all

[1] Leonard Henry Trent was awarded the DFC in July 1940 and went on to command B Flight of 487 (New Zealand) Squadron in 1942. He won the Victoria Cross for his part in a raid on Amsterdam on 3 May 1943. He was shot down and became a prisoner of war.

returning safely, although due to the failing light, they landed at Abbeville as the squadron had been ordered to move again, to Crécy. Three more of the squadron's u/s machines were abandoned at Goyencourt, making five in two days.

The order to evacuate also went to 105 Squadron, as by 6 p.m. they were on their way to Echimines. Obviously Wing HQ had finally got their way.

Then at 7.30 six aircraft of 57 Squadron at Poix made a bomb raid on Le Cateau, having three of them shot up. As the order to move to Crécy came while they were in the air, these damaged aircraft had to be abandoned at Poix together with one other, when they moved the next day.

In reality these operations were armed-reconnaissances, for as the air war changed, so did the tactics of the Air Component recce Blenheim squadrons. Eric Nind recalls:

> After the 10th May, photographic reconnaissance ceased, and was replaced by low and medium level armed reconnaissance, to locate, bomb, and report back positions of the advancing German armoured columns. Few of these could be carried out, because we were retreating at the same time, and had difficulty in keeping in touch with our own HQ., Air Component, Field Force.
>
> On 18th May, I took off from Poix satellite in the early evening to lead six aircraft on such a reconnaissance of Le Cateau and Avesnes, only to find on our return that the squadron had once more retreated, to Crécy. It was too late for us to follow them that night. We also knew that the Germans were then in Amiens, so we stayed the night, continually running up our engines, until we could take off for Crécy at dawn. That evening, 19th May, we evacuated Crécy, for Lympne in Kent. We were particularly fortunate compared with some squadrons in being able to fly out thirteen aircraft.
>
> *Flying Officer E.F. Nind, 57 Squadron*

CHAPTER ELEVEN

The Rush to the Sea

Sunday, 19 May
Air Marshal Arthur Barratt was handed another problem early on 19 May, not that he needed any more. The French sent a message at around 5 a.m. that two enemy columns together with mechanised infantry were moving north towards the Neufchatel-Montcornet road. A special reconnaissance sortie was ordered which reported back to BAFF HQ at about nine o'clock, indicating that the territory immediately north of the Rethel-Blanzy stretch of the Aisne River, was full of troops.

Unfortunately, this author could not find which squadron carried out this mission. The Component Blenheim squadrons' records are incomplete and, in any event, they were all busy moving back. Perhaps it was flown by one of the Lysander units.

The fact remained, however, that the Germans were now pushing hard into Flanders, with the obvious intention of cutting the Allied forces in two, with a rush towards the coast, along the Somme River. This would leave a large part of the BEF cut off and in retreat to the coast between Boulogne, Calais and Dunkirk.

It couldn't have come at a worst time for Barratt. Following 2 Group's losses over recent days, the Air Staff were so alarmed that they also thought future raids should also now only be flown at night. But now, Barratt requested support yet again because of the new threat. However, this was refused. 2 Group needed a rest and time to repair several damaged aircraft. With his Battle squadrons now mostly relocated and ready again for operations, Barratt had no choice but to call on them for a day mission, their first since the disastrous 14 May.

A maximum effort was called for. Orders were despatched

although with the state of communications, some squadrons received their orders by despatch rider! The orders were sent out by BAFF HQ at 9.20 a.m. and by 10.40, the first Battles were over the target area! It is difficult to establish how many aircraft were involved due to the poor records. Some say 33, others 23 or 17. The following units sent aircraft:

    12 Squadron – 6 Battles
    88 Squadron – all Battles! (timed at 7.30 but this is probably
                                incorrect)
    103 Squadron – 6 Battles
    142 Squadron – 3 Battles
    150 Squadron – 6 Battles
    218 Squadron – ?
    226 Squadron – 2 Battles

This shows 23 with others from 88 and 218, so 33 might be correct. For the most part, however, the target proved to have gone 'stale', for the area was not particularly crowded with enemy troops, although some villages were reported to be worth attacking. Fighter escort was provided by no fewer than 26 Hurricanes but six Battles were lost. The following squadrons make mention of the morning raids. 12 Squadron:

F/O B.G.F. Drinkwater	Sgt Seymour	LAC J. Aitken	K9377
P/O J.J. McElligott	Sgt B.C. Long	LAC T.O. Burgess	L5538*
Sgt W.H. Kellaway	Sgt E.T. Bunt	LAC F. Walker	L5249
F/O P.R. Barr	Sgt E.J. Belcher	LAC K.D. Rawlings	N2178*
P/O R.A.D. Meharey	Sgt G.J. Batty	AC G. Purslow	P5237
S/L B.E. Lowe	Sgt A. Morris	AC C.G. Landon	P6597

These crews met Me109s after bombing the village of St Fergeau. James McElligott's Battle had its port petrol tank set on fire and he was badly wounded in the arm. Both crewmen fired their guns at the 109s, and Burgess claimed one shot down. But the Battle was going down, and then it crashed into a wood. McElligott and Burgess were taken to a French hospital where McElligott later died of his injuries. Tom Burgess, suffering from shrapnel wounds, later received the DFM. Sergeant Long returned to the squadron.

Flying Officer Philip Barr was also shot down, wounded in the leg and taken to a French hospital, with his gunner, wounded in the thigh. Their observer was killed. The French later reported two Me109s had been shot down in the scrap and the wreckage located.

No. 88 Squadron recorded an attack on Hirson, their only casualty being one of their air gunners as wounded – LAC E. Wigglesworth. 103 Squadron noted an attack on troops in a village in the Condé-sur-Aisne area. 142 Squadron:

P/O H.H. Taylor	Sgt S. Lang	LAC H. Long	K7696*
Sgt A.J. Godsell	Sgt B.A. Hopgood	LAC W.D. Boyle	L5226*
Sgt G.H. Ebert	Sgt T. Jones	LAC R.S. Utteridge	P5238*

None of the three returned. Howard Taylor, from Perth, Australia, and his crew were all reported prisoners, Sergeant Godsell and his observer were also captured but LAC Boyle was killed. Sergeant Ebert, who had joined the squadron from 226 Squadron in October 1939, force-landed ten miles south of Epernay and returned with his gunner, although his wounded observer, Tom Jones, later died.

On the way to the target, 150 Squadron's six Battles ran into heavy AA fire from the town of Rethel, and this, plus bad weather, made finding targets difficult. Squadron Leader R.M. Bradley dropped his four bombs on an AA battery of four guns and scored a direct hit. The others bombed whatever they could find but few results were seen. One Battle failed to return:

P/O D.E.T. Osment	Sgt G.W. Clifford	AC W.G. Slade	P5235*

All three were later reported to be prisoners of war. Allan Frank's Battle (L5583) was also damaged and he had to make a forced landing at a French airfield at Sommesousse.

The pilots of 226 Squadron attacked cross-roads on the road from Ecly to Seraincourt. Concentrations at Hauteville and vehicles at the east end of the Château Porcein road junction, west of Condé. Bombs were seen to fall on the west side of the crossroads, and the convoy at Hauteville seemed to be well on fire as the pilots flew away.

A column of tanks were seen near to Hauteville and reported. Heavy ground fire was experienced but all the Battles got home safely. The crews had made shallow dive attacks from around 7,000 feet, released their bombs from between 2,000 and 4,000 feet, along rather than across the roads. Condé village, too, seemed to be on fire as they flew off.

The tanks which these pilots reported, were an obvious target, but Barratt had no forces available until well into the afternoon, by which time they might be anywhere. 2 Group had promised to hold two squadrons at one hour's notice during the afternoon, but Barratt decided not to call upon them.

These were the only operations of the day, except for a 59 Squadron recce in the late afternoon. 18 Squadron had been ordered back to England, having flown to Crécy that morning. One Blenheim had crashed on take-off, possibly L9191, but the crew were unhurt; Flight Lieutenant Wheldon, Sergeant Craig and Sergeant Hawkins DFM. From Crécy, the squadron aircraft began to leave for Lympne at around 4.30 p.m. while the road convoy moved off to Boulogne. The squadron regrouped at RAF Watton.

Other squadrons on their way home were 57 and 59. 57 were ordered to move to Crécy; at 5.30 on the 19th it moved again to Boulogne. On the 20th it would board the SS *Mona's Queen* to England, while its aircraft went to Lympne, led by Squadron Leader Denis Rogers, before being based at Wyton. 59 Squadron sent its road convoy off towards Crécy while five Blenheims took off for the same base. The ground personnel then left for Cherbourg while the aircraft were flown over to Lympne the next afternoon.

At Lannoy, 139 Squadron (what was left of it) flew its remaining Blenheims to Amiens, handing them over to 57 Squadron to fly home. Then the ground party left for Nantes, making camp at Pithiviers. On the 20th they reached Angers.

Before it left, 59 Squadron were ordered to send out a recce machine, at 4.30 p.m. on the 19th:

P/O C.R. Wylie	Sgt Liddiard	AC Houlihan	L4856*

They had flown to Merville, landed and were met by the Army Liaison Officer who requested them to report on enemy movements. They took off again, returning at 7.30. They tried to locate the Advance GHQ in order to give their report, and were also informed that the squadron was returning to England. Clive Wylie decided to fly back to Crécy to refuel, before he too would leave for England. However, in the now darkening sky he became lost, although he felt certain he was over the Somme area. Off to the west he could see Abbeville in flames. Setting what he hoped was a new course for Crécy Wood, he was still unable to find it and finally had to land in a stubble field at ten o'clock.

Sergeant Liddiard had contacted Beauvais by radio but they kept challenging him as they were unable to give the correct signals. They gave up and slept by the machine until 3 a.m. when they decided to walk to the village of St Vast, which was six miles north-west of Amiens. Before they could do this they watched a dive-bombing attack by over 40 German Stukas, and then six German aircraft, spotting the grounded Blenheim, flew over and machine-gunned it. Hurrying to get under cover in a nearby wood, Aircraftman Houlihan fell, hitting his head and was unconscious for some 12 minutes.

After the raid, they returned to the machine, removed maps, papers, the observer's compass, and taxied the damaged Blenheim to the lee of the wood. It appeared to be still flyable but they needed fuel, so they decided to get to Crécy. They reached Picquigny but all traffic was being diverted from Abbeville. Enemy aircraft were bombing there and Dieppe. Still walking, they covered 13 miles but were then given a lift in a French Airforce lorry, travelling through several towns before joining up with 52 Wing's road convoy, arriving with it at Rouen at 7 p.m. on the 20th.

They reached Cherbourg early the next morning, boarded a ship and were in Southampton that evening. Houlihan was taken to hospital to have his head injury seen to, while Wylie and Liddiard finally got back to the squadron at Andover on the 22nd.

*

With the relocated Battle squadrons now operational again, they had again to prepare to fly night missions. This brought its own problems, now that most of the squadrons had now gone to new airfields. 103 Squadron for example, who had already changed its bombing tactics, a high approach of around 8,000 feet on daylight ops, with a dive to around 4,000 before bombing (they also decided when possible to abandon the sub-formation of three machines, and fly singly to provide freedom of movement), found problems at their new base. The height of nearby crops that helped to camouflage the airfield, prevented the pilots seeing the glim lamp flarepath, so an electrically controlled flarepath had to be rigged, from the generator of the Chance light. This was designed with shielded lamps in small wire stands which could be dimmed by the use of a rheostat in the generator, turned off from a master switch.

Allan Frank recalls how pilots were selected for night raids:

> The system for dividing crews was simple. If you had ever flown a Battle by night you went by night, if not you went by day. Since I had the splendid night flying record of three landings in a Hawker Hart, I went out by day!
>
> *Pilot Officer A.D. Frank, 150 Squadron*

Monday, 20 May

2 Group were back on the line. With the Germans now pouring through the Gembloux Gap, the Belgian and BEF forces would have to retreat further, the BEF to the Somme. French forces were holding a line Douai–Valenciennes–Condé–River Sensée–Maulde. The enemy armour swept round Péronne to reach Amiens and Abbeville, forcing a retreat across the Escaut. The Blenheims must be sent out.

Escorted by no fewer than three Hurricane squadrons of Fighter Command, 21 and 107 Squadrons sent out formations, led by Squadron Leader Pryde and Wing Commander Embry respectively. They made rendezvous over Wattisham, and picked up the Hurricanes over Hawkinge. Once over the French coast, they headed for targets of columns on the Arras–Cambrai–Albert road. Heavy gunfire greeted them and a number of aircraft were damaged, but all returned safely.

A 142 Squadron Battle had to make a recce sortie at 11 a.m., taking vertical photographs of Troyes, which Pilot Officer Ian Chalmers (P2177) completed successfully.

A repeat mission by 21 and 107 Squadrons was flown towards late afternoon, again led by Pryde and Embry. 107 attacked motor transport passing through Ervillers, the town being set on fire by the bombing. Again several machines were damaged by ground fire but yet again all aircraft returned. Obviously the strong Hurricane escort had prevented enemy fighters interfering, but when the Air Staff saw the reports, and discovered that not one single German fighter had been shot down, they considered this a waste of fighter effort! They again felt it better for the bombers to operate at night, leaving the fighters to score kills. Accordingly, 82 Squadron, now back at full strength, 110 and 40 Squadrons, put up raids that evening.

Led by the Earl, Paddy Bandon (P6925 'Z'), six aircraft took off in sections at 9.35 p.m. and 10.05. The target was AFVs in Audenarde–Graumont areas. Two aircraft failed to locate targets, and one machine returned to base with mechanical trouble. 40 Squadron also put up six Blenheims to bomb in the Arderard area, acting independently. Some columns were attacked and everyone got home, but the total night's effort was disappointing – as was to be expected. 110 also sent out six independently to the west of Brussels at twenty minute intervals beginning 00.25 a.m. but again nothing concrete could be claimed.

Little wonder that Arthur Barratt requested an immediate return to daylight operations. Night raids would achieve nothing and be of no help to either the BEF or the French. Nevertheless, his Battle squadrons began to fly night operations that night. They were still considered too vulnerable for daylight raids.

Five Battles of 12 Squadron flew out and bombed Montcornet and Mezières between 11.17 and 11.55 p.m., harassing enemy columns. 88, 103, 142 and 226 also flew night raids. 103's target was Fumay, over the border in Germany itself (five aircraft). Only one Battle was lost, from 226 Squadron. They put up seven aircraft, and of the missing crew, the observer was killed, the pilot and gunner taken prisoner:

| Sgt Annan | Sgt A. Livingston | AC R.J. Jonas | K9176* |

However, 142 Squadron did lose an aircraft on this night. Four Battles had been assigned but a parachute flare went off in one of them as it was being prepared. The machine caught fire and the fire crew arrived but were told to pull back as the bombs were on board. Later the fuel tanks exploded but not the bombs, so the fire crew closed in, but then the bombs went off. Five men died instantly, four of the fire crew and one of the squadron's instrument repairers, who was watching. The driver of the fire tender was seriously injured, and was later captured in hospital when it was over-run by the advancing Germans. Another Battle was damaged by flying splinters. The dead were Corporal Passey, LAC McGrath, AC1 Bird, ACs Jenkins and Knowlton (I/R). The driver was LAC Jarvis.

Tuesday, 21 May

With the German Panzer spearhead reaching Abbeville, Arras, Amiens and Hesdin – at an amazing speed – and with reconnaissance becoming a problem, 40 Squadron sent out two Blenheims at 7.30 a.m. to take a look at the areas around Amiens and Audenarde. Their findings would help compile targets for another 2 Group raid, but when they (Pilot Officer Bell in N3552 and Sergeant S.I. Tonks in P4927) put down at Merville in order to give their reports, they found the aerodrome abandoned, so quickly took off again.

At 8.15 a.m. Basil Embry led 12 aircraft into the Etaples–Abbeville area, finding, attacking and scoring hits on MT in the village of Auxi-le-Château. Some bombers were damaged and again Hurricanes escorted them, and all returned.

Three other 40 Squadron Blenheims, took off at 11.30 to bomb an AFV convoy at Montreuil, near Abbeville, led by Flight Lieutenant Batt. All returned at 2.07 p.m. At 2 p.m., 15 Squadron sent out six Blenheims, led by Squadron Leader John Glen, the OC A Flight. All these 2 Group ops now were designed to impede German columns, or at least slow them down, as they made the rush to the coast in order to cut off the BEF. The crews were briefed to locate and bomb AFVs approaching Boulogne from the direction of Montreuil.

S/L J.G. Glen	Sgt Taylor	P/O Gordon	L9413
F/O L.H. Trent	Sgt W.J. Stephens	Cpl J. Sutcliffe	L8855
P/O C.H. Robinson	Sgt S.C. Readhead	LAC Horton	N6156
F/Lt P.F. Webster	Sgt R.A.M. Stone	LAC R.E. Hunter	R3706*
F/O R.B.G.E. Clarke	Sgt B.S.J. Piff	LAC Murphy	L9024
Sgt Day	Sgt Phillips	LAC Hewlett	R3704

The Blenheims reached the target area and raced across the French countryside right down on the deck. They were literally lifting over hedges and trees. Then ahead they spotted enemy columns on two roads. Flight Lieutenant Webster saw the first convoy then the second a short distance further on at which he flew. But the second bunch had had a few more moments to see the Blenheims coming and as most of the squadron bombed the first, Webster, going for the farther road, met a hail of light flak.

His aircraft was hit, and LAC Robert Hunter felt a bang under his seat and then he saw a stream of fuel seeping out from the port wing. He told his pilot right away but the imperturbable Webster merely dismissed this problem by saying that he thought the engine was on fire. And so it was.

Webster then began discussing with Ray Stone whether he should try to climb and bale out or should they crash-land or try to get home. Apart from a burning engine, all aileron control had been shot out. Finally Webster elected to put the Blenheim down. After flying for some way, he eventually bellied in a field somewhere between Etampes and Boulogne. As the crew clambered out of the mess, they saw that one 40 lb bomb had jammed under the tail wheel, while others were littered about along the track they had made in landing.

Satisfied that the burning Blenheim would be of no use to the Germans, the crew set out for the coast, managing to get a lift in an Army ambulance. They arrived in Boulogne where Webster talked his way onto a ship despite an army officer telling them that they should grab rifles and help fight. The three men arrived in Dover, where Webster received treatment for an injured foot (the other one this time) and Hunter for some splinters in his left thigh and a cut ankle, received when the shell had exploded under his seat.

At mid-day, an 18 Squadron Blenheim made the unit's first recce mission from its new English base at Watton, intending to have a look at the Douai–Arras–Amiens and Abbeville areas. It failed to return:

P/O C. Light　　　　　Sgt A.E. Craig　　　　Sgt G. Hawkins DFM　　L9325*

Cyril Light and George Hawkins both died, but Craig seems to have survived.

Three more 2 Group squadrons operated that afternoon. 21, 82 and 107 Squadrons put up 23 Blenheims, 9, 3 and 11 respectively. The formations flew out via Gris Nez and Boulogne, searching for tanks and troop convoys. The leading section of 21 Squadron attacked three tanks north of Etaples and scored direct hits, while the others bombed targets at Hesdin and Montreuil. 82 Squadron's section, led by Flight Lieutenant T.M. 'Joe' Hunt, made a shallow dive from 5,000 to 2,500 feet against MT and AFVs at Capelle, Marcouvillle and Hesdin, while Embry's 107 Squadron, who couldn't find any tanks, hit MT in the village of Austreberthe.

As these aircraft were coming back, 82 Squadron put up another six Blenheims with three of 18 Squadron, plus six from 110 Squadron, to attack columns between Etaples and Boulogne. This was 18's first operation in a new role, from reconnaissance to light bomber, after its return from France. 82 were led by Squadron Leader W.P. Sutcliffe, recently awarded the DFC for an important photo op he flew over Sylt back in March:

S/L W.P. Sutcliffe	Sgt A.J. Scott	AC G. Whitehead	P6895
P/O E.J. Keeble	Sgt Avery	AC Elliott	P4843
Sgt A.E. Merritt	Sgt Carlisle	AC L.D. Nineham	L8829
F/O C. Breese	Sgt Williams	Cpl Harris	P6910
P/O D.M. Wellings	Sgt Macfarlane	AC Beeby	R3619
Sgt Kenton	Sgt Harbord	AC Crozier	P4828

18 Squadron:

F/Lt R. Langebear	Sgt A.J. Gulliver	LAC D.C. Moore	L8866
P/O V. Rees	Sgt N.V. Pusey	LAC K.E. Murray	L9185*
Sgt Holland	Sgt Chatterton	LAC Haydon	L9472

They bombed columns on the Boulogne–Etaples road after meeting up with their fighter escort over Boulogne. Sergeant Holland of 18 Squadron had to abort the mission when his gunner found his gun turret not functioning, but Pilot Officer Vivian Rees ran into totally unexpected trouble.

Nearing the rendezvous point with the fighters, Rees saw six RAF fighters pass across the front of the formation and turn in behind. The leading fighter suddenly opened fire on the Blenheim shooting away the aircraft's engine cowling, and holed all the fuel tanks. Flap and undercarriage were also damaged and smoke streamed back from the damaged port engine. Rees had no alternative than to put the bomber down on its belly, which he did successfully at Wimereux. They got down safely and they got back the next day via Boulogne, having set fire to their machine before abandoning it.

Only Richard Langebear bombed with 82 Squadron, giving them the impression that their escort had shot down two of the three machines. Squadron Leader Sutcliffe:

> We had a fighter escort. Targets were German transport on roads leading out of Boulogne. This was a low level operation and after we had dropped our bomb load on German transport, we returned and used the aircraft's machine guns against vehicles on the roads. Our bombs consisted of two 250 lb and twelve 40 lbs. One Blenheim of 18 Squadron was shot down.
>
> *Squadron Leader W.P. Sutcliffe, 82 Squadron*

The final Blenheim raid of the day was carried out by six machines of 110 Squadron which took off at 6.55 p.m., led by Squadron Leader L.F. Sinclair (L8749), its new CO from the 16th, bombed the same areas and returned at 9 p.m.

Night ops for the Battles were again the form and 88 and 226 Squadrons made sorties without loss or major incident. Further planned sorties were suddenly cancelled by AASF HQ.

Wednesday, 22 May

The day's first operation was flown by the AASF following a request the previous evening from GHQ that Battles should look for and attack tanks in the Amiens, Abbeville and Arras areas. Air Marshal Barratt protested that this sort of task was most unsuitable for his light bombers in view of the large area in which German AFVs might be. He also said that identification of such vehicles was difficult, especially with the poor view from Battle aircraft, and so was hitting such targets, not only because of their size but also, once again, the heavy defensive fire they would encounter at low level. And they would have to bomb at low level to have any chance of putting a bomb on one.

But GHQ were adamant and they were supported by Air Ministry, so Barratt had reluctantly to comply, hence the cancellation of the previous night's planned raids.

At 5 a.m. the first Battles took off, 142 Squadron sending off six aircraft, while 103 sent four. 103 now had some 31 aircraft on strength as the previous day they had been given the aircraft of 218 Squadron which had moved to Nantes. With its heavy casualties, 218 were being sent home to England. (88 Squadron may have sent a couple of Battles but this is uncertain.)

Of the six 142 machines, led by Squadron Leader William Wight, one was unable to find a target and returned after having to land and refuel at Rouen while the fifth and sixth machines away were recalled by radio because of bad weather. Flying Officer A.D. Gosman did find a tank which they bombed, then became lost in low cloud and had to force-land near Paris, returning the following day. 103 had little to report either, and Sergeant Critch was hit by light flak and had to force-land but he and his crew were unhurt.

Thus Barratt was later told that in total, four Battles had returned owing to bad weather, three had been forced to land elsewhere, one had returned with its bombs and one had been lost apparently (one assumes one of the forced landed aircraft was unrecoverable). Two or three attacks had been made on tanks seen near Doullens, Amiens and Bapaume but none of the pilots involved were able to report positive identification, attacks merely being made because vehicles opened fire on the aircraft. (A very dangerous state of affairs considering most ground people at this stage were firing on anything with wings, Germans, British and French!) Barratt of course was not in the least surprised with the morning results, particularly as the weather, until recently quite good, had turned to rain and low cloud, and BAFF cancelled further ops at 9.30 a.m. Barratt then telephoned the Deputy Chief of the Air Staff, informing him that the net result had been one tank bombed.

*

With 52 Recce Wing now back in England, along with the recce Blenheim squadrons, any operations called for were flown over France from UK bases. On the 22nd, 57 and 59 Squadrons flew sorties, the former unit, operating from an advanced base at RAF Hawkinge, losing a crew:

| P/O R.L. Saunders | Sgt S.F. Simmons | AC1 G.R. Price | L9184* |

All three were later reported as killed. Flying Officer G.H.D. Evans of 59 Squadron, flew a successful sortie in the afternoon, although his aircraft was damaged when it hit a bird. David Evans:

On the 22nd we flew from Andover to Hawkinge, having run through a bit of dirty weather, and carried out again what was termed a strategic reconnaissance around the Abbeville–Amiens–Aumale areas, which indicates that the German forces were cutting down towards Paris. I gather the F.540 records us hitting a bird on this trip but have no such recollection. Doubtless there was plenty else to think about!

Flying Officer G.H.D. Evans, 59 Squadron

The squadron was also operating from a forward base in southern England, RAF Lympne, and lost a crew, who were also all killed:

F/O F.D. Bird	Sgt C.J.W. Brinn	AC2 G.D. Coles	L9266*

Afternoon 22 May
The Blenheims of 2 Group were again active on the afternoon of this day in attempts to support the Allied armies against the German armoured thrusts directed towards Boulogne. It is of interest to note that as at 9 a.m. this day, the Group had just 73 Blenheims ready for operations.

The Group's activities began with a recce sortie by 107 Squadron:

F/Lt H.P. Pleasance	Sgt R.D. Cook	LAC P.E.F. Adams	P6894

They made a successful report covering the areas of St Valéry, Abbeville, Poix and Neufchâtel, landing at 4.25 with much valuable information. Meanwhile, 107 and 110 Squadrons at Wattisham had begun to take off between 4.15 and 4.30.

Wing Commander Embry led six aircraft into the area covered by Harold Pleasance. They found numerous targets, all well defended, which badly damaged one aircraft:

P/O J.A. Miller	Sgt R.J. Saunders	LAC W. Stokell	P4925*

One engine was knocked out, the hydraulics went u/s and the second motor was also damaged. Pilot Officer Miller, who together with his observer had been injured by shrapnel, decided not to force land in France and headed out over the Channel. He got to within seven miles of the English coast when the second engine finally failed and he had to ditch. He and his crew clambered out and within half an hour they were picked up by a British patrol boat. Meantime the squadron had successfully bombed road convoys and inflicted considerable damage on MT.

The six Blenheims of 110 Squadron also met serious gunfire:

S/L G.F. Hall	Sgt K.F. Quarrington	LAC C.S. Torrance	L8761*
F/O G.O. Lings	Sgt Martin	AC Bingham	N6207
P/O N.N. Ezekiel	Sgt Chaplin	LAC Young	L8749
S/L J.S. Sabine	Sgt W. Evans	Sgt J.V. West	P4858
F/Lt P.H.A. Simmons	Sgt Friendly	LAC Smith	L8755
Sgt Miller	Sgt Duffy	AC Greenwood	P4860

They found troops and transport vehicles on roads in the vicinity of Henschel and St Pol, but came under heavy ground fire. Squadron Leader George Hall was shot down and he and his crew were killed. The other five Blenheims were all damaged. Flying Officer George Lings had to belly land at base as his undercarriage had been shot away.

An hour after these two units had taken off, 15 and 40 Squadrons were lifting off from Wyton. Over the Boulogne area and towards Abbeville, 15 Squadron bombed from a high level pattern at 6,000 feet, returning with just one damaged machine, piloted by Pilot Officer Henderson, N6177.

Squadron Leader Paddon led 40 Squadron, bombing convoys in the same general area, all returning safely at around 8.30 p.m. Meanwhile, four more raids had been mounted, aircraft from 21, 82, 107 and 110 being on their way well before seven o'clock. This was followed by yet another effort by 107 Squadron, who sent out another small formation, led by Embry, at 7.40. This was a special raid on a reported German HQ of their 9th Division at Ribencourt. They arrived just as the light was failing, but bombed the village successfully.

Several Blenheims were damaged by ground fire, but only one was lost on these latter missions. 82 Squadron, with 21, had bombed enemy columns in the Samar–Hesdin areas, going for tanks and MT they found on a bend just north of Hubertsent. One 82 Squadron aircraft was shot down and the crew killed:

Sgt J.L. Hartfield	Sgt F. Phillipson	AC A.W. Elliott	P4828*

That evening the Battle squadrons were on night ops. 142 sent out four aircraft but only one found a target to bomb. Pilot Officer Edwards had to make a forced landing near Paris and returned by rail.

The other squadrons' activities were unremarkable, although two of the crews of 103 Squadron, piloted by Flying Officer Dermot Kelly and Flight Lieutenant Ingram were initially reported overdue, but they both had to force land at dawn and later flew back.

Thursday, 23 May
The British Expeditionary Force was still retreating, leaving the Belgian forces on the north of the River Lys, from Menin to Courtrai and the Escaut. During the night a salient at Arras had fallen but it was hoped that French forces could close the gap remaining, although in the event, this proved impossible. Information from the French was little or non-existent, and when 2 Group did hear something, it was that the Germans had managed to get across the vital canal which ran from St Omer to Aire.

Two Group, following the previous day's air efforts was now down to just 60 operational aircraft, but another full effort was being laid on for mid-morning.

At 4.30 a.m., 53 Squadron put up a recce Blenheim. Flying Officer Samuel Pepys, who only arrived on the squadron on the 16th, failed to return and he and his crew were later confirmed as prisoners:

F/O S.G.L. Pepys	Sgt A. Haygreen	AC H. Spear	R3691*

Another recce Blenheim, this time from 18 Squadron, was also lost, during a mission over the northern French Channel ports. This pilot survived but his crew, including the veteran Sergeant Frank Miller, were killed:

P/O D.S. Dickens	Sgt F. Miller DFM	Cpl B.M. Harding	R3598*

At ten minutes after ten o'clock, the first Blenheims of 2 Group began to take off. Their target was the southern exits of Arras. Six aircraft of 40 Squadron were led by its CO, John Llewellyn:

W/C J.G. Llewellyn	Sgt J.A.D. Beattie	P/O W.G. Edwards	P4909*
P/O Bell	Sgt Salvage	LAC Foreman	P4908
Sgt J.S. Morton	Sgt A.D. Kelso	AC Rodgers	N3552
F/Lt R.H. Batt	Sgt Bloodworth	LAC F.H. Jones	L8757
F/O R.H. Jacoby	Sgt P.A.M. Burrell	LAC P.R. Whittle	L8834*
P/O F.R. McAuliffe	Sgt A. Spencer	LAC E.G. Neville	L8836

Above Gareth Clayton and Basil Embry, 107 Squadron. (*R.C. Rotheram*)

Below The damaged wing of Embry's Blenheim (L8777), 23 May 1940.

Bottom Flying Officer Eric Nind in his Blenheim. Note the ring of the ring-and-bead gunsight. (*E.F. Nind*)

Six Blenheims of 107 Squadron, led by Gareth Clayton, hooked up with the 40 Squadron boys, made rendezvous with their Hurricane escort then crossed the sea for the Arras locality. They met bad weather and heavy cloud, and, already late after waiting over Hawkinge for 32 Squadron's fighters, they mostly had to bomb alternative targets.

No. 40 Squadron lost two aircraft, including Llewellyn. He and his gunner were killed, although his observer baled out and returned three days later. Flying Officer Reg Jacoby was taken prisoner, but his crew died. 107 bombed troops in woods west of Boulogne, and some of the machines were damaged including Embry's L8777. Because of the clouds, the formation had broken up, Embry threading his way through the clouds but finding no gaps. Knowing he was asking for trouble, he hung around too long trying to find the target and as expected, was hit. A terrific explosion blew his Blenheim upside down but he regained control. Looking out at his port wing, he could see a hole '…as big as a grand piano.' Just keeping control by flying with the aileron of the damaged wing fully depressed into the airstream, he flew away, still surrounded by bursting AA shells, heading for the coast. He made it back and landed at Hawkinge, scattering some workmen as he came in who failed to see him.

At one o'clock, six Blenheims of 15 Squadron flew out, picking up an escort of Spitfires before heading for Arras. Weather was still bad and almost every one of the six Blenheims had to bomb the Woods at Boulogne. One aircraft failed to return; the crew had been killed.

| P/O J.G. Masters | Sgt E. Tucker | LAC C.W. Thompson L9403* |

Towards the end of the day, 82 Squadron put up three Blenheims, led by Joe Hunt, taking off at 6.05 p.m. Their target was the Fort de la Creche which they believed they damaged. This was despite heavy AA fire from British destroyers off the coast, which continued to fire even when recognition signals were fired off.

2 Group were certainly taking a pounding. Since the Blitzkrieg had begun, nearly 50 Blenheims had been lost together with over 120 members of aircrew dead plus others wounded or taken prisoner. Many more aircraft had been

damaged, written off, or simply pressed back into service to keep the operational numbers up. Could the pressure be maintained, was one question being asked. The Group, at this rate of attrition, would soon just drain away.

*

In the late afternoon, 12 and 150 Battle Squadrons were given targets. Flight Lieutenant Drinkwater (L5537 'K') led four Battles of 12 Squadron to bomb roads and tanks but the low clouds continued to prove a major difficulty in finding and bombing suitable targets. Some flak was met and Drinkwater had to force-land at Cry when his radio failed.

Over the same target area – around a convoy west of Beaumetz – 150 Squadron saw 12 Squadron bombing and also saw AFVs parked in the village of Ransart. Squadron Leader Bradley dropped his bombs on a copse and road near this village and later machine-gunned a convoy on the Arras–Doullens road.

Pilot Officer C.H. Elliott reached the target area at 8.15 and located stationary AFVs parked in the village, the head of the column at the western exit, the tail at about half a mile out of it on the Blairville road. More AFVs could be seen in the copse bombed by Bradley. Total strength of the convoy appeared to be some 100 vehicles. Elliott bombed from between 4,000 and 2,000 feet, scoring three direct hits on the copse and another on the road. The second aircraft in his section also dropped his bombs in the copse and on the road.

Just on eight o'clock, Flying Officer A.D. Frank was having difficulty seeing targets because of cloud and poor visibility. Then coming out of cloud he saw a 12 Squadron Battle bombing a convoy. Looking down he saw about 25 vehicles on the Arras to Doullens road. With gunfire engaging the other Battle, Frank dive-bombed the convoy and registered four near misses along the side of the road, as his gunner shot up vehicles with his rear gun. As he pulled away he saw the other Battle's bombs blast the convoy.

Both of these Battle squadrons, plus 88, operated that same night. 12 Squadron sent two aircraft to bomb revictualling yards at Florenville and the town of Charleville, although cloud was again a problem. 150 Squadron sent eight machines to attack troops and AFV columns near Mezières. 88 Squadron's targets are not recorded but two Battles failed to return. One was later reported only to have force-landed and was safe but out of petrol. The other machine was lost and its crew killed:

P/O A.E. Wickham	Sgt E. Hibbert	AC1 M. Whelan	P2356*

Friday, 24 May
The German invasion of the west was now exactly two weeks old. The Allied armies had been cut in two, with the bulk of the BEF surrounded, its back to the sea. In the south the French and other British units faced the Germans across the Somme. This day saw Boulogne fall after a spirited rearguard action by the French, and earlier by the British Guards who had evacuated to England. With nowhere to go, the BEF had to be rescued. An evacuation from the remaining French ports, Calais and Dunkirk, seemed likely.

With Boulogne lost, everyone expected German panzer units to press quickly towards Calais. 2 Group were again needed to attempt to stop them by bombing either them or the approach roads they might use.

Nine Blenheims of 110 Squadron, led by Wing Commander Sinclair, took off at 8.55 a.m. (in R3741) to bomb the Calais–Englebert road. They found about 40 AFVs near St Inglevert and bombed them. When they returned, without loss, at 10.40 with the news, 21 and 82 Squadrons were alerted and sent off shortly after 11.

The six Blenheims of 21 Squadron found AFVs between Calais and St Inglevert and scored some hits and near misses. Pilot Officer Rogers' machine (L8743) caught some flak in the bomb bay and his gunner, LAC Lang was wounded by flying shrapnel. Flight Lieutenant L.V.E. Atkinson led 82 Squadron's six machines, making shallow dive attacks down to 1,500 feet, hits and near misses being scored on the road. Fighter escort had been provided and all aircraft returned.

These returning crews were reporting an estimated 100 plus tanks and armoured vehicles on the move. This immediately prompted a further mission, this time given to 107 Squadron. Embry led in his 'new' Blenheim, L9391, taking off at 2 p.m., but they were unable to locate the vehicles they were told to expect. He therefore led a bomb attack on AA batteries in woods to the west of Calais. When he landed at 3.40, the camera pictures were developed and these showed that enemy AFVs had indeed been around, well camouflaged or in woods and under trees. Cameras had been expressly carried for the last few days in order to bring back any sort of information the optic eye might reveal. In consequence 15 and 40 Squadrons were bombed up and briefed.

In between this activity, 57 Squadron sent a Blenheim out from RAF Hawkinge to Amiens:

| P/O W. Hutchings | Sgt Whitlam | Cpl A. Daley | ? |

Over France they ran into a formation of 18 Me110s which began to chase the now rapidly retreating recce plane. In the turret, Daley kept up a spirited return fire, and one Messerschmitt appeared to be hit at the beginning of the fight. The British machine was severely damaged, its hydraulics were shot out, and Hutchings was wounded in the arm, but the gunner nailed the leading 110 over the Channel which went diving towards the sea. Helped by his observer, Hutchings made it back to a crash landing at Lympne, at 5.45.

At this precise moment, 15 and 40 Squadrons were taking off. 15 were led by Flight Lieutenant Len Trent (L8855), with Pilot Officer D.S.R. Harriman (P6913), Flying Officer W.H. George (L8848), Pilot Officer Henderson (R3614), Sergeant Megginson (L9413) and Sergeant Day (N6196). They bombed the road from Cap Gris Nez to Calais from 8,000 feet. On their return Pilot Officer Henderson was on his final approach to land when his port engine cut. As he put down his flaps the Blenheim spun in and crashed. Henderson and his crew, Sergeant Holmes and LAC Austin, were all killed.

By this time we were forced to use hastily supplied inexperienced replacement crews whose chances of survival were slim indeed. Our policy was to operate where possible in sections of three, each section being led by one of the few experienced survivors of the original squadron. Each wingman was briefed to maintain close formation at all time and to do whatever his leader did and nothing else. This worked reasonably well but not always. On 24th May, having

got my section safely back to Wyton after a successful attack
on AFVs at Calais, I instructed them to change over tanks for
the approach and landing as our main tanks were a bit low.
They both acknowledged and confirmed that they had
changed over. A minute or so later, the No. 2 lost an engine
and spun in. It transpired that due to inexperience he had
turned the wrong tap.

Flying Officer W.H. George, 15 Squadron

No. 40 Squadron's six Blenheims, led by Squadron Leader
Gerald Gleed bombed enemy convoys around Arras and were
back by 8 p.m., without loss. The main problem, however, was
that with the elapse of time, the AFVs previously seen were now
well dispersed.

And the Group had not yet finished. Between 7.20 and 8 p.m.,
21, 82 and 107 Squadrons mounted further raids. 21 Squadron,
led by Squadron Leader Petley, were also sent after the tanks but
as the others had found, they were well dispersed, but the six
aircraft bombed roads and anything else they could see.

The Earl led his 82 Squadron (R3618 'N') to the same locality
– Oye and Gravelines – but they failed to find tanks either but
hit the road. Finally Embry led the same 12 crews from the
morning raid against convoys and bridges at Calais Marck.
Direct hits were observed and an AA gun site knocked out,
which had to be some satisfaction. Their fighter escort, they
could see, were mixing it with a number of enemy fighters, and
the Blenheims landed at 9.20 without casualties.

*

That afternoon, the AASF squadrons were ordered to prepare
every available bomber for night ops. By 3.40 p.m., the
following list was submitted to AASF HQ:

75 Wing:	88 Squadron –	10 Battles
	103 Squadron –	8 Battles
	150 Squadron –	8 Battles
76 Wing:	12 Squadron –	9 Battles
	142 Squadron –	6 Battles
	226 Squadron –	6 Battles
Total:		47 Battles

Seven night ops were finally flown by 12 Squadron, going to the towns of Givet, Fumay and Bouvignes. They had also been ordered not to bring any bombs back over enemy territory, and they were to cause the maximum disturbance to the enemy's lines of communication. All bombed and met moderate flak and searchlights. One crew saw a Me110 but no attack was made by it.

The other squadrons all flew night ops, but the only item of interest is that 150 Squadron, for the first time, used a mixed bomb load in their Battles. They carried two 250 lb bombs and eight 25 lb incendiaries. One aircraft carried the 250 pounders plus eight 40 lb GP bombs.

Plans had now been made to attempt to evacuate BEF troops from Dunkirk which would indirectly cause a problem for 2 Group. It had been trying to stem the advancing German Panzers which seemed poised to engulf Dunkirk. These would now be halted by the German High Command while the Luftwaffe bombed the BEF into submission. Yet with the net closing around Dunkirk, the closeness of the defenders and attackers made it almost impossible for the Blenheims to give full support for fear of hitting Allied soldiers.

The now famous evacuation officially began on the 26th.

CHAPTER TWELVE

Behind Dunkirk

Saturday, 25 May

South of Dunkirk the River Lys was under direct threat, the Germans bringing up pontoon bridges and rubber boats. In the north, Belgian forces were being forced back leaving the BEF to plug the gap which this fall-back created. On the coast, Calais was now under direct attack, and were so closely threatened that 2 Group could no longer bomb the enemy because of the risk of inflicting casualties on the defenders.

Wing Commander Sinclair led his 110 Squadron (six aircraft) to bomb a canal bridge and to make a recce between Calais and Boulogne. The attack was not a success but the recce proved of value. They all landed at 7.45 a.m.

Also out at dawn was a 57 Squadron Blenheim:

F/O E.F. Nind	Sgt A.G. Logan	Cpl F.T. Russell	?

Flying over Belgium, they met heavy ground fire, and Sergeant Logan was hit in the leg by an explosive bullet when near Ypres. Despite severe blood loss and pain, he continued to navigate, and when they got home, gave his report before being sent off to hospital. Flying Officer Nind:

> When we got back to England we continued to carry out reconnaissances from Hawkinge, flying down on each occasion from Wyton where we were based. On 25 May I took off from Hawkinge to carry out a reconnaissance of Ypres, Lille and Hazebrouck. On completion I turned for home and sighted three Me109s. I was flying at 2,000 feet so I put the nose down and went for the deck to try and avoid them. When I got to about 200 feet, a lot of light flak came up from a wood and my observer, Sergeant Logan, was hit in

215

his left shin by what appeared to be an explosive bullet, as there was a strong smell of cordite in the cockpit. There was a hole about the size of a golf ball in the front of his shin and he was losing a lot of blood.

He was sitting alongside me, so as soon as I had shaken off the 109s I took his helmet off and used his intercom cord to tie a tourniquet round his lower thigh. I then put the throttles on maximum boost and headed for Hawkinge. Despite this, by the time we got back blood was swilling around the floor of the cockpit.

He had a rough time for a month or two. The surgeons took the leg off below the knee, but then gangrene set in and they had to take the knee off too. Later I got down to see him at his home in Christchurch and in about nine months he had returned to the squadron on light duties. His RAF trade was that of Fitter I, so I recommended him for a commission in the engineer branch, which was subsequently awarded. About two years later I ran into him again when visiting a Pathfinder squadron to find Logan had become the Squadron Leader Station Engineer.

Flying Officer E.F. Nind, 57 Squadron

By mid-morning, 2 Group had briefed 15 and 40 Squadrons at Wyton to bomb MT on a road between Guimes and Rety, two miles north of Calais. 15 were led by Flight Lieutenant A.R. Oakshott – six aircraft, while Brian Paddon led the six of 40 Squadron.

F/lt A.R. Oakshott	L8851	S/L B. Paddon	P4908
P/O R.S. Gilmour	R3704	F/O C.W. Bromley	N6236
P/O K.S. Roberts	R3603	Sgt J.S. Morton	L8827
P/O C.H. Robinson	N6156	F/Lt R.H. Batt	L8836
P/O D.S.R. Harriman	P6913*	F/O G.D. Hill	P4927
Sgt R.R. Megginson	L9413	Sgt S.I. Tonks	P4920*

They met heavy opposition, including at least nine Me109s. Flak and fighters shot down two Blenheims, one from each squadron, while four others of 40 Squadron's machines were all damaged, except Paddon's. The missing crews all died except Sergeant Tonks who was taken prisoner:

P/O D.S.R. Harriman	Sgt P. Bloomer	P/O J.H. Gordon	P6913*
Sgt S.I. Tonks	Sgt J.L. Alexander	LAC D. Goffe	L4920*

The Blenheims did have a 'loose' fighter escort, but they became embroiled with some Stuka dive-bombers over the French coast.

The general situation, having become increasingly serious, prompted AASF to send out its Battles in daylight in the late morning. 12 Squadron had two aircraft available, which headed north and bombed Panzers on the Cancy to Hesdin road. Pilot Officer R.A.D. Meharey and Sergeant F. Field found no tanks but bombed some MT north-east of Blangy.

Some Battles of 88 Squadron bombed targets near Abbeville, and 150 had two of its bombers attack MT moving north along the Abbeville road, despite heavy gunfire from the Forêt de Crécy. 226 also made two daylight sorties and 103 also sent out aircraft. This latter unit lost one machine when Sergeant G. Beardsley, flying with just a WOP/AG LAC Lewis, was shot down. For the second time these two found themselves on the ground in the forward area, this time they had to walk 27 miles before they were picked up, being then given a lift by a motorcycle and sidecar. They finally got back to the squadron on the 27th. George Lewis was later to receive the DFM.

During the afternoon, 2 Group sent out 21 and 107 Squadrons. Six of 21, led by Scottie Pryde (L9269), went for pontoon bridges across the River Lys between Menin and Courtrai with a fighter escort. Only near misses were seen. Only slight AA fire too but one Blenheim was lost, just the pilot surviving, as a prisoner:

Sgt H. Rawson	Sgt A.K.R. Keates	LAC D.V. Cleaver	L8734*

Basil Embry led 107 to the same targets and they claimed some damage inflicted but didn't see any troops. They did meet heavy flak and some of their aircraft were damaged but all returned.

The 25th's bombing effort, small by comparison to recent days, was ended by further night sorties by AASF Battles. 226 put up seven aircraft but three returned with engine trouble. 88 Squadron sent out aircraft too but lost one crew who were all killed:

P/O C.C.R. Anderson	Sgt R.W. Butler	AC1 E. Wilks	L5467*

Sunday, 26 May

By this day, the BEF were holding a pocket around the coastal port of Dunkirk, soon to become one of the most famous towns in the annals of WW2. German troops simply overwhelmed the Belgian forces, holding a mere 30 miles of a 127-mile perimeter and they were near collapse, short of ammunition and supplies. There was now no possibility of linking up again with the French in the south across the Somme.

Bomber Command Blenheims were out early that morning: 21, 40 and 82 Squadrons took off soon after dawn. 21, led by Squadron Leader R.D.C. Gibson, went out with 82 and 40, and expecting enemy fighters, Fighter Command gave them an escort of 32 Squadron from Biggin Hill. The 18 bombers flew out over Manston, 21 successfully bombing columns, troops and a railway junction, while 82 went for pontoon bridges south-west of Courtrai and another to the north-east, as well as the railway north-west of Marck. 40, led by Squadron Leader Gleed, also went for bridges. No German fighters were seen and all returned.

Reconnaissance Blenheims did not fare so well. 53, 57 and 59 Squadrons all sent out aircraft, mostly to try to gather vital information about what was happening to the Belgian forces. 59 Squadron sent out one at 9.15, flown by Flying Officer David Evans, with Sergeant Whiting and AC Finlayson as crew.

> On the 26th we flew to Hawkinge again and we flew off to the area of Dunkirk and carried out a tactical reconnaissance this time. The area over which we operated was to the south and west of the town starting from a place called Berques and including St Omer. I have a note that the aircraft was hit by shrapnel or a bullet but we still landed back at Hawkinge, reported then flew back to Andover, so clearly the damage can't have been too bad or very extensive.
>
> *Flying Officer G.H.D. Evans, 59 Squadron*

Later in the day, the squadron lost Pilot Officer Shaw on a recce, but it was Pilot Officer Reynolds who had quite an adventure:

| P/O Reynolds | Sgt G.E. Kirk | AC Bryde | R3695 |

Reynolds' Blenheim was hit by small arms fire over France and a cannon shell smashed his elevator controls, with the exception of the extreme end of the travel of the control column. Almost out of control, Reynolds ordered his crew out and Kirk went. Then Reynolds realised he still had some sort of control and grabbed the gunner and pulled him back. They made it across the Channel to land at Andover, but the unfortunate Kirk was taken into captivity. Later the squadron reported Pilot Officer R.E. Shaw missing (in R3613) (with Sgt Schwinol and AC2 Brogan) and the loss of Pilot Officer Carruthers' Blenheim. He'd been forced to land at Boos and returned without it. Richard Shaw was killed.

No. 53 Squadron lost one crew, who were all killed.

| P/O G.M. Bailey | Sgt J.K. Evans | AC1 A.A. Gillmore | L8853* |

Of the two recce ops flown by 57 Squadron, one got back badly shot up, flown by Squadron Leader J.A. Roncoroni. In total, therefore, three recce machines had failed to return, with others damaged. 52 Recce Wing recorded on this day that during the period 19 to 26 May, only four crews had been lost although the wastage of Blenheims had been far higher. Most of the returning aircraft had been found to have received damage from ground fire, especially small arms. Some of these aircraft could be repaired quite quickly on the units, others had to be sent to MUs while others had to be written off. The wing also noted that the Blenheim IV was standing up very well to battle damage, many returning with severe damage, but they'd got home.

*

The day was still young when orders went out for the Battles to once again fly daylight sorties. It was a special target. Four Battles from 103, four from 142 Squadrons, and two from 150 were assigned.

At the Château Roumont, near Ochamps aerodrome, the Intelligence people had discovered that there was going to be a meeting by about 20 senior German Luftwaffe officers. Time over the target was 10.18 a.m. and an escort of 1 and 73 Squadrons was provided.

The Battles of 142 were the first to arrive, in driving rain, but they dived to 2,000 feet and dropped 12 × 250 lb bombs, which one observer said he saw bursting all around the château, one appearing to burst right in the building. The last Battle did not release soon enough, so continued on until he found another suitable target. Flying over a railway loop north of Recogne, he bombed the junction, claiming a definite hit.

With the rain still lashing down, 103 Squadron, which had been led by John Havers, reached the château two minutes after 142. As initially only one Battle returned, it was only known for certain that four bombs had been dropped, and those in a dive attack from 9,000 to 4,000 feet. To the crew the château still appeared intact but the heavy rain made observation difficult.

As this crew made their way back, they passed over Ochampes aerodrome, seeing at least five aircraft on the ground. They were fired on by light and heavy flak, but got away. Later, a second Battle reported back that they had also bombed, at 10.15, hitting the château and seeing smoke coming from the foot of it. Heavy flak met this machine and this, plus the rain and poor visibility, had forced the pilot to make a landing at Verdun. The pilot had also flown over the aerodrome – on his way to the château – and was able to confirm seeing a large number of aircraft around the edge. At one point there were about 20, stacked nose to tail. They had also seen aircraft on the airfield at St Hubert, but due to heavy gunfire, had not stayed around to count them. Later the third Battle was located. Its pilot had been forced to crash land when its undercarriage failed to come down. This left just one as missing:

F/O J.N. Leyden	Sgt E.G. Heyward	AC W.F. Hubbard	L5514*

James Leydon was later reported a prisoner, his crew dead.

The two aircraft of 150 Squadron took off at 9.25 and were over the target at 10.15:

P/O C.H. Elliott	Sgt Gupwell	LAC Kirk	P6602
P/O J.E. Vernon	Sgt G. Busby	LAC A.W. Rutland	L5459*

Before he bombed the château, Elliott lost sight of Vernon and returned on his own. Later the French army reported seeing a British aeroplane attacked by four Messerschmitts over Thionville and shot down in flames at about 10.50, although two parachutes had been seen. However, James Vernon got back and made the following report:

At 9.25 on the 26th May I took off as leader of one half section to attack a target five miles north-west of Recogne. At approx 10.05, while flying at 10,000 feet near Montmédy, a severe storm was encountered and aircraft dived to 5,000 feet. Whilst diving we lost touch with other aircraft. Considerable difficulty experienced in locating target which was attacked between 10.20/25. Visibility was poor but rear of building was observed to have been hit. Bomb craters were observed in edge of wood close to southern end of building. My own attack was made by dive-bombing from south to north from 6,000 to 3,000 feet. Bombs observed to burst in building although very little smoke seen. Considerable AA fire encountered from three batteries, one at Libin, one at Ochampes and one east of the target.

As I was leaving vicinity I observed at least four Me110s circling Recogne between 2,000 and 3,000 feet. I dived to ground level, followed by the four enemy aircraft who attacked us half a mile south of Recogne. One Me110 was observed to be on fire at 1,500 feet, two miles south of Recogne flying at a very low level. Attacks appeared to be from rear and beam. Beam attacks were evaded by turning towards the attack.

In vicinity of Florenville, I observed an enemy aircraft landing on an aerodrome. I attacked with the front gun and observed several hits along its fuselage. Soon afterwards, Sergeant Busby reported a painful wound in the leg and then LAC Rutland reported his reflector site shot away by enemy fire. Enemy fire appeared to be both cannon and ball, which caused much damage to the airframe, fracturing rudders and trimming control making aircraft tail heavy. Later the rudder bar was shot away.

This combined with engine trouble, fractured oil pipes, oil pressure NIL, the engine cut and we force landed near Avioth in the German lines. Set fire to aircraft and in company with Busby and Rutland, commenced to travel towards a small wood. Somehow I was separated from the other two when taking cover from machine gun fire, who are believed to be prisoners of war, and I eventually located an outpost of the Maginot Line and then in turn, the Fort itself.

Pilot Officer James Edward Vernon was later awarded the DFC, but by that time he was himself missing in action. Who the French saw is unclear, unless the parachutes came from one of the 110s. Busby and Rutland were indeed later reported as prisoners.

In the latter half of the afternoon saw 2 Group back in action. Squadron Leader Hunt led six aircraft from 82 Squadron in another attack on pontoon bridges over the Lys, between Menin and Courtrai, claiming one bridge hit and a roadway blocked.

These six landed home at 6.13 p.m., but already 107 and 110 Squadrons were well on their way out. Escorted by three Hurricane squadrons, Wingco Embry led 12 of 107 and six of 110 on an armed recce to the St Pol area, to try to locate the aircraft seen earlier by the Battle crews. However, they saw no sign of the aircraft, thought by the Intelligence staff to be Ju52s bringing in fuel supplies for MT and Panzers. With orders not to bring bombs home, Embry attacked MT in the Forêt d'Hesdin, several vehicles being hit. On the way back no fewer than 11 of his 12 Blenheims were damaged by ground fire as they ran the gauntlet back to the coast. Five of 110's crews claimed direct hits on the same wooded area.

One 110 pilot who did not fly on this raid was Flying Officer G.O. Lings, who went to RAF Feltwell to receive his DFC.

That night, 12 and 88 Squadron flew night sorties without loss.

Monday, 27 May
At 5.30 a.m., 18 Squadron, who the previous day had moved to the airfield at Gatwick, flew a recce mission. Squadron Leader D.D. Rogers, using good cloud cover, had no opposition to his trip around Boulogne (R3734) and he was back safely by 7.15.

This was just about the time that 15, 21 and 40 Squadron were taking off for 2 Group's first effort of the day. 15 was led by Leonard Trent (in L8855) – six Blenheims bombing anything German around Dunkirk and Boulogne. 21 Squadron's six Blenheims bombed four houses near the village of Belle St Boullefort, about four miles east of Boulogne, used by the Germans as a HQ. Led by George Pryde, the buildings were demolished. Flight Lieutenant Robert Batt led 40 Squadron's six, bombing enemy positions near Courtrai. These and all the other bombers returned without loss or serious damage.

Reconnaissance missions were still proving difficult. 53 Squadron had a particularly trying day with three crews detailed for sorties:

P/O P.F.C. Villiers-Tuthill	Sgt A.H. Payne	AC D.B. Mearns	L8735*
P/O Aldridge	Sgt McRae	AC Trafford	R3703*
P/O Robinson	Sgt ?	AC Couchen	R3733

The first two appear to have been sent out during the morning. Percy Villiers-Tuthill simply failed to return and he and his crew were reported killed. Aldridge was attacked by an enemy fighter and his Blenheim damaged. They tried to get back over the Channel but were forced to abandon the machine over St Margarets, north of Dover. Aldridge and his gunner were injured.

Robinson took off at noon to fly a sortie over Hoogstade, Poperinghe and St Omer. They were assailed by 11 Me109s, which badly damaged their aircraft and wounded all three men, but they got back at 1.15.

By the afternoon 2 Group were ready once more, and at 1.35 Squadron Leader Sutcliffe led six Blenheims of 82 Squadron, meeting up with six of 21 Squadron. They attacked MT in the St Omer area. A Me110 attacked Pilot Officer R.C.D. McKenzie's machine (R3707 'O') and his gunner, Aircraftman Crozier, fired 1,000 rounds at it. The 110 half rolled and fell away into a cloud. During the approach to the target, German Stukas and their fighter escort could be seen attacking Calais.

An hour later six aircraft of 110 Squadron led by Wing Commander Sinclair, attacked MT in the same area, again returning without loss. The final effort was made shortly after six o'clock when 40 and 107 Squadrons flew out. Gleed led six of 40 against convoys near Dunkirk, while Basil Embry led 12 Blenheims of 107, to St Omer. 107's take-off time was 5.45:

W/C B.E. Embry DSO, AFC	P/O T.A. Whiting	Cpl G.E. Lang	L9391*
F/O J.W. Stephens	Sgt W.J. Barrett	LAC E.C. White	N6190
P/O W. Carter	Sgt S. Clayton	LAC J.R. Browning	N6237
S/L L.R. Stokes	Sgt L. Graves	LAC D.S. Barnes	R3737
Sgt H. Warman	Sgt W.C.H. Paish	LAC J. Mahoney	N6192*
P/O K.D. Taute	Sgt L.S. Fearnley	LAC J.R. Waterhouse	P4919
F/Lt H.P. Pleasance	Sgt R.D. Cook	Sgt P.E.F. Adams	P6894
F/O C.P. Bomford	Sgt R.A. Bowman	AC H.T. Dennison	L9323
F/O D.J.A. Roe	Sgt D. Haigh	LAC E.W. Gimson	L9306
P/O G.B. Murray	Sgt G.A. Wilson	LAC A. Moses	L9468
P/O R.H.M. Bennett	Sgt C.F. Plimmer	LAC D.S. Harrison	R3740
P/O H.F. Mitchinson	Sgt L. Charnock	LAC J. Bartley	R3739

The previous day, Wing Commander Embry had received a signal that he was to take command of RAF Station, West Raynham, effective the 28th. 107 would be taken over by Squadron Leader L.R. Stokes, on his promotion to wing commander. Embry tried to postpone the date of appointment not wanting to leave his squadron at this particularly busy time, but was refused. With another raid already scheduled for the 27th, Embry decided to lead one more show while Leonard Stokes flew as a section leader to see how it was done. Stokes thought this a good idea, and would take over command when they had returned.

The squadron flew out via Ramsgate, but the flak began at the coast and was with them all the way to St Omer. They bombed columns passing through St Omer amidst heavy ground fire, which hit Embry's Blenheim just after his bombs had gone down. He felt a stab of pain in his left leg, and with his machine still being hit, it completed a turn but, with the controls gone, it was time to leave. Signalling to his observer, Tom Whiting, (the R/T was u/s) he motioned him to bale out which he did. With the Blenheim now totally out of control and diving earthwards, Embry looked back for his gunner but he appeared crumpled in his turret – dead. Embry then left the doomed aeroplane, his parachute opened, and as it did so, his Blenheim hit the ground below.

Although captured shortly afterwards, Basil Embry eventually escaped from a German column and following various adventures, helped by a number of French men and women he reached Paris. Then, helped by various people, he got away to the south of France, then into Spain, Gibraltar and finally home to England at the beginning of August.

Meanwhile, 107's Blenheims all bombed St Omer, several crews seeing their CO go down, but saw two parachutes open so were encouraged that at least two of them had got out. Then some Me109s came on the scene, two attacking one Blenheim flown by Sergeant Warman, who began to trail smoke and did not return. He and his crew all perished.

I was leading the second box behind Wing Commander Embry, who was on his last flight before handing over 107 Squadron to Randall Stokes. I must be one of the very few who saw one squadron commander hand over his command to his successor in the air!

One of my most vivid memories of those hectic three months is the force of Basil Embry's leadership and the tremendous spirit he engendered in 107 Squadron at a time when the Blenheims of 2 Group were suffering massive casualties. He was a superb leader sans pareil.

Flight Lieutenant H.P. Pleasance, 107 Squadron

Embry was leading and we were flying either as his No. 2 or No. 3. We'd just bombed and had flak burst all around us. Then I saw Embry's aircraft suddenly go straight up in the air; he'd obviously been hit in the elevators. As it stalled I saw the bottom escape hatch come open. As one later read in Embry's book *Mission Completed*, he put his foot up against Tom Whiting's back and booted him out. I saw Tom drop down and moments later Embry followed. The Blenheim seemed to me to be stationary as we flew past it. It was a terrible thought, thinking, there goes our CO, as Embry came out of that aircraft.

Sergeant L.S. Fearnley, 107 Squadron

That night the Battles returned to the night sky. No losses are recorded, although one 88 Squadron machine hit a tree on take-off. All three members of the crew were injured – Sergeant D. Haywood, Sergeant J.R.A. Jones and LAC E.C. Williams. 142 Squadron's target was St Hubert aerodrome, which would be part of the Battle's daylight target programme on the morrow.

Tuesday, 28 May

The Dunkirk evacuation had begun, and 11 Group of Fighter Command was fully committed to providing cover for the beaches and town, and for the myriad of tiny ships and larger vessels who would be engaged in getting the BEF away to England.

Another major event on this Tuesday was that Belgium finally gave in and King Leopold capitulated on behalf of his country. The weather wasn't good restricting 2 Group efforts although with fewer fighter squadrons now available, they were reluctant to head inland too far. However, they did try to keep advancing German troops back from the beach-head.

Shortly before dawn, 82 Squadron sent out six Blenheims led by Squadron Leader Hunt, picking up an escort from RAF Northolt before making for the St Omer area. Flak tended to break up both the bombers and the escorting fighters, but targets were bombed and then Hunt (P6925 'Z') carried out a recce of an area ten miles west of a line St Omer to Aire, despite heavy AA fire.

The Group's next raid was not until after 11 a.m. 15 Squadron, led by Alan Oakshott attacked troops behind Dunkirk, in the area of Quest-Mont, which was followed in quick succession by nine Blenheims from 21 Squadron, who bombed MT in the Forêt de Clairmarais, to the east of St Omer. The first section bombed through cloud but the rest were uncertain of results due to 10/10ths cloud which was down to 600 feet, together with heavy rain. AA fire came up at them over the coast east of Dunkirk and brought down one machine, before Squadron Leader 'Jock' Gibson turned for home. What happened to the pilot is uncertain, but the observer was killed and the gunner later returned:

Sgt Bailes   Sgt G.E.D. Twamley   AC S.C. Thompson   L8744*

Nine Blenheims of 40 Squadron were next, heading out from England after 3 p.m., led by Robert Batt, attacking enemy convoys on the Arras–Menin road without loss. Finally 107 and 110 Squadrons (nine and six machines) also went for columns on roads leading to St Omer. Stokes led 107 for the first time, while Sinclair led his 110 against columns in Clairmarais forest and in the Forêt Eperlecques.

Perhaps the most eventful sortie of the day was carried out by 59 Squadron:

P/O J.F.H. Peters   Sgt T.W. McDonagh   Sgt J.A.S. Finlayson   R3664*

John Peters' Blenheim was hit by AA fire at around 4.15 p.m. near Dunkirk when at 3,000 feet. There was a tank battle going on below at the time. The Blenheim had obviously had it. It became uncontrollable and began to roll over onto its back. It was thought that the gunner was also wounded. Peters ordered the bale out and soldiers on the ground did see three people leave the aircraft but only two parachutes deployed. The wounded gunner seems to have hit his head on leaving and was then unable to operate the rip cord. The observer was seen to drift away towards the German positions and both he and the gunner were later confirmed as being killed.

As he drifted down, Peters was fired at from the ground, one bullet ripping through a section of his 'chute making his descent more vertical and more rapid! He hit the ground so hard he was knocked out but on recovering, he made his way on foot, joined up with the army and was given a lift on a tank into Dunkirk. From there he was lucky enough to get onto a British destroyer, HMS *Pangbourne*, arriving at Margate the next morning.

Both 12 and 150 Squadron flew night raids, the former sending nine Battles to bomb St Hubert and Ochampes aerodromes as well as the railway at Libramont.

At least one Battle squadron flew some day ops during the day. 103 were operating in the Abbeville area and one aircraft, flown by Flying Officer R.D. Max, was caught in a valley commanded by German flak positions. Roy Max had his Battle damaged and its engine hit, making it impossible for him to climb. He had continued to fly through heavy ground fire collecting more damage as he did so. His gunner, LAC Dubois was wounded, but Max finally got through and landed his severely damaged machine at Chalons.

F/O R.D. Max   Sgt D. Allen   AC Dubois   L5515

We were sent out to bomb pontoon bridges the Germans had built and we had to try and hit this darned thing. I came around at about 6,000 ft. and started to dive down and as I did so I found enemy guns on three sides. It amazed me because the German convoy was still moving up and hadn't yet got near to the bridge. Obviously their engineers had come ahead to put the bridge across and had placed those guns all around.

I dropped my bombs and then came out low. I could see this one gun on top of a hill, which seemed to be doing the most damage, so I gave him a good burst with my one wing gun. Unfortunately they'd hit us before that and the engine started to back-fire and make funny noises. Then I saw the engine temperature rising so obviously glycol was leaking out and it was getting hotter and hotter. I headed back as far as I could, saw an airfield which had French aircraft on it and poor old 'Trunky' Allen, my observer, was cursing. Dubois, my gunner, had been wounded and I'd been hit with a bit of shrapnel in the left knee. I thought I'd lost my knee because I couldn't feel a thing, it was completely numb. All I could see, looking down, was blood dripping off my heel. Anyway, when I landed I'd all but decided I'd lost my leg, it was terribly sore and stiff. But I got out and all there was was a little cut at the side and it was bruised. Obviously the shrapnel's momentum coming through the side of the aircraft to hit the leg, had slowed down just enough to give the leg a nasty cut.

Flying Officer R.D. Max, 103 Squadron

Two members of 110 Squadron had their names in the *London Gazette* on this day. Flight Lieutenant H.D.H. Cooper had been awarded the DFC for his part in the Maastricht bridges attack on 11 May, and his observer, Sergeant John Stewart Robertson received the DFM for his valuable photos taken during the attack.

Wednesday, 29 May
2 Group Blenheims continued to give support to the evacuation by attacking German positions beyond the perimeter. 15 and 40 Squadrons were out at dawn. The nine of 40 Squadron led by Gleed bombed targets at Calais, Dixmude, Thorgart and Nieuport. Trent led eight of 15 Squadron (L8855) against AFVs and MT columns in the forward areas,

but they ran into fog on the return flight and the Blenheims split up and landed at various aerodromes: Abingdon, Bassingbourn, Alconbury, Hawkinge and Wittering!

Squadron Leader Sutcliffe led nine of 82 out at 10.20, also bombing AFVs in the Dixmude area. Sutcliffe himself bombed a column of vehicles in a village and hit a house. It fell across the road, effectively blocking it. A lone Me110 was seen but it did not attack.

This morning also saw the return of 114 and 139 Squadrons to England. The remnants had made their way to Cherbourg where they boarded the SS *Bruge*, and SS *Ghent*, sailing for Southampton.

It was 2 Group that was in action during the afternoon, 107, 110 and 21 Squadrons going out at approximately two hour intervals. Only 21 ran into trouble. Led by Scottie Pryde, they bombed AFVs, MT and troops between Dixmude and Thorout; the Blenheim pilots searched independently for targets because of extensive low cloud patches. Pilot Officer L.M. Blanckensee (P6886), with his crew of Sergeant Williams and AC Jack Guest, was spotted by a roving Me109 which attacked them repeatedly. Finally Guest got in a telling burst and the 109 was shot down, but not before the Blenheim's hydraulic system had been knocked out. Reaching base, Lewis Blanckensee had to make a wheels-up landing. Jack Guest received the DFM and this was the second Me109 he had shot down during May.

Despite bad weather, 88 Squadron attempted night sorties, sending six Battles to bomb Charleville. The first aircraft crashed on take-off and the crew were killed when one of their bombs exploded:

| F/O H.G. Evitt | Sgt E.W.J. Chapman | AC1 Edwards | P2313* |

The others bombed the target but the weather forced Flying Officer H.G. Marriott to force land at Avord and Flying Officer D.L.R. Halliday to force land at Vitry, but both crews were back the next day. Bombing results were uncertain, as due to the bad weather, the target was difficult to see even when they dropped parachute flares, so the Battles bombed on an ETA.

On the 29th – my birthday – we again flew a tactical reconnaissance to the south west of Dunkirk and on this occasion we chased an Hs126 which probably was directing artillery onto the beaches. My crew were Sergeant Wyse and AC Cleland.

It was a very unpleasant sight down below as I recall bomb and shell craters and all the columns of black smoke and AA bursts. It really looked like something out of Hell from above, so what it must have been down below I shudder to think. The trip only lasted an hour and a quarter and having reported back found that we had been hit so when I flew back to Andover I left my wheels down lest, having got them up I couldn't get them down again.

There must have been reasonable communication between Dunkirk and Hawkinge since the ALO had commented when I mentioned chasing away the Hs126, that this had been much appreciated by the troops on the ground as its direction of artillery fire had made him a blasted nuisance.

Flying Officer G.H.D. Evans, 59 Squadron

Thursday, 30 May
Even the bad weather couldn't keep 2 Group on the ground, although they only managed two raids on the morning of the 30th. At 9.50, 11 aircraft (the 12th had to abort with engine trouble) bombed targets at Nieuport and Dixmude, but clouds curtailed the bombing. 15 Squadron, led by Squadron Leader P.F. Webster, bombed MT columns, three vehicles being seen to overturn on the Furness road, while other bombs fell on a road and canal north-east of Nieuport. Flying Officer Robertson (N6156) was wounded by ground fire but he got back and landed at Martlesham, where he was taken to hospital.

Shortly after four o'clock that afternoon, 2 Group sent out four squadrons – 40, 82, 107 and 110, followed at around 6.30 by a further raid by 110 in company with 21 Squadron. All aircraft had varying degrees of success or failure, failure due mainly to weather conditions. The good news was that the Blenheims suffered no losses.

Ronny Rotheram of 107 Squadron, who had been brought down over Belgium on the 12th, had returned to the squadron:

I was back on operations on the 22nd May, when we flew two sorties from Wattisham; the second sortie finished in some confusion when we landed at dusk at RAF Manston – from all directions! We did one sortie on 23rd May and two sorties on the 24th, followed by single sorties thereafter. By the end of the month we were operating just past Dunkirk and we could tell where we were by the different coloured flak and AA that met us. We were rescued several times from the attentions of Me109s by the timely arrival of Spitfires and Hurricanes. The smoke from the burning oil tanks in Dunkirk was actually drifting over Ipswich.

Flying Officer R.C. Rotheram, 107 Squadron

The Battles of 103 Squadron flew night sorties to complete the day's bombing.

In the occasionally odd way of bestowing decorations, and who should receive them, 103 Squadron were informed on this day, that the French had allocated three French decorations to the squadron. This was all very fine, but who should they go to? Finally it was decided that certain pilots, observers and air gunners should be selected, the final recipients made by the toss of a coin! Thus the three recommendations were forwarded in the names of Flying Officer Roy Max, Sergeant J.A. McCudden, and Corporal Madkins.

What happened to the decorations? Probably the paperwork got lost in the works due to the subsequent French collapse. Strangely though, Roy Max's parents in New Zealand, received a message before this happened, saying their son had been awarded the Croix de Guerre. The family 'leaked' this to the local newspapers, of course, but Roy never received his French medal.

During the day, Air Marshal Barratt and Air Vice Marshal Playfair visited 103 and 226 Squadrons. Although the BEF were evacuating from Dunkirk, with the Germans poised to attack south, across the Somme, everyone knew that the AASF squadrons would soon be back in the thick of the action. Everyone hoped that perhaps the French and the remaining BEF units to the south of the Somme, might yet halt the German onslaught. The Germans had failed to reach Paris in the First World War, would the threat of occupation now help galvanise the French into a heroic defence of their first city?

Friday, 31 May

Three weeks since the Blitzkrieg began, the BEF were evacuating, while the French waited for the next round. Meantime, 2 Group mounted another dawn attack with eight aircraft of 82 Squadron which attacked MT and the bridge over the Yser at Dixmude. They missed the bridge.

15 and 40 Squadrons were out a few hours later, attacking MT on the Furnes–Ypres road or around Ypres itself.

Later that morning, AASF HQ sent out 12 Battles to attack enemy aircraft seen parked on Laon aerodrome and on the nearby racecourse. 12 Squadron put up six aircraft, which took off at 10.50. (The squadron which put up a further six aircraft is not readily identified, or perhaps the second six failed to go because of the weather.) The weather was terrible. 12 Squadron's crews found 10/10ths cloud down to 3,000 feet. The cloud was meant to act as cover for a surprise attack, instead it totally foiled it. Four Battles came back with their bombs, unable to find the target, while another, intending to bomb on ETA, then found his bomb release gear not working. The others bombed various targets on ETA, and one gunner was wounded by AA fire from south east of Laon.

All 2 Group squadrons, except 15, operated during the afternoon, between 12.30 and 8 p.m. 107 Squadron were attacked by some 109s, and one was shot down by an observer firing a gun from his blister position. Escorting Hurricanes bagged a couple of more.

No. 40 Squadron managed to hit a pontoon bridge under construction, and blocked the road to the permanent bridge near Nieuport. Again no losses were sustained by the Blenheims. Night raids by 88 and 150 Squadrons ended May, and as the last of 150s Battles landed at five minutes past midnight, June had begun. But what would June bring for the Battles of the AASF and the Blenheims of 2 Group?

CHAPTER THIRTEEN

War on the Somme

The first week of June

The Germans' main objective was the destruction of the BEF around Dunkirk, and the ground forces which had pushed the British back were keen to finish the job. However, Hitler directed, following promises by his boastful Luftwaffe supremo, Hermann Goering, that the Luftwaffe should bomb them into submission or destroy them. Hitler was mindful that he still had the rest of France to vanquish and was husbanding his armour and troops for this task. If the Luftwaffe could accomplish the destruction of the BEF or cause them to surrender, he would save his army for the next task.

However, with surprisingly calm seas, and the determination of the Navy, ably supported by many civilian seamen or weekend sailors, over 338,000 Allied soldiers were taken off the beaches or from the harbour of Dunkirk between 26 May and 3 June. If the German Generals had had their way they would have captured an army and still been more than strong enough to take the rest of France.

While the last few days of Operation Dynamo ran their course, 2 Group continued its support.

On the 1st, 15 Squadron put up three missions of six Blenheims each. Peter Webster led the first at 6 a.m. Hugh George led the second around an hour later, while Alan Oakshott headed the third that evening. All were directed against AFVs and troops around the Dunkirk perimeter. Hugh George's log book records the destruction of a bridge at Hondschoote.

All squadrons, bombed MT, AFVs, tanks and troops around the diminishing perimeter, virtually without loss. The only damage sustained came on 2 June, when 107 Squadron led by

Top Blenheim 'J' (P4919), 107 Squadron, which crash-landed on 2 June. (*R.C. Rotheram*)

Above Sergeants W.G. Brinn DFM and Dickie Gunning DFM, 107 Squadron, with their upside-down Blenheim (R3683), 2 June. (*R.C. Rotheram*)

Left Flight Lieutenant H.P. Pleasance DFC, 107 Squadron. (*H.P. Pleasance*)

Gareth Clayton, attacked an enemy battery firing at shipping off Gravelines. Twelve Blenheims attacked in section, but flak was severe and three machines were hit badly enough for the three pilots to have to make forced landings at base on their return. These were Pilot Officer K.D. Taute (N6191), Flight Sergeant H.J. Ratcliffe (P4919) who made a belly landing, and Sergeant Gunning DFM (R3683). The last was a most spectacular crash, with the Blenheim turning turtle to finish up on its back.

> At Gravelines it was low level. We just hedge-hopped across the Channel and my main memory is seeing the oil tanks burning at Dunkirk which went on for days. The smoke stretched as far as Kent and East Anglia.
>
> It was amazing that we survived this attack for the Germans were really pooping stuff at us. We got hit by a bit of flak but were not seriously damaged.
>
> One of the problems always with low level jobs was the blast from other aircraft's bombs that were going in ahead of us.
>
> *Sergeant L.S. Fearnley, 107 Squadron*

On one mission to Dunkirk at dawn on the 3rd, Sergeant Albert Merritt of 82 Squadron (in P6895) searched for German gun positions. It was a dangerous place to be at any time considering the amount of German aircraft around, despite Fighter Command's air patrols. Merritt was chased by both Me109s and Ju88s and his gunner, George Whitehead, who usually flew with Philip Sutcliffe, recalls: 'Took refuge in the black smoke over Dunkirk from burning oil tanks. Eventually bombed German guns and returned home.'

As for the Battle squadrons, they stood ready. 103 moved its base to Herbouville on the 3rd. Three of its pilots were also decorated at this time. Flight Lieutenant C.E.R. Tait and Flying Officer T.B. Fitzgerald received DFCs, Sergeant C.D. Perry the DFM. In 107 Squadron came the announcement that Embry's old crew, Whiting and Lang had been awarded the DFC and DFM respectively. Sadly, Lang was dead.

Other squadrons were on the move. 150 moved to Houssay on the evening of the 2nd while its crews were on night ops. The road convoy began the 186-mile trek which took them 19 hours. The squadron's 19 machines flew to the new airfield on the morning of the 3rd. 88 Squadron (whose Flight Lieutenant D.L.R. Halliday had just been notified of his DFC) left for Moisy early on the 3rd, and its road convoy arrived at 5.30 that evening. 142 Squadron had a fire in one of its tents, destroying a number of parachutes and helmets as well as instruments and maps. It had to borrow some from 105 and 226 Squadrons.

On the night of the 3rd, Flight Lieutenant J.M. Hewson, was one of five Battle pilots that flew a raid to Trier, and he scored a direct hit on a railway line after releasing a parachute flare.

A crew of 12 Squadron was lost on the 3rd, although the circumstances are not recorded. All three men died:

P/O C.S. McIntyre   Sgt G.H. Hudson   AC1 D.L. Leonard   P2269*

The squadron then moved on the 4th to Souge. It was installed just in time for the German offensive which began the following day.

The Blenheims of 59 Squadron were now at Eastchurch, having moved there on 1st June.

> We set out on the 4th but after about ten minutes had to return as the aircraft had gone u/s. I then transferred to another aircraft with my own crew and then took off to fly another tactical recce, to the area Rue-Crécy Auxi-Aumale, again north of Paris. That trip was a bit longer, about two hours and a quarter. I have a vague recollection that we were told that the 51st Division had got themselves shut in between Dieppe and Le Havre, north of Rouen, and that we were covering any attacks that might come in their direction.
> *Flying Officer G.H.D. Evans, 59 Squadron*

Wednesday, 5th June
With Dunkirk over, the Germans turned their attention to the Somme. The attack was expected and when it came it covered a wide area, but particularly at these points:

1. An advance south-west from St Valéry and Abbeville, which by the evening had pushed the British 51st Division nearly back to Bresle.
2. An advance south from Amiens by a Panzer attack by some 300 tanks.

3. An advance south-west from Péronne by 400 tanks.
4. An advance south-west from Lafare-Chauny.
5. An advance south-west from Laon.

They made other crossings of the Somme and the Aisne but these five advances constituted the main threats, and all were pointed at the Lower Seine region, or the Germans' key prize: Paris.

The attack was so vast it was difficult to know where to bomb and it was well into the afternoon before information could be sifted. Immediately the report of tanks on the Péronne–Roye–Amiens and Montdidier roads was received, AASF had to launch an attack.

They had been on stand-by for most of the day; 150 Squadron had even flown nine of its bombers to 12 Squadron's base in readiness, at 11.30 that morning. 12 and 142 Squadrons sent out aircraft to attack the tanks at 7.30 p.m. but although they did not see any great numbers of troops, they did bomb two roads and various vehicles.

But then they spotted some tanks heading towards Tricot. The Germans had not advanced as far south as this, so the tanks must have been French. This led the three Battles of 12 Squadron, led by Flight Lieutenant Peter Hunt, to come under attack by two French Morane fighters, damaging two of the Battles, piloted by Pilot Officer J.F. McFie (L5458) and Pilot Officer G.M. Hayton (L5568) who had to force land at Vaux–Villecerf.

At the same time as these Battles took off, 2 Group sent out 107 and 110 Squadron – 24 Blenheims in total. Their target was also tanks and AFVs on the various roads from Albert, Bapaume and Péronne. Near Etaples, 107 Squadron came under attack from four Me109s, and a Me110 which appeared to be hit by fire from the Blenheims. It turned on its side and fell away with its port motor on fire. During the encounter, one Blenheim was hit:

| P/O K.D'A. Taute | Sgt L.S. Fearnley | Sgt J.R. Waterhouse | N6191 |

Keith Taute and Sergeant Waterhouse were both wounded but Taute flew the aircraft back and landed at Hawkinge to allow his gunner to be taken to hospital. Not so badly hurt himself,

Taute then flew back to Wattisham. Len Fearnley remembers this day very well.

Things had really come to life again following the fall of Dunkirk. We were twelve aircraft flying in four sections of three and the usual drill was for us to get to a road in the target area, then follow it until we came to a village where usually we'd find enemy concentrations. We were pretty freelance as we couldn't fly in tight formation because we'd be under bofors fire etc, and we didn't want to stay in the bombing run for too long. It was always a case of getting in and then getting out.

We approached the target area. It was evening time after a lovely warm June day, very pleasant, but a little too warm in our 'glasshouse'. The flak was disturbing because we didn't have so precise a target area but we wanted to get as near to our target before breaking formation. When finally the radio signal came to spread out, that's when we began to reduce height.

We bombed and were immediately hit after releasing our bombs. The shell hit the bomb bay just as the bombs went down, which was quite good timing really, I suppose. It exploded on hitting the aircraft and disabled our air gunner, John Waterhouse, although we didn't know at that time because we'd lost the intercom. I'd just come up from the nose and was sitting next to Keith Taute which observers usually did after dropping, so as to keep a lookout for enemy fighters.

We went into a bit of a dive because the tail was thrown up into the air, but Keith sorted that out, although we were dropping way behind the rest of the squadron. A good deal of shrapnel came forward. I could hear it rattling on the armour plate behind Keith and my seat, and although I didn't realise it at that moment, Keith took shrapnel in both legs.

We were now virtually on our own and that's when fighters came in. They attacked and also shot up our already wounded gunner, so he had bullet holes as well as shrapnel wounds. Keith said that he couldn't get through to Waterhouse, so could I get back and find out how he was.

There wasn't too much room to get through to the back of the Blenheim and dusk had now come upon us making it quite dark in the rear fuselage. As I clambered through, I stumbled on the gunner, who had fallen out of his turret.

In the pitch dark I felt around, my fingers going through his torn Irvin suit and into his arm where shrapnel or bullets had caught him, right down the muscle of the right arm. There was a First Aid kit somewhere in the back which I found with difficulty, gave him a shot of morphine and hoped I'd done some good for him.

I could hear that we were still under attack and got back into the front of the Blenheim, and down to the blister gun in the nose. This was a bit of a scatter gun which we fired backwards with the aid of a rearview mirror and I blasted away at anything I saw, including one fighter which came up underneath us.

We'd slowed down considerably by this time due to our battle damage, and bullets were still going over my head. We crossed the coast and got down to sea level, weaved about a bit, and finally the fighters left us – probably out of fuel or ammo. We flew on at wave-top height and landed – we both thought at Manston. (The squadron diary records Hawkinge.) I got out but Keith stayed put. Despite his wounds he wanted to get back to base and his wife in Ipswich and knew if he got out someone would send him off to see the doctor. An ambulance was already waiting for us and I helped get our wounded gunner, now unconscious, out from the hatch under the fuselage. He was quickly in the ambulance and away.

I got back in the Blenheim, Keith took off and headed for Wattisham, dodging one or two balloons over the Thames Estuary I remember. When we landed at Wattisham, Keith was looking very pale. He must have been in some pain, having a number of shrapnel splinters in both calves, but he got us home. He was in hospital for some weeks but later returned to the squadron. We'd been in the air for 3½ hours, 1½ hours in daylight and two hours in the dark. Without doubt the armour plating saved both our lives that day.

Sergeant L.S. Fearnley, 107 Squadron

The other squadron, 110, was reduced to 11 bombers when

Flight Lieutenant H.D.H. Cooper DFC crashed on take off, then they were down to ten when another returned with engine trouble. It was Sergeant Palmer, observer to Squadron Leader Stephens (R3738), who was 110's B Flight Commander, who claimed the 110 shot down.

It will be noted that air gunners in 2 Group had now all been promoted to sergeants, although the WOP/AGs in the Battle squadrons in France continued to fly as corporals and aircraftmen.

The Battle squadrons were now using Echimines landing ground as an advance airfield for night operations. Squadrons sent aircraft almost daily to this field for nocturnal forays against the enemy or even into Germany.

Thursday, 6 June
The gallant British 51st Highland Division fought back and began to delay the enemy thrust along their section of the front line. Elsewhere, the French began to fall back. They had been talking of an armistice for some days. It looked again as if the British forces would be pushed into a coastal pocket around St Valéry.

No. 40 Squadron sent out recce aircraft to see what was happening. At 3 a.m. Flight Lieutenant Robert Batt and his crew headed out:

| F/Lt R.H. Batt | Sgt A. Spencer | Sgt E.G. Neville | L8826 |

He was followed by Flying Officer Joe Stevenson (L9412). Batt flew at less than 200 feet to observe accurately the troops movements, so necessary to plan raids against them. Not surprisingly the Germans were not anxious to let the British see too much and they were met by heavy ground fire and patrolling fighters. The Blenheim was hit by flak and Alan Spencer was wounded but he could still operate his gun, which was just as well when the fighters began to chase them. Edward Neville also kept up a spirited fire and possibly shot down one fighter. They escaped and brought back valuable information. Later all three men were decorated with the DFC and DFMs. Stevenson also returned from his mission.

They landed around 6.15, and by 8.30 the squadron had prepared for a raid against enemy concentrations south of St

Ricquier. Twelve Blenheims took off to try to stem an advance towards Bresle:

S/L G.W.C. Gleed	Sgt Burge	Sgt A.F.W. Sammells	L9326
Sgt Cowman	Sgt Bloodworth	Sgt F.H. Jones	P4918
Sgt D.J. Rice	Sgt R.C. Moffatt	Sgt D.E. Peters	P4927*
F/O G.D. Hill	Sgt Jeffery	Sgt A.F.H. Barber	R3682
P/O V.G.W. Egstrom	Sgt M.R. Chouler	Sgt D. Liddle	R3692*
Sgt Newton	Sgt Fitton	Sgt McCreary	P4908
S/L B. Paddon	Sgt V.C. Salvage	Sgt T.A. Foreman	L8827*
P/O P.F.T. Wakeford	Sgt Wallace	Sgt Baker	P4917*
P/O B.B. James	Sgt J.E. Garcka	Sgt W. Furby	L9410*
F/O C.W. Bromley	Sgt Main	Sgt Gamble	R3689
P/O C.B. Best	Sgt Howarth	Sgt G.D.P. Quinn	R3778
Sgt J.S. Morton	Sgt A.D. Kelso	Sgt Rodgers	L9270

Two Hurricane squadron escorted the bombers, 17 and 111, and Me109s were engaged. Flak and fighters hit the bombers hard, and five were shot down. Pilot Officer James and his crew were killed. Pilot Officer Wakeford force-landed and returned later by air while his observer got back by ship. The gunner was wounded and kept in hospital in France. Vaughan Egstrom force-landed in 'No Man's Land' with his crew wounded. He tried to get help for them but due to the rapid advance of enemy forces, they were taken into captivity. He was also wounded but got home to England before going to hospital. Brian Paddon and Sergeant Rice, with their crews, were all taken prisoner.

It had been the old story. The Germans were defending their advancing troops in the immediate Battle area as they had done at Maastricht and at Sedan. After several days of light or no casualties, the light bombers were going to be up against it again, even with fighter escorts.

The next efforts were not until the afternoon when the AASF sent out Battles of 88 and 103 Squadrons (five and four respectively) to attack concentrations of German troops at Sancourt–Matigny. These enemy units were part of an advance from the Péronne loop of the Somme. One machine returned with a defective ASI but the rest carried out their assignment, although little was seen so they bombed MT and tanks near Chaulnes, covered by the Hurricanes of 73 Squadron. All returned safely although not without some moments of drama.

The crews saw large numbers of Luftwaffe fighters over the battle front and two Battles were attacked by Me109s but in each case, gunfire from the rear gunners forced them to shear off. German air activity was much in evidence; large formations of Ju87s were observed bombing in and around Roye, as well as Dorniers and Messerschmitt 109 and 110 escorts.

As this was going on, the Blenheims were again leaving their English bases. At 5 p.m., 21 Squadron sent 11 aircraft, 15 Squadron seven, meeting their fighter escort at Le Tréport at 5 p.m. Their targets were road bridges across the Somme at Abbeville and troops at Abbeville and St Valéry. Three direct hits on bridges were claimed and all the bombers got home, although one pilot, Sergeant Parker, had his machine hit by ground fire. He was wounded in the leg by shrapnel and the hydraulics were severed, forcing a belly landing back at base:

Sgt Parker	Sgt Walters	Sgt Burt	R3761

This raid was again led by Squadron Leader George Pryde of 21 Squadron, who had flown around a dozen such raids over the last month. Scottie Pryde had joined the RAF in 1932 and by this date had around 1,600 flying hours in his log book. Strangely this raid on the 6th does not feature in an otherwise well kept flying log. He suddenly disappears from 21 Squadron's diary and his log book is blank after an entry dated 1 June. Further investigation revealed that Pryde was killed on 19 June while at No. 4 Ferry Pilot Pool. His DFC was announced in August.

The day ended again with some night ops by the Battles, while 142 Squadron were busy moving bases, this time by Villiers–Vaux. It would be operating again by the night of the 7th.

At the Battle's ALG at Echimines, enemy raiders were in strong evidence during their night sorties. Tracer fire zipped across the landing ground just three yards from 103 Squadron CO's car as he drove to the flarepath area with the Medical Officer. 53 bombs were then dropped, 23 falling on the airfield. Two aircraft on the ground were slightly damaged.

Friday, 7 June
The Luftwaffe were also active shortly after midnight, when the luckless 88 Squadron were bombed again just 20 minutes

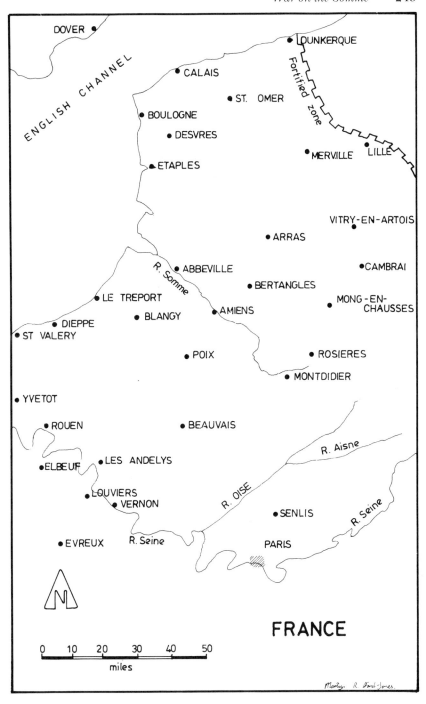

FRANCE

into the morning. They too were in the middle of night operations and one Battle was damaged by splinters. During the confusion, one WOP/AG – LAC Lewis, was caught by a turning propeller blade while running for cover, and so seriously injured that he died at 7.a.m. Meanwhile, the Battles had bombed the St Valéry area.

As dawn came up, 107 Squadron were sending three Blenheims on a low level recce to obtain information on where the Germans were crossing the Somme between St Valéry and Abbeville, and also what activity could be seen along the Montreuil–Hesdin–Auxi–le–Château roads. Once over France the three machines acted independently to cover the maximum area.

Wing Commander Stokes went down to 100 feet and completed his task in spite of heavy ground fire. He was then spotted by some Me109s and he went down to 50 feet while he took evasive action. Hugging the ground, his rear gunner kept up a spirited return fire and succeeded in shooting down one Messerschmitt which was seen to crash into the ground. The other two 109s broke away. Stokes landed at just on 9 a.m. without a single hit on his aeroplane.

The second Blenheim, piloted by Sergeant Gunning, landed a few minutes before his CO, having carried out his recce without encountering any opposition at all. The third Blenheim was not so fortunate.

Flight Lieutenant H.P. Pleasance went to the Auxi–le–Château–Abbeville road area and to the Somme Estuary but failed to return:

F/Lt H.P. Pleasance	Sgt G.A. Wilson	Sgt P.E.F. Adams	R3686*

However, they had quite an eventful mission. They spotted a column of MT near Hesdin and strafed them and then seeing about 30 German aircraft on an obvious advanced landing ground, proceeded to shoot them up too. Then they encountered three Ju87s which they attacked, Sergeant Adams dispersing them with his turret gun. However, they had now attracted the attention of an estimated 17 German aircraft, but Pleasance evaded and eventually shook them off. As if this was not enough, they then found another road column at Bernaville, strafing this in the face of intense ground fire.

Now their luck ran out. Pleasance was hit in the leg and his Blenheim was badly damaged, making it necessary to force land. This was accomplished without further injury and they then set fire to the Blenheim before making their way to Rouen to make their report. For his efforts on this day, Harold Pleasance was to receive the DFC. Harold Pleasance recalls:

Our instructions were to report on German troop movements in the Abbeville area. We took off in the early morning after a briefing by the CO, and in no time at all, so it seemed, we were over France.

I decided, being on my own, we should fly low, occasionally climbing to 2,000 feet. We flew along a number of roads and saw a lot of German transport. We were shot at from time to time and my air gunner replied in kind. After flying around for what seemed a hell of a long time we saw a lot of transport. They threw up a lot of flak and we were hit a number of times. I felt a pain in my right leg and then I think the starboard engine was hit and packed up. The aircraft was becoming difficult to control and to keep in the air. I had thought of climbing up to bale out but could not climb high enough. I decided to land as best we could and picked on a sizeable field and landed wheels up in a cloud of dust.

We clambered out. My crew was unhurt but I had some shrapnel in my right leg. However, I could walk fairly well. We were debating what to do when we saw some of our own troops on a road nearby. (We had come down at Longueville–sur–Scie, about 15 miles south of Dieppe.) I decided I must destroy the Blenheim and this we did with the help of the soldiers. Then we joined up with them and set off towards Rouen.

I was dropped off at a Field Hospital where I gave a report on what I had found, hoping that it would get to the right quarters. The Army put me in an ambulance and I said goodbye to my crew, wondering whether or not we should meet again. I eventually arrived in Rouen, but my time of being frightened was not over yet. We came to a halt in the middle of a bridge over the Seine to allow an ammunition convoy to go north. I could not help thinking to myself what a perfect bombing target I was parked on, and how bloody unfair it would be if I finished the war here. We eventually moved off the bridge and arrived at La Rochelle where I boarded a hospital ship for Portsmouth. I was in hospital for a few days and then returned to the squadron at Wattisham.

Flight Lieutenant H.P. Pleasance, 107 Squadron

Two recce missions were also flown later in the morning by 82 Squadron, piloted by Pilot Officer R.C.D. McKenzie (R3731 'Y') and Sergeant A.E. Merritt (P6915 'A'). Both were attacked by a number of Me109s but both got back shortly after 2 p.m.

From these missions and other information, it was obvious that the enemy advances were now driving from the Somme towards the River Seine. A second German thrust which was moving south from Péronne was left for the French to attend to. 21 and 82 Squadrons were briefed for a raid planned for soon after midday.

Wing Commander Bennett led nine aircraft of 21 off at 12.30, and Squadron Leader Hunt headed nine of 82 at the same time. The objective was to bomb and block targets and roads at Airaines to cause traffic jams, if reported AFVs could not be found. They couldn't, so Airaines caught it. Several Blenheims were damaged by flak – and fighter attack, despite a fighter escort, which 82 Squadron was to describe as 'remote'.

Philip Sutcliffe recalls:

We met up with a Henschel 126 reconnaissance plane and approached him from the rear. I had him lined up and pressed the front gun firing button, whereupon the air hose came adrift. The Henschel pilot saw the Blenheim almost alongside him. He turned on his back and dived away before Whitehead could get his guns to bear. This was not the end of the story. On the way back to England, Lewis in R3709 and another Blenheim – R3701 – joined our Blenheim. South of Le Tréport we were attacked by two Me109s. This pair made four or five attacks opening fire each time. Every time they attacked and they opened fire Whitehead called up on the intercom and I turned the three Blenheims towards the direction of attack. After the last attack they departed. Our three air gunners had a field day. The three Blenheims crossed the Channel at sea level.

Squadron Leader W.P. Sutcliffe, 82 Squadron

By this time the fact that we badly needed fighter escorts had penetrated and these were provided by Hawkinge, etc. But they were a mixed blessing as they seemed to be incapable of keeping station across the Channel and to be intent on amusing themselves with mock attacks on our formations. We did not appreciate this or the drain on our nervous energy keeping an eye on them and satisfying ourselves that they were not 109s – so much so that I recall landing at Hawkinge after one raid and having a set-to with them. Webster did so as well. I left them with the thought that in future we would open up on anyone coming within range in a belligerent manner – which we did, and that put a stop to it.

Flying Officer W.H. George, 15 Squadron

By mid-afternoon, 15, 40, 107 and 110 Squadrons were on their way to France. 15 and 40 sent 12 and six Blenheims to bomb AFVs and MT in the village of Mianney without loss. 107 and 110 (six and 12 aircraft) were close behind them bombing Airaines again to block off the town. 107 saw their bombs hit the west and east exits and the town centre. Moderate AA fire damaged five of their Blenheims, 110 recording no damage, although one aircraft was forced to abort at Abbeville with engine trouble.

The Battles of 12 Squadron took off at 5 p.m. – nine in number – to attack tanks and AFVs in the Poix area. They ran into 109s:

Sgt G.R. Wheeldon	Sgt J. Shone	LAC J. Taylor	L5415
P/O J.F. McFie	Sgt C.S.G. Beevers	LAC J.G. Thompson	L5458
P/O C.N. McVeigh	Sgt E.N. Odell	LAC C.G. Landon	L5420
Sgt F. Field	Sgt H.C. Bevan	LAC McKrill	P2162*
P/O P.H. Blowfield	Sgt J.J. Batty	LAC J. Grant	L5237
Sgt A. Preston	Sgt Spiller	LAC Tracy	L5328
Sgt J. Wilcox	Sgt A. Emery	LAC Hislop	L5249
P/O J.S. Shorthouse	Sgt N.C. Cottrell	LAC Copley	L5451
P/O G.M. Hayton	Sgt Simpson	Sgt J. Harvey	L5568

Pilot Officer C.N. McVeigh was attacked by six Messerschmitts and Sergeant F. Field by two, the latter falling in flames followed by their deadly opponents. Sergeant Odell confirmed that LAC Landon shot down at least one 109. Pilot Officer Blowfield saw eight 109s pass 600 feet below him on his way to the target but luckily they failed to see him. Sergeant Wheeldon was seen and attacked, but he escaped although damaged in the port wing, elevator and tail.

Six Battles of 150 Squadron were also out from Echimines into the Abbeville area, ordered to return to Houssay upon their return. Flying Officer Vernon, who had been lucky to get back after being shot down on 26 May, went down on a convoy, bombing it from low level but was hit and brought down. He and his crew all died. Jim Vernon's DFC was gazetted in July:

| F/O J.E. Vernon | Sgt G.W. Clawley | LAC J.E. Atkins | L5288* |

In his new Battle, which he collected on the 3rd (L5579), Alan Frank remembers this raid, for this, his second Battle, was also damaged.

> We had no trouble on the way out and reached the target area. It was rather easier than usual as it was a very hot, dry day, and the Germans had stirred up a very considerable dust cloud which drew our attention. I spotted, behind the dust cloud, and in its vicinity, a crossroads where there was something of a traffic block.
>
> On this occasion I quite clearly saw the crossroads as a good target, dive-bombed it, releasing at our usual height of 2,000 feet, and certainly dropped the bombs in the area, although it was quite impossible to see the damage or anything else.
>
> I pulled away and as I set course I was hit in the wing by a 20 mm shell. I had thought I was clear of the flak but obviously I wasn't. I lost my airspeed indicator but nothing much else and flew home safely and landed with no further trouble. This was one of the few occasions one found the target – one we were supposed to be looking for, and possibly hit it!
>
> *Pilot Officer A.D. Frank, 150 Squadron*

Also out were 103 Squadron, and they too ran into 109s. Sergeant Brams and Pilot Officer Roberts both had to force land but got back, Roberts' crew claiming a 109 destroyed. Pilot Officer A.R.D. Barratt was set upon by nine 109s but successfully evaded and escaped.

The Battles also operated that night. For the first time, 103 Squadron carried an additional four 25 lb incendiary bombs, carried loose in the cockpit, for use over the target! 142 Squadron sent one aircraft to bomb a bridge near Abbeville, and another to bomb St Hubert aerodrome. One crew failed to locate the base when they returned and when their fuel gave out were forced to take to their parachutes. The Battle crashed near Châteauneuf and the three men returned to the airfield the next morning:

P/O H.L. Oakley	Sgt Martin	AC Ledson	?

No. 150 Squadron operated six machines against German lines of communication.

Saturday, 8 June
On this day came the announcement that Donald Garland and Tom Gray of 12 Squadron, lost in the squadron's heroic attack on 12 May, had been given posthumous awards of the Victoria Cross, gazetted the previous day.

The first 2 Group sorties were delayed because of fog, but finally 21 and 82 Squadrons got away at 10, and 10.22 a.m. Making rendezvous over Watton, the two squadrons headed for North Weald where they picked up their fighter escort before setting course for France.

In the Horroy area they bombed troops and MT as well as tanks and houses, the latter, as was usual, in attempts to cause falling masonry and rubble to block roads which ran through villages – now deserted. Intense flak came up to meet them, and one Blenheim was shot down from each squadron. Hugh Dunford-Wood of 21 Squadron, and his crew were killed, Robert McKenzie (82 Squadron), who had escaped the 109s the previous day, was taken prisoner with his gunner, his observer being killed:

F/O H.D.S. Dunford-Wood	Sgt E. Jones	Sgt D.R.C. MacLagen	L9023*
P/O R.C.D. McKenzie	Sgt J.M. Cooper	Sgt Crozier	R3618*

Squadron Leader Sutcliffe, who had led 82 Squadron's formation, spotted a German Henschel 126 over the front line, and attacked it. They were quick, nimble little observation machines, difficult to hit, but Sutcliffe and his crew felt certain they had shot it down. (Sergeant Scott and Sergeant Whitehead were his crew, in P6895). Philip Sutcliffe:

> Raid on AFVs on road south of River Somme. Came across a Henschel 126 which George Whitehead had a go at with his twin turret guns. He believed he shot it down.
>
> *Squadron Leader W.P. Sutcliffe, 82 Squadron*

At 1.30 p.m. 12 Battle aircraft were ordered against German columns in a more northerly area to the Blenheims, around Abbeville, Longprés, Poix and Aumale. They were, however, given seven Hurricanes as escort, provided by 501 Squadron.

Three aircraft from each of 12, 142, 150 and 226 Squadrons had been set on stand-by during the morning, knowing that once again they would be facing flak and possible fighters in yet another daylight operation.

In the event, 12 Squadron were able to put up four aircraft, led by Squadron Leader Brian Lowe (L5580). Lowe found a column of MT south of Avesnes and the Battles attacked. Germans scattered, and four bombs hit the head of the column, destroying the road, but one aircraft was hit by ground fire and crashed. Tom Brereton, who because of defective aircraft had not been able to fly the fateful 12 May mission, when Garland and Gray had earned their VCs, survived the shoot down as a prisoner. His crew were killed. It was a strange coincidental twist of fate that he should be shot down on the day the squadron received the news of the VC awards:

| F/O T.F.S. Brereton | Sgt P.J. Boddington | LAC C.S. Burt | L5546* |

Operating from an ALG at Decima, 150 Squadron's section of Battles also found road targets which were attacked. They too lost a Battle, and a crew, to ground fire:

| F/Lt R.A. Weeks | Sgt W.D.P. Pittar | LAC L.O. Grant | L5112* |

Records of 142 and 226 Squadrons do not indicate what they achieved on this day; indeed, 226 lost all its June records in the evacuation. However, the AASF did lose three Battles on these early afternoon missions.

Their Hurricane escort ran into a force of 30 Ju87 Stukas and an estimated 80 Me109s ten miles to the south-east of Abbeville; the Hurricanes had the worst of the exchange.

Also out over the Poix area were six Battles of 103 Squadron. Pilot Officer G.W. Thorougood was flying his first mission (P2315).

P/O G.W. Thorougood	Sgt Asson	P/O Webber	P2315*

Gordon Thorougood, with his crew, saw some 50 dive bombers at a lower altitude, attacking a village. Thorougood attacked, diving right through the German formation and shot down one Ju87, but he was then attacked by some 109s. Webber in the rear position, claimed one 109 shot down, but they got away with their audacious attack, although Webber was wounded three times. They had also been badly shot-up and they had to force land at Maudie, south of Paris. Webber was immediately evacuated to England.

The squadron also lost the veteran Sergeant Beardsley on this day. This NCO had been shot down on 14 May and walked back, a feat he repeated on the 25th. It was third time unlucky this time, for he and his crew were all captured.

Sgt G. Beardsley	Sgt G. Avery	LAC G.F. Lewis DFM	N2259*

At around 3.15 p.m. 11 more Battles were sent to attack columns in the Poix–Aumale area. It is difficult to know which units were involved or if some of the raids referred to above were actually flown later. All that is recorded is that yet another Battle was lost, making a total of four for the afternoon sorties.

The German columns were vast in size, with numbers running to some 300 lorries, 200 tanks and AFVs over a column five miles in length. In truth what could a mere handful of Battles do, and the defensive gunfire must have been horrific. Luckily on the second raid, there were no reported German fighters, for the promised RAF escort failed to materialise.

The afternoon continued with yet more raids by 2 Group. Since 30 May, 2 Group had not been totally available to Air Marshal Barratt but on the 8th, the restrictions were lifted. Barratt once again had the full resources of the Group's Blenheim squadrons. Now, 15, 40, 107 and 110 sent a force of 36 Blenheims out to try and hit the ever advancing German columns, that it seemed impossible to stop or even slow down.

No. 15 and 40 Squadrons went for AFVs in the area of Loimer,

Molliens and Poix, led by Squadron Leader Webster, and
Squadron Leader Gleed. Sergeant Alfred Box, observer in
Flying Officer Hugh George's machine (R3704), was wounded,
while one Blenheim failed to return. Squadron Leader Wilfred
Burke and his crew were all killed:

| S/L W.I.H. Burke | P/O R. Moffatt | Sgt G. Thompson | R3746* |

This attack on AFVs in the Poix area was a hairy one as far as
I was concerned. We dive-bombed and I recall seeing my
bombs hit a group of AFVs, three of which overturned and
were destroyed, and simultaneously being myself hit by one
of their 20 mm shells, which exploded in the cockpit,
severely wounding my navigator, Sergeant Box, and
knocking out most of my instruments. I have no recollection
of pulling out of my dive which was a steep one at full
throttle from 6,000 feet. My next memory is of finding
myself flying a badly crippled aircraft just above the stall at a
very low altitude and of being quite unable to improve on
either speed or altitude.

We staggered across France in this helpless fashion, inad-
vertently at one point crossing an airfield – which may have
been Poix – with a squadron of Me110s on it with crews
rushing towards their aircraft, none of which however, got
into the air thanks to my gunner, Sergeant O'Donnell. We
eventually reached the French coast whereupon the aircraft
decided to climb without any assistance from me. Meanwhile,
Box, who I thought was dead, had had to be left unattended as
I had the greatest difficulty in keeping the Blenheim in the air
and O'Donnell could not be permitted to leave his guns. Over
the Channel, however, we managed to get a tourniquet on
Box's leg and to stem the bleeding and he recovered consciousness. I was aiming to land at the first available airfield to
get him to hospital but he would have none of this and insisted
on working out a course to Wyton. We finally landed safely
at Wyton and Box finally recovered after a long period in
hospital and in due course resumed flying with the squadron.
Flying Officer W.H. George, 15 Squadron

No. 40 Squadron saw their bombs hit one column of vehicles
and troops and their six aircraft all returned, landing at 6.12
p.m.

Squadron Leader Stephens led 107's six aircraft, Wing Commander Sinclair, 110 Squadron. 107 also saw their bombs burst amongst tanks and troops, but they all got home with just three aircraft damaged. 110 also bombed successfully, but lost one machine while Sergeant Sims had to land his damaged bomber at Le Havre. Both crews later got back to England; Pilot Officer Philip Arderne lost his Blenheim, but got back on the 13th:

P/O P.V. Arderne	Sgt G. Robson	Sgt J. Tippett	R3670*

Once again the promised fighter escort failed to make rendezvous, or at least most of them did. Me109s were encountered which impeded the bombing effort and one 109 was apparently claimed destroyed. Records indicate that one force of six Blenheims was detailed to attack a petrol dump in the Bois Watte area, north-east of Abbeville. One aircraft only claimed a hit on this target.

Despite the RAF's efforts, nothing was stopping the onward rush of the Germans. They had begun to encircle Allied forces around Rouen and by the evening a general retreat from Bresle commenced.

The Battles were out that night. 12 Squadron bombed Trier aerodrome and the exits from Laon. Mist made the location of targets impossible but Pilot Officer McVeigh bombed an AA battery north-east of Trier, while Sergeant Wheeldon dropped his bombs on some searchlights that were obviously annoying him.

Also operating from Echimines were 142, 150 and 226 Squadrons.

Sunday, 9 June

Only 2 Group operated on this day, one raid in the morning, one in the afternoon. The morning show saw Wing Commander Stokes lead 12 Blenheims of his 107 Squadron, with Wing Commander Sinclair taking six of his 110 crews, to attack German AFVs near Poix. They took off at 10.30 and although the two formations were in close proximity, it was 107 which suffered all the casualties:

W/C L.R. Stokes	Sgt L. Graves	Sgt D.S. Barnes	R3737
F/O H.L. Atkin-Berry	Sgt L. Charnock	Sgt B.P. Collins	R3688
Sgt R.S. Gunning, DFM	Sgt W.G. Brinn, DFM	Sgt A. Moses	R3740

F/O D.J.A. Rose	Sgt D. Haigh	Sgt E.W. Gimson	L9467
P/O D.J.S. Warren	Sgt J.T. Waterfall	Sgt W.E. Law	P6894
F/S H.J. Ratcliffe	Sgt P.J. Crowley	Sgt C.A. Bartlett	R3810
F/O J.W. Stephens	Sgt W.J. Barrett	Sgt E.C. White	N3593
F/O C.P. Bomford	Sgt R.A. Bowman	P/O F.E. Frayne	L9323*
Sgt E.H. Sarll	Sgt G.D. Drew	Sgt R. Jeffcoat	R3815
F/O C.Y. Buckley	P/O C. Campbell	Sgt E.H.B. Cotton	R3739
P/O R.H.M. Bennett	Sgt A.E. Langford	Sgt H.T. Denison	R3685*
Sgt J.H. Cater	Sgt S. Clayton	Sgt J.R. Browning	N6228

As the Blenheims raced in towards their targets, moderate but accurate flak began to feel for them. Their fighter escort flying above and behind could do nothing for them although when some Me109s did turn up, they did decline to engage the bombers. With flak bursting amongst the 107 machines, first one, then two and then three dropped away. Two were seen to crash land with engines in flames. Pilot Officer Frayne, gunner to Charles Bomford, was later reported in a French hospital with severe burns. He was thrown clear as the burning Blenheim hit the ground but his two companions were killed. Flying Officer Cyril Buckley also died, but his crew were later confirmed as prisoners. Pilot Officer Bennett and his crew escaped serious injury in their landing and later got back.

Targets in and around the Forêt de Boray were bombed, hits being seen amongst the columns and transport vehicles, many of which were completely wrecked.

The city of Rouen fell during the day, and with no bridges left intact across the mighty Seine, all British forces were thus cut off. With Rouen in their hands, the Germans turned north to cut off Le Havre. Meantime, on the Bresle front the British fell back, leaving just two regiments to hold the line while the main force fell back to the Seine.

2 Group followed up their morning raid with a raid by 15 and 40 Squadrons followed by 21 and 82 Squadrons. 15 and 40 bombed columns of MT and AFVs in the Poix–Formerie area claiming many vehicles smashed, while 21 and 82 went for similar targets around Poix-Grandvilliers, also hitting villages in the area which contained troops and transport. Three of 82 Squadron's aircraft were damaged, and Pilot Officer D.M. Wellings' gunner, Sergeant Thripp, was slightly wounded (P6925 'Z').

That evening, 88, 103 and 150 flew night ops. 103 lost one

Battle – possibly N2253 or L5246. Squadron Leader Harold Lee AFC suffered engine failure and he and his crew had to bale out. Lee sustained a compound fracture of the right leg and was evacuated to Le Mans. Sergeant Derrick Norrington DFM and LAC Werner were unhurt. Squadron Leader Lee was later mentioned in despatches for his work in France.

CHAPTER FOURTEEN

Messerschmitt Skies

The desperate situation continued. With the Seine bridges down, the Germans were bringing up their tried and tested pontoon bridges. On the Channel coast, Le Havre was now cut off and the gallant 51st Division was making for St Valéry-en-Caux where the Royal Navy planned to take them off.

A sign of just how bad the situation was, was that Barratt had once again to call upon his Battles to fly daylight operations. Paris was now under direct threat and the unthinkable was fast becoming a reality. It had taken the Germans just one month to achieve what they had failed to do in the four years of the Great War 1914–18

Monday, 10 June
The two Wattisham squadrons, 107 and 110, set off at 6 a.m. to attack columns and transport as well as AFVs in the areas around Gournay and Fleury. They did not find too much activity, but bombed again the Forêt de Boray hitting some columns. Flak was slight and inaccurate and when some Me109s were seen, they stayed well clear when they saw the Hurricane escort.

By mid-morning it was clear that the AASF must have a go at columns and bridges. At 10.45, 12 Battles were sent off to bomb columns approaching Vernon on the Seine, just north-west of Paris. 88, 103 and 142 Squadrons were given the job.

Squadron Leader P. deC, Festing Smith led the 88 Squadron sortie and reached the target area at 12.13 p.m. Festing Smith, who had retired from the RAF as a flight lieutenant but had returned when war came, dived at the bridge from 13,000 feet, releasing his bombs at 3,000. One bomb scored a direct hit. After more bombs had fallen, a fire was seen to have started in the adjacent town on the north bank. Heavy AA fire was experienced near the Vernon road, and as the pilots took in the sweep of the river, they could see no bridges still standing, except the railway bridge at Vironvay.

Flying Officer Roberts led 103 Squadron's Battles. Sergeant Brams also saw that the target bridges were down, so dropped his bombs on the nearby cross-roads. Sergeant Adair bombed the north pier of the broken Vernon bridge and then the town, diving from 8,000 to 3,000 feet. Pilot Officer Stubbs bombed the railway line east of the town.

Flying Officer Dermot Kelly's task was not helped when he was attacked by a Hurricane and his Battle was so badly damaged that he had to return to base. Sergeant W.R. Critch's machine was also badly shot about by ground fire, but despite this, he made determined attacks and bombed German columns. William Critch was recommended for the DFM which was duly awarded. A Me109 was seen by some of the pilots, chasing a Battle some miles north of Vernon but it appeared to evade it. However, 103 lost one two-man crew; both were killed:

P/O C.V. Thomas   LAC P.I. Blyth   P2328*

The six 142 Battles raided bridges over the Seine in the St Pierre area. Several bridges were seen to be destroyed, so bombs were dropped on troops and villages. Pilot Officer Martin attacked and hit a pontoon bridge he found under construction.

When the pilots returned, they reported that all the bridges between Rouen and Nantes were down, with the possible exception of a railway bridge at Vironvay, although it was in fact burning.

As these aircraft were landing, 12 Squadron were sending out six Battles to attack AFVs reported around Poix, Aumale and Abbeville. Pilot Officer Blowfield (L5420) scored a near miss on a convoy of trucks in the village of Saisseval.

In the early afternoon, 2 Group sent out a force of Blenheims from 15, 21 and 82 Squadrons, escorted by 20 Hurricanes. They sought and found enemy troops and MT between Rouen and Les Andelys as well as on the Forges–Rouen road. All aircraft returned, and one pilot, Pilot Officer Percival (R3708 'D'), even claimed to have attacked and shot down a Henschel 126 observation aircraft with his front gun. (Engaging Henschels was becoming a habit with 82 Squadron.) Philip Sutcliffe records:

> Raid against AFVs and troops in Fleury village. Attacked with bombs and machine guns, front and rear. We passed over a French airfield and counted at least 12 Morane fighters on the ground. We returned to England south about, and spent some four hours 20 minutes on this flight – the longest during the period 12th May to 18th June.
>
> *Squadron Leader W.P. Sutcliffe, 82 Squadron*

With the earlier report of a possible bridge still over the Seine at Vironvay, not to be ignored, the AASF sent out another 12 Battles shortly before 5 p.m. and the light traffic bridge at Pont Delage, reported being in use by the advancing Germans. Other targets were columns reported heading for Pont Delage and Vernon.

Three of the Battles were of 88 Squadron, but the other units are not readily identifiable, because of unclear or missing records. However, the Battle pilots reported that both target bridges were destroyed, so besides bombing them for good measure, they also hit MT near Vernon, and other bridges seen over the Andelle and Pont St Pierre, and another over the Seine at Courcelles, which had previously been reported down. Either the report was wrong or the Germans had effected repairs.

Tuesday, 11 June
The Seine crossings again dominated the bombing efforts on this day while further to the north-west, the Germans began assaulting the St Valéry perimeter. Unfortunately for the 51st Division, sea fog had delayed their hoped for evacuation.

South of the Seine, the Germans were content at this moment to enlarge and consolidate this foothold on the south side, rather than push further south. The Germans now had firm bridgeheads at Rouen, Elbeuf, Louviers, Vernon and Les Andelys.

At dawn, 12 Battles, including three each from 12 and 88 Squadrons, were sent to a new crossing point reported near Vezillon to the south of Les Andelys. In the event, haze or smoke made it difficult for the crews to find even the river. Three crews did find a clear patch but could see no sign of any bridge, so they dropped their bombs in the town and nearby forest of Les Andelys, although one pilot reported what he took to be a crossing south of Vernon.

Nos. 15, 40, 107 and 110 Squadrons were out in the late morning, 15 running into trouble. Their target was concentrations of troops and vehicles in the woods at Les Andelys, St Clair and Vernon. Hits were scored in some woods at La Mare and fires were started, but three aircraft failed to return, two not being to enemy action.

While on their way to the target area, the Blenheims flew through a heavy patch of cloud and Pilot Officer R.H. Werner must have increased his speed slightly for on coming out of it, his machine was suddenly right in front of Flying Officer Clarke's machine. Werner quickly turned his machine to the left but collided with the other Blenheim, the wing of his Blenheim being ripped off. The aeroplane dived into the ground, killing all three men aboard.

Flying Officer Clarke struggled to keep his crippled aeroplane in the air but it was obviously useless. Then the starboard engine began falling to pieces. Keeping the Blenheim on an even keel for as long as possible, he ordered his crew to bale out. This they did, but then the bomber went down out of control and crashed, the gallant pilot being killed. His crewmen got down safely and later returned to the squadron.

The third Blenheim was damaged by flak and had to make a forced landing at Cherbourg:

F/O R.B.G.E. Clarke	Sgt B.S.J. Piff	Sgt T.J.W. Mahoney	L9024*
P/O R.H. Werner	Sgt. M.G. Jones	Sgt R. Spencer	L8851*
P/O Hyland	Sgt Pirks	Sgt Petrie	N3588*

On the 11th June we paid the price for having to operate with inadequately trained crews. My great friend Ronnie Clarke was heading the usual section of three when his No. 2 collided with him in cloud, losing a wing and spinning in. All were killed. Ronnie's aircraft was badly damaged and barely

Above Hugh George (*centre*) 15 Squadron, with his friend Ronnie Clark (*right*) who died after a collision in the air, 11 June. Clark stayed at the controls of his crippled Blenheim to allow his crew to bale out. On the left is F/O Shannon. (*W.H. George*)

Below Blenheim IVs of 82 Squadron. UX-A (P6915) was badly damaged by Me109s on 7 June and had to be written-off. (*via RAF Museum*)

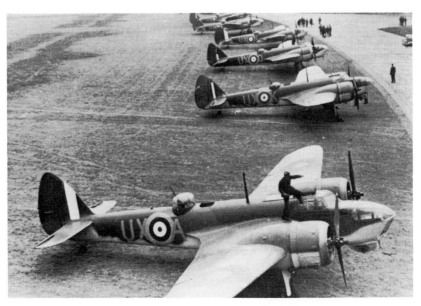

controllable but he insisted on hanging on until he was sure he was over unoccupied France when he ordered his crew to bale out which they did successfully, thereupon he lost control, crashed and was killed.

Flying Officer W.H. George, 15 Squadron

Everyone else got back except Pilot Officer N.N. Ezekiel of 110 Squadron who had to land at Lisieux to refuel. Indeed, several of 110 had to land at aerodromes on the south coast of England when fuel ran low.

As these Blenheims were reaching their English bases, the Battles were out once more. The report of a bridge across the Seine south of Vernon, made by one of the morning Battle pilots had to be attended to. Six Battles of 88 and 150 Squadrons were sent with fighter cover. Two of the crews not only found a bridge but hit it, leaving a large gap in the middle. Two other crews then found and bombed a pontoon bridge at St Pierre (variously reported as at Vironvay). Work was in progress at this bridge, men being clearly seen laying a large girder across a missing arch.

At 2 p.m., 59 Squadron sent Pilot Officer R.W. Ayres over France to carry out a recce, but they were chased by three Me109s and one 110. The chase lasted for 20 minutes but Sergeant Webb in the rear turret, had some satisfaction, shooting down the 110.

Mid-afternoon saw further Battle ops, sixteen being sent to harass the German bridgehead at Vernon, around the Forêt de Bizy on the south bank of the river. Cover was supplied by AASF Hurricanes, some of which, according to the Battle crews, were seen attacking some He111s that were bombing Pacy-sur-Eure.

Six Battles of 150 Squadron took off at 2.50 to attack a bridge at Le Manoir. Alan Frank was on this sortie (L5593) and remembers it because when they found the bridge there were no Germans to be seen, no flak, no fighters, in fact no opposition at all. And they missed the bridge!

During the day, the Battle squadrons did not go unscathed. In the afternoon, 88 Squadron lost a two-man crew, who were killed, their Battle being seen to fall in flames:

P/O J.D.W. Gillam   Sgt R.C. Caldwell (obs) L5519*

An observer in another 88 Squadron machine was wounded. An observer in 142 Squadron, Sergeant Hall, was also wounded while one Battle was lost. It too was seen to fall in flames, but the pilot was later known to be a prisoner although his crew were killed:

P/O B.W. Perriman   Sgt J.N. Fraser   AC J.H. Ledson   L5200*

One crew from 226 Squadron were also shot down, the crew being killed:

Sgt G.F. McLoughlin   Sgt E. Marrows   LAC J.A. Russell*

One good note as far as the Battle units were concerned, was the announcement on the 11th, of awards to 218 Squadron personnel. Acting Flight Lieutenant John McM. Hughes received the DFC, while Corporal J.A. Drummond and AC2 E.J. Evans received DFMs and promotion to sergeants.

*

In the afternoon, 2 Group sent out 21 and 82 Squadrons. 21 flew to attack troops and AFVs in the woods at La Mare, five miles to the south west of Les Andelys.

S/L R.D.C. Gibson	Sgt Barnes	Sgt Norton	P6959
P/O J. Harrison-Broadly	Sgt B. Williamson	Sgt Thompson	L8759
Sgt Bain	Sgt Aldridge	Sgt Charles	R3755
F/O F.C. Gibbs	Sgt Edwards	Sgt Chrisholm	L8737
F/O S.L. Sigurdson	Sgt Bailey	Sgt Trew	L8745
P/O Rogers	Sgt Huckins	Sgt Bradshaw	L8743*
F/Lt S.F. Coutts-Wood	Sgt Swan	Sgt Burt	R3687
Sgt J.J. Outhwaite	Sgt J.P. Waters	Sgt J.M. Sculfer	R3674*
P/O D. Macdonald	Sgt G. Lewis	Sgt A.G. Murray	L8746*

They took off at five o'clock and were due to pick up their promised fighter escort over the target. The leading sections bombed successfully but Me109s went for the following six, shooting down three. Flying Officer Sigurbjorn Sigurdson had his Blenheim badly shot up forcing him to jettison his bomb load. He was forced to return, got home safely and crash landed with wheels-up. Three other Blenheims were damaged.

Hurricanes of 73 Squadron had been assigned the job of escort and were in the vicinity but they appeared to be engaged in the destruction of a Dornier 17 and not to have encountered any enemy fighters.

Harrison-Broadly's crew claimed two 109s shot down, one each by the observer and the gunner. Macdonald was later reported a prisoner but his crew had been killed. Sergeant Outhwaite, who had survived being shot down on 14 May, was killed with his crew.

By contrast, 82 Squadron, which Squadron Leader Hunt led to look for AFVs on roads between Le Havre and Etretat, saw no sign of movement so all nine aircraft brought their bombs back.

So important was the information that tanks were in this area, that 12 Squadron were ordered to send six Battles to attack them. They took off at 6.10 p.m., but only two were spotted by Sergeant Wilcox (L5568) near Goubert which he bombed.

This attack had been specially requested by the French Admiral in Le Havre, in charge of evacuation efforts from that port. The Battles had received fighter cover, but very little was seen and the other five Battles returned with their bombs. These efforts, and those of 82 Squadron, would have been better spent had they been sent to the nearby area between Etretat, Fécamp and St Valéry, for the Germans had broken through to Fécamp and were concentrating on destroying the main body of the 51st Division and IX Corps rather than advancing straight to Le Havre.

Night ops were mounted by 142 and 150 Squadrons. Squadron Leader Wight was 142's sole representative, and he bombed woods near Vernon. 150 sent out six night sorties.

Wednesday, 12 June

This day saw the last combatant existence in France of the gallant 51st Division. After holding out for as long as possible, Major General Fortune finally had to order the cease fire and surrender at 10.30 a.m.

The bombing efforts for the 12th were mostly directed against targets in the vicinity of the Seine crossings or support for St Valéry. At dawn, nine Battles were sent to attack a reported pontoon bridge south of Les Andelys but a bridge could not be seen so they bombed roads and woods in the locality.

In the area of the Oise River, the French requested urgent attention to bridges north of Senlis. A number of Battles were sent out and given cover by French fighters. Pontoon bridges were found at Verberie Pont Pointe and to the south of Chevrières and later the destruction of all three bridges were claimed. One Battle was shot down and another had to make a forced landing. The squadrons involved are uncertain, but possibly one was 103. 88 was certainly involved for they lost two aircraft.

At 8.30 a.m. they sent a force to St Valéry, part of the wing's effort against pontoon bridges at Pont Pointe. The first section of two ran into trouble:

F/Lt A.L. Pitfield DFC	Sgt J. Ballantyne	L5334*
P/O J.M. Talmon	?	?*

James Talmon saw Pitfield attack the northern end of one bridge but then he disappeared below the level of the nearby trees amid a torrent of ground fire. Alan Pitfield and his gunner were both killed.

Talmon followed, diving to 700 feet on to the southern end of the bridge and released his bombs which blew this portion of it apart. Continuing his dive to the northern end he opened up with his gun on troop concentrations on the river bank, then turned and machine gunned troops on the south bank.

Intense light and heavy AA fire surrounded his Battle and its fuel tanks were holed and the hydraulics were put out of action. The engine began to falter and soon Talmon was forced to land on a well bombed French aerodrome at Mitry Moray.

The French occupants were burning their remaining aircraft and busily preparing to evacuate so Talmon set fire to his crippled Battle and he and his gunner left with the French. He finally caught up with 88 Squadron at Brest on the 16th. He was later to receive the DFC for his determined attack.

Soon after 9.30, 107 and 110 Squadrons were off to attack large troop concentrations at Le Mare, escorted by two fighter squadrons from RAF Tangmere. Flying Officer Stephens led the six of 107, Wing Commander Sinclair led the 12 of 110 Squadron. Over the target the bombers came under heavy AA fire and one of 107's Blenheims was seen to fall in flames over La Mare. The crew all died:

P/O B.D.G.H. Reid	Sgt R.W. Lawrence	Sgt C.A. Bartlett	R3810*

At 11.30, it was the turn of 15 and 40 Squadrons. Oakshott and Trent led the two 15 Squadron sections; the six Blenheims made a high level bomb run over Le Bourquet, successfully bombing MT. Again flak claimed a victim, and again the crew perished.

| P/O A. Takedeli | Sgt F.V. Gunning | Sgt D.H. Peulove | R3747* |

The six Blenheims of 40 Squadron had mixed fortunes. One section of three failed to find any targets due to low cloud and brought their bombs back to England. The second section bombed but again one aircraft was hit by flak and went down. The other two crews, led by Flying Officer C.W. Bromley (in R3611) saw two parachutes appear and indeed the pilot and gunner of the doomed bomber did survive as prisoners. The navigator was killed.

| Sgt C.D.W. Barton | Sgt D.L. Dorris | Sgt E. Rodgers | R3893* |

Four Fairey Battles of 142 Squadron flew out to find and attack bridges near Le Manoir at 11.30, found and bombed them successfully. Pilot Officer L.H. Childe scored a direct hit on one (P6600) and Sergeant 'Dagger' Spear (L5252) scored a hit from 5,000 feet.

Shortly before three o'clock, 21 and 82 Squadrons took off. Wing Commander Bennett led six of 21 to bomb AFVs reported in a wood situated in a loop of the Seine near the Forêt de la Mare. They picked up a BAFF fighter escort at Honfleur at 4.25. They bombed the target amid heavy flak fire which damaged several of the Blenheims.

Squadron Leader Hunt led nine of 82 to bomb AFVs in woods near to Bernières, returning without casualties.

At about the same time, twelve Battles were directed against the pontoon bridge at Vesillon that had been searched for at dawn. 88 and 103 were two of the squadrons involved. They found a railway bridge that was under repair by German engineers near Le Manoir which was hit, the working party scattering, while dumps of repair materials were destroyed. Meanwhile, the Battle crews over Versillon were hampered by bad visibility and several failed to see any targets. Three pilots did see what they thought was a completed bridge at Courcelles and this was bombed. 103 Squadron claimed success, but other results were uncertain as several Me109s appeared, one Battle being lucky to escape into cloud when chased by three of the fighters.

The recce sorties of 59 Squadron were interrupted on this day. Pilot Officer C.M.M. Grece (with Sergeant Ryan and AC Gillard) took off to fly over Chartres. He found heavy cloud but this saved him when he was found and attacked by four Me109s. He made three attempts to get through and dived so fast into the cloud on one occasion that his observer's window and his own port window blew in!

Pilot Officer A.D. Hopkin of the same squadron, had trouble from French fighters rather than German. He was to fly a recce, between the Marne–Châlons–Paris but even before he reached the area his Blenheim (P3631) was forced down by nine Moranes.

Two Battles of 12 Squadron flew a night op into the area of Pavilly but both were forced to return due to low cloud over the target area.

No 142 Squadron sent out three Battles to Gisors and one failed to return.

All three members of the crew died, and were buried in Les Tys Cemetery, Eure–et–Loire.

F/Lt G.D.J. Martin   Sgt E.F.W. Curtis   LAC G.H. Kettlewell   ?*

Thursday, 13 June

With the surrender of St Valéry–en–Caux on the 12th and the completion of the evacuations from Le Havre that night, the only remaining British forces in France were all south of the River Seine. Those immediately concerned in the continuing struggle had their positions between the Rivers Risle and Iton.

The disastrous situation from the military viewpoint was reported to the Chief of the Air Staff by Air Marshal Barratt in a signal timed at 1200 hours.

The progress of the Battle of France has so far given no indication that the French armies can check the German advance, even where the former have been assisted by the formidable water obstacles of the Aisne, Somme, Marne and Seine. Information up to 0900 hours today, shows that

German elements have crossed the Seine in three pockets west of Paris, and that one pocket is probably being rapidly extended towards Dreux by armoured formations. There has been an enemy advance on a wide front south of St Lys and the enemy appear to be crossing the Marne in some strength between Meaux and La Ferté on the Aisne. Breakthrough by armoured formations was made on the 11th June, east of Château Thierry (Marne) and these elements are now believed to have travelled east and re-crossed the Marne at Châlons–sur–Marne, where the bridges had not been blown. My impression in regard to the various French liaison officers attached to my staff, is that they regard the situation as virtually hopeless and that they hourly expect a decisive breakthrough. Evacuation of the civil population from Paris and the threatened areas have been proceeding at great pace and for the past three days there has been intense congestion on all roads leading south.

The British and French Armies had been contending with congested roads since the start of the Blitzkrieg. Many returning soldiers and airmen would long recall the pitiful sights of refugees trying desperately to reach an area of safety. Pushing their few possessions and essential items on carts, bicycles, sometimes cars or trucks, they had, in reality, nowhere to go. They were often bombed or strafed by German planes whose main intention was to force these refugees away in order for the Panzers and road convoys to proceed at full pace.

Roy Max remembers one bi-product of these refugee columns. Often the cars and motorcycles ran out of petrol and had to be abandoned. The boys of 103 Squadron – and probably others – would 'liberate' these, bring them to the airfield, fill them with fuel and be seen to be driving about in all manner of vehicles for a few days. As they moved bases however, these too had to be left behind.

*

The RAF's scale of effort intended for the 13 June, was very large and as an indication of this effort are the words of a message from Winston Churchill to the French Premier, M. Reynaud and to General Weygand:

The RAF will make a further increased effort to render assistance to your valiant, hard-pressed forces from 13th June onwards. During the daylight hours of the 13th, all available Blenheims, to the number of 60, will be ready to attack targets indicated by General Georges through Air Marshal Barratt. Ten squadrons of fighters will also work from England within the limits of their range. For the night of the 13/14th June, 182 heavy bombers will be available to attack targets as desired by General Georges. In addition to the above support from this country, you will of course, have the six bomber and five fighter squadrons of the AASF, under the orders of Air Marshal Barratt. Special instructions have been issued to ensure that these squadrons are kept to full strength in aircraft, pilots and crews.

It is not clear if the pilots and crews of the Battle squadrons were informed of the last sentence of this message. They had not been kept up to full strength since 10 May, German flak and fighters had seen to that. It was obvious now, that the long suffering Battle crews were now to be thrown once more into the battle front in something of a desperate attempt to stop what in reality had become unstoppable.

Winston Churchill was obviously in a difficult situation. He desperately needed to keep France in the fight. He knew that if France fell, Britain would be alone to face Hitler's might and that an invasion of the British Isles must surely follow.

Barratt knew too, that they had to try and support the French, but he was only too aware that for his AASF bombers, supported by 2 Group, and even with help from the 'heavies' of Bomber Command, it was too few aircraft and far too late.

Sixty Blenheims, Churchill had said, an average of ten each of 2 Group's six squadrons. During the initial stages of the French Campaign, the Group had averaged only 70 bombers available for operations. Their losses too had been tremendous and not just in aeroplanes. Around 130 air crew were dead or missing with more than 30 more wounded. The Group had already lost the equivalent of their daily operational average and all squadrons had a number of Blenheims unable to operate through severe battle damage. One thing was clear, the situation was not going to improve, and would it achieve

Top Blenheim 'J' of 107 Squadron (R3816) which replaced P4919 written-off on 2 June. (*IWM*)

Above Flying Officer Derrick Franklin of 142 Squadron in his Battle. (*J.M. Hewson*)

Right Flight Lieutenant John Hewson, 142 Squadron, who won the DFC for his actions on 13 June, staying with his burning bomber because his gunner was unable to bale out. (*J.M. Hewson*)

anything to continue to try and support the battle anyway? The next few days would tell.

The bombing effort on the 13th began at dawn. 142 Squadron sent out six Battles at 5 a.m. to fly an armed-recce over the areas of the Seine–Vernon–Pacy–Evreux and the Forêt de Bizy. It was carried out in bad visibility but what enemy columns they saw seemed mostly small and unimportant.

With this limited information, however, a raid was organised for this area, as reports continued to come in. These were mounted by 150 Squadron, at 10.05 and 142 themselves at 10.45.

Six Battles of 150 flew out to the Vernon and Poix areas. Two of the six failed to return when 109s attacked them:

P/O A.R. Gulley	Sgt Berry	LAC D. Phillips	L5524*
Sgt R.G.B. Beale	Sgt H.J.F. Tutt	Cpl D.B. Carter	L5437*

As the Battles came into the battle area and saw enemy columns on the roads, they split into sections, before dive-bombing. On the return flight, Gulley and Beale saw about 30 aircraft over Vernon–sur–Seine and thought they might be Hurricanes. Five of these aircraft dived on them and they quickly saw they were not Hurricanes but Me109s.

Leading Aircraftman Donald Phillips, who had been with 52 Squadron before the war, engaged the 109s and shot one down, but their Battle was quickly set on fire. Alfred Gulley tried to get the burning Battle down, crash landed in a field and bounced into another. he was killed in the crash and the two airmen temporarily knocked unconscious. When they came round, they scrambled clear but it was too late for their pilot. Berry was burned about the face and hands.

Both airmen were taken prisoner but Phillips managed to escape and although he was last heard of in a French hospital in Amiens, by November the squadron heard he had got away and was safe in Gibraltar. He later returned to England at the beginning of December, promoted to sergeant and awarded the Military Medal. Roy Beale and his crew all died.

Three Battles of 142 Squadron bombed the bridge over the Seine at Rouen across which enemy troops and transport were moving along the Vernon–Rouen roads. Approaching the target at 4,000 feet through 7/10th cloud, Me109s and Me110s found them.

F/Lt J.M. Hewson	Sgt R.V.T. Kitto DFM	LAC R.S. Utteridge	?*
P/O W.D.K. Franklin	Sgt Pollock	LAC Pounds	?
P/O K.R. Sutton	Sgt Rudd	Sgt B.J. Rowe	?*

John Hewson's machine was set on fire and he ordered his crew out. Sergeant Richard Kitto, who had been with John Hobler when they were shot down on 14 May, parachuted to safety but Utteridge, who had been blazing away at the 109s and claimed two shot down, was wounded. Hewson brought the burning Battle down to a crash landing, despite a damaged port aileron and flames streaming from his port fuel tank. After Kitto had jumped, Hewson himself was about to go but when he stood up, he saw his gunner was in no condition to bale out so quickly took control of the aircraft again and brought it down close to a wood.

Getting out of the burning machine, Hewson helped Utteridge out and they just got clear before the petrol tanks exploded. While all this was going on, they were repeatedly attacked and machine-gunned by some of the 109s. Hewson later got his wounded gunner into a French hospital and eventually got himself back to the squadron. He was recommended for the Distinguished Service Order but received the DFC. Kitto made his way to St Malo and returned to England by sea. Utteridge later received the DFM but was taken prisoner when the hospital was over-run by advancing German troops. John Hewson relates:

> I went in first and then the other two – each then made their own way home. I was caught by two Me109s and one Me110 which was the one to do the damage with a cannon shell which hit the port fuel tank. The flames were going well past the tail plane. It looked as though the port wing would come off so I gave the order to bale out. Kitto went out through the bottom trap. I took my straps off, opened the hood to bale out when I saw part of a parachute around the rear gun. I knew then that Utteridge was still in there and probably wounded. I got back in and put the straps on, cut the motor, flaps down and fancy flying with the wheels up, landed it in a field close to the Rouen–Chartres road. I got him out, he had

been hit in the head and was in a bad way but I managed to get him away from the aeroplane and near the road. I was lucky to stop a French truck full of soldiers. They were very good, put him in the back of the truck and looked after him. My French was not very good but I sat next to the driver who told me there was a new hospital just built outside Chartres. When we got there they took him in straightaway and that was the last I saw of him. It took me 24 hours to get back to the squadron, travelling with the refugees. I was lucky to stop a car with a man, his wife and two kids going to the south. When we got back I told our sergeant to give him all the petrol he needed. I would say Utteridge must have been in that hospital when the Germans arrived.

Flight Lieutenant J.M. Hewson, 142 Squadron

Derrick Franklin had his Battle severely shot up by the Messerschmitts and his observer was wounded in both legs but he got home. Pilot Officer Sutton was shot down and crashed in the Evreux–Preux area. His observer was wounded in the right eye and head by shrapnel, while Sergeant Rowe received shrapnel wounds to his left leg. He did, however, claim one of the fighters shot down but his spirited fire helped to deter further attacks, which allowed Sutton to get the crippled machine onto the ground. Rowe too received the DFM.

The other squadron concerned in these actions was 103, but no details of their mission survive. In fact this day they flew two raids.

The bombers of 2 Group were also directed against these road targets, and 40 Squadron sent out nine Blenheims at 11.40. The squadron suffered no casualties. At mid-day, 142 sent out further Battles, and Pilot Officer Childe (L5434) bombed a convoy in the area of the Seine with 16 × 40 lb bombs.

2 Group kept up the pounding by despatching six aircraft of 15 Squadron at 1.30 p.m., led by Squadron Leader Webster. The weather was still extremely bad and enemy fighters were still reported in the area. Several crews bombed the woods – the Forêt de Gault, where reports had indicated no fewer than 500 tanks were concealed.

This report of 500 tanks, perhaps more, sent a shock wave

through AASF HQ, and suddenly everyone was galvanised into hitting this target. An urgent French request indicated that the forest would prove to be a 'fruitful' target, and the number of tanks gradually increased till it was thought the total was nearer to 1,000!

2 Group therefore mounted two further raids, one to the Seine area and the second to the Marne and the tanks. Six of 107 Squadron led by Wing Commander Stokes and 12 of 110 led by Sinclair, bombed the river crossings and approaches to the Seine at Pont de L'Arche and Vernon. They were attacked by Me110s which shot down one Blenheim, the crew being killed. The rest returned after flying through heavy AA fire.

P/O A.F. Stidtson	Sgt F.C. Higgins	Sgt J.R. Browning	R3616*

The twelve of 110 Squadron faired better, although one aircraft had to abort with an airframe problem and another had to force-land at Shoreham with engine trouble.

The second raid, to La Gault, was undertaken by 21 and 82 Squadrons. They suffered casualties. 21 Squadron:

F/Lt L.V.E. Petley	Sgt Hart	Sgt Norris	L9269
F/O J.C.G. Sarll	Sgt Jennings	Sgt K. Meyer	L8872
P/O L.M. Blanckensee	Sgt Williams	Sgt J. Guest	R3676*
F/O S.L. Sigurdson	Sgt Bailey	Sgt Trew	L9029
P/O W.A. Saunders	Sgt W.H. Eden	Sgt C. Webb	R3742
Sgt Bain	Sgt Turnbull	Sgt Thompson	R3675

82 Squadron

F/Lt L.V.E. Atkinson	Sgt Reece	Sgt M.C. Cleary	R3619
P/O Ritchie	Sgt A.A. Stanley	Sgt A.M. Clark	R3731
P/O D.M. Wellings	Sgt Howard	Sgt Thomas	P4839
F/Lt J.C. Breese	Sgt Williams	Sgt I.T. Harris	R6910*
P/O Percival	Sgt Oliver	Sgt Bristow	R3712
P/O Craig	Sgt Hutcheson	Sgt Doughty	R3708
P/O Lewis	Sgt Robertson	Sgt Clarke	P4843
P/O R.E. Williams	Sgt D. Carbutt	Sgt A.S. Beeby	P6925*
Sgt A.E. Merritt	Sgt Carlisle	Sgt L.D. Nineham	L8829*

Pilot Officer Lewis Blanckensee and his crew were killed, while Flight Lieutenant Petley had to make a forced landing. In 82 Squadron, Charlie Breese was shot down; he and his observer were captured, but his gunner was killed. Pilot Officer Eyton-Williams and his crew survived, but Sergeant Albert

Merritt and his gunner were killed although his observer seemed to have survived.

Now it was the turn of the Battles to attack the tank concentrations. 88 Squadron was the first to go although it had received orders at mid-day to move its base that evening. The formation of Battles went for the Forêt de Gault although they had to fly through a number of Me109s. At least three Battles were attacked, and one was shot down; its two man crew, Sergeants Hayward and Jones, were wounded and taken to Sens hosptal.

Later, 12, 142 and 150 were sending off Battles for the Forêt de Gault. 142 lost one aircraft, and the crew were taken prisoners:

| Sgt D.J. Holliday | Sgt D.A. Whiting | AC T. Greenall | * |

These were followed by 150 Squadron with six Battles. Four of whom were:

S/L R.M. Bradley	F/Sgt Leitch	LAC Rickard	L5591*
P/O A.D. Frank	Sgt Wilson	LAC Bailey	L5593
P/O C.H. Elliott	Sgt Gupwell	LAC Kirk	?
Sgt S.E. Andrews	Sgt N.J. Ingram	LAC H.R. Figg	L5543

The weather had not improved and the Battles had to make their way through low cloud and poor visibility to the target area. Squadron Leader Bradley arrived over the area and made a recce to see if he could see any of the reported tanks. All they could see for certain were tank tracks where they entered the woods. With nothing else in sight, he bombed this part of the wood and after circling for some time, set off for base.

Almost immediately they were attacked by five Me109s and Bradley dived to ground level, his gunner shooting down one of the attackers. He was then wounded in the leg and arm. Meanwhile, the 109s riddled the Battle which caught fire and Bradley had then to make a crash landing, which he did successfully, two miles north of Ribais. The three men got clear and after Bradley had got his wounded gunner to a hospital, he and his observer made their way by road and rail to Nantes on the 18th, where arrangements were made for their return by air to England.

The other Battles were also engaged by 109s. Sergeant Sidney Andrews bombed some tanks and then had to fight off several 109s, one of which his gunner, Henry Figg, shot down. They were badly shot about but they got back; all three men later received DFMs.

On 13 June, Tiny Elliott and myself were briefed to attack tanks alleged to be refuelling in a wood near La Gault. When some 20 minutes short of the target we were attacked by two Me109s. I waved Tiny away to break formation and we both dived from our cruising height – about 6,000 feet – to tree-top level. I managed to lose mine but regrettably lost myself in the process and ultimately returned without finding the target. Tiny had more trouble with his 109 but he managed to get home with the damage confined to his aircraft. Not a very successful sortie!

Pilot Officer A.D. Frank, 150 Squadron

At 6 p.m., 12 Squadron put up six aircraft to hit the forest area. No tanks were seen but a large concentration of MT seen moving north towards Gourgaivaux but it was presumed friendly. After another look round, bombs were dropped on the south side of the forest and other nearby woods. They met intense AA fire, then the 109s appeared. Three Battles were shot down:

F/O B.E. Moss	Sgt B.E. Long	LAC Radley	L5451
P/O G.M. Hayton	Sgt Simpson	LAC J. Tracey	?
Sgt G.R. Wheeldon	Sgt H. Batty	LAC J. Taylor	L5396
P/O J.S. Shorthouse	Sgt N.C. Cotterell	LAC Copley	L5324*
P/O R.C.L. Parkhouse	Sgt A.R. Morris	LAC D.A. MacDonald	L5580*
P/O J.F. McFie	Sgt C.S.G. Beevers	LAC J.G. Thompson	L5531*

Sergeant Wheeldon (L5396) was also attacked but succeeded in driving off the 109s. Of the missing, Parkhouse and McFie with their crews were all taken prisoner. Shorthouse and Copley ended up in hospital with burns, Norman Cotterell was reported missing, and later his death was confirmed.

Despite the efforts of the afternoon, results were disappointing. Few tanks had been seen, although part of the forest had been set on fire. It seemed obvious considering the number of enemy aircraft in the area, not to say the ground fire, that the enemy's presence was there and that an offensive seemed likely. In total, 26 Battle sorties had been despatched, of which 17 had bombed. Although something like an ammo dump had been hit, the effort cost the AASF six Battles. Four Blenheims had also been lost.

As the French had requested the raids, they promised to provide fighter cover. Little if any was seen, and the RAF losses suggest that if it was provided it certainly was not very effective.

One of the Battles had landed near Prissy after bombing three tanks the pilot had seen at a crossroads in a wood. Two fires were started and then more tanks were seen on the road between Charleville and La Gault. La Gault village was burning but the arrival of a 109 made further reconnaissance a secondary function.

The Battles would be back looking for the tanks the next day, for it seemed obvious now that with such a large concentration of enemy armour and troops, a final thrust was about to be made.

CHAPTER FIFTEEN

The Fall of France

Friday, 14 June 1940

By this date it was quite clear that the French line was ceasing to exist and that the armies were beginning to split up into isolated groups. The Germans would enter Paris today. Bombing operations continued none the less, in the Seine area.

The weather was terrible which seemed only to add to the misery of such forces that were trying to stem the German tide. At dawn, 75 Wing were ordered to mount a raid against targets in the area south of the Seine, near Evreux. Ten Battles were briefed but the weather prevented any attacks.

The Blenheims of 110 Squadron fared little better, although twelve Blenheims did make an appearance over AFVs south of the Seine, at around 8.30 p.m. Only a handful of crews managed to find targets through the low cloud.

Most of the Battle squadrons were now moving. 88 Squadron's main road convoy had left for Nantes an hour after midnight. They had now finished in France. At noon, all aircraft left for England, landing at Abingdon before flying on to RAF Driffield in Yorkshire. At 12.30 the ground people left for Brest.

Sixteen Battles and two Magisters of 103 Squadron evacuated to Souge, while at 9.30 150 began to head for Nantes. 226 Squadron at Artins began to evacuate.

At 10.30, 15 Squadron sent out a force of nine Blenheims, led by Oakshott and Trent, making a high level attack around Vernon despite the bad weather and low cloud. MT and AFVs were bombed and an AA battery was also hit. One Blenheim flew back on one engine.

No. 142 Squadron were active. They flew an armed recce south of the Seine and then at one o'clock three aircraft, piloted by Sergeants A.N. Spear, and G.H. Ebert and Pilot Officer R.H. Edwards, also out on an armed recce, found the Germans had got aircraft on the airfield at Le Caudray, near Evreux. Enemy fighters were now being met as far south as Chartres and no wonder. It is evidence of the speed and organisation of the enemy, that the Germans were already using aerodromes so recently vacated by the French. Several Me109s were seen and bombed as they sat at dispersal. Meantime the rest of the squadron packed for the move to Rennes, while waiting for the order to go.

Nine Blenheims of 40 Squadron took off at 1.45, led by the veteran, Squadron Leader G.W.C. Gleed. Their target included MT and a bridge over the River Eure:

S/L G.W.C. Gleed	Sgt Burge	Sgt A.F.W. Sammells	N3592*
P/O Bowler	Sgt Coburn	Sgt Shawyers	R3745
P/O Lewis	Sgt Currie	Sgt Johnson	R3693*
F/O C.W. Bromley	Sgt Usher	Sgt Gamble	R3811
P/O C.B. Best	Sgt Howarth	Sgt Corney	L9412
P/O Traill-Smith	Sgt Fry	Sgt G.D.P. Quinn	R3778
Sgt Higgins	Sgt Cody	Sgt Liggins	L9270
Sgt J.S. Morton	Sgt A.D. Kelso	Sgt Winston	L9402
Sgt Newton	Sgt Fitton	Sgt McCreary	R3611

Gerald Gleed had flown some dozen raids during the campaign, ever since 10 May. He was shot down and so was Pilot Officer Lewis. Pilot Officer Bowler's Blenheim was hit in the oil tank and he had to make a forced landing at RAF Bicester having had to return before reaching the target. Flight Lieutenant Robert Batt took over the flight commander post.

Activity became quite intense from the middle of the afternoon. At 3.40, 12 Squadron sent three Battles out to bomb the woods south-east of Evreux where large columns of MT had been reported, as well as the airfield at Le Courdray, attacked earlier by 142 Squadron:

P/O P.H. Blowfield	Sgt J.J.C. Batty	LAC J. Grant	L5396*
Sgt J. Wilcox	Sgt A. Emery	LAC Hislop	L5383*
Sgt D.H. Preston	Sgt Spiller	LAC Harvey	L5249

Sergeant Preston was unable to find any targets so returned. The other two ran into fighters and neither returned. LAC Grant was killed in the air fight before the Battle was shot down. Sergeant Batty later returned to England, where he reported that Pilot Officer Blowfield had been killed on the ground by German tanks.[1]

Between 5 and 5.30, 2 Group sent out 21, 82, 107 and 110 Squadrons. For once the Blenheims ignored troops, convoys or AFVs, their assigned target being the recently occupied aerodrome at Merville.

Wing Commander Bennett led his 21 boys in with 82 in close company, bombing from 9,000 feet. Slight AA fire greeted them and one Blenheim of 21 fell out of formation and was last seen going down, chased by a 109. Later information confirmed the pilot had died but his crew were prisoners:

P/O W.A. Saunders	Sgt W.H. Eden	Sgt C. Webb	R3742*

No. 40 Squadron, led by Hunt, suffered no casualties, for the fighter escort kept away any 109s that tried to elbow their way in. They saw their bombs fall and explode amongst German aircraft on the ground.

The crews of 107 and 110 Squadrons, as they bombed, counted as many as 40 Ju88s on the ground, with some Me109s. They too saw their bombs fall in and around the dispersed aircraft, destroying many.

As this raid finished, 150 Squadron were sending out three Battles to bomb targets of opportunity in the main battle area. Sergeant R.A.C. deC. White bombed a wood in which he saw some motor transport vehicles, while Sergeant W.C. Pay also bombed MT before he was spotted by seven Me109s. However, taking the Battle's usual evasive action of flying down onto the deck, he managed to shake them off.

Flight Lieutenant Hugo Beale bombed a convoy and later, when south of La Loupe, he too was attacked, by nine Messerschmitts. His gunner, LAC Burrows, hit one from a range of 50 yards and it poured black smoke. The rest of the 109s then also broke away. Raymond White was to receive the DFM shortly afterwards.

Four Battles of 103 Squadron were also sent out, at 6.45 p.m. but two failed to return:

---

[1] Sergeant Batty was killed in a flying accident on 8 February 1941, in the same crash which killed Sergeant R.T. Tomlinson DFM.

| P/O R. Hawkins | P/O J. Hugill | | ?* |
| Sgt Brumby | Sgt Hedley | LAC Werner | ?* |

Ronald Hawkins and Hugill were taken prisoner. Hawkins, however, later escaped, reached Vichy France and then Spain. He was known by his comrades to carry every conceivable aid to escape with him when he flew, and it seems they certainly came in handy. He eventually got back to England after a period of internment in Spain. He later became a squadron leader, and commanded 3 Squadron, flying Hawker Typhoons. He was later killed in action in October 1943.

The other Battle crew crash-landed in an orchard at Laval, but were back with the squadron that same afternoon. There were other Battles out at this time but records are missing. P2335 of 226 Squadron was certainly lost on this day.

*

This day saw almost the last of 2 Group's participation in the French campaign, although its Blenheims would start a new phase of operations similar to the afternoon raid on Merville.

The Battle squadrons of the AASF too were almost finished. Their work, so gallantly carried out over the recent weeks, was now coming to an end as France collapsed. The task now, was to get away – get back to England.

At around 5 p.m., several German bombers attacked the base of 103 Squadron still busily packing. The enemy aircraft suddenly appeared over the brow of a nearby hill which boarded the airfield. The aircraft, reported as either Dornier 17s or Me110s, delivered what the RAF grudgingly admitted was 'an excellent attack.' Several aircraft were hit and set on fire, and a Sergeant Bone was wounded. Three hours later came the order to move the next morning.

The base of 12 Squadron was also raided that night, and a Battle was destroyed on the ground.

By this time, 59 Squadron and its reconnaissance Blenheims were back in France. On 13 June, five or six crews had flown from Odiham (where it had moved on the 10th) to Le Mans, as David Evans remembers:

We operated out of Le Mans and then various other airfields as we were chased out of France. I can't remember who briefed us or indeed what we were told to look out for, except, of course, for any enemy forces becoming evident. On 14 June we did 1½ hours on a tactical recce in the area of Nantes–Evreux, in other words, to the north west of Paris and south of the Seine. I noted that we saw, but luckily were not seen by, two Me110s.

Flying Officer G.H.D. Evans, 59 Squadron

Saturday, 15 June
The final missions of the AASF Battles were flown on this morning. Those who were still able to operate had been in almost constant action for the past 36 days. All had suffered considerable casualties, but none had refused to continue to the end.

These last missions were confined to armed recce sorties into the Dreux and Evreux areas soon after dawn, followed by raids to the same areas beginning at 9.45. Fighter cover was provided by 67 Wing.

No great enemy concentrations were discovered, although some MT and trains being used by the Germans were bombed. The area seemed full of very hostile and very intense AA fire, and two Battles failed to return.

Two of the squadrons flying the dawn recce were 142 and 150. 150 sent a total of 10 Battles out, bombing in the areas Louvières–Vernon–Viry–Danville–Evreux, but lost one aircraft:

P/O Benjamin	Sgt Armstrong	LAC Hillyard	L5541*

The crews had flown out in pairs; Benjamin flew in company with Pilot Officer Elliott at 4.30 a.m. Nearing the battle zone, Benjamin headed for the east of Evreux where some troops had been reported. He met heavy ground fire and seeing no sign of the troops, decided to bomb a village from which some of the AA fire was coming from. As he was about to go in, three Me109s attacked.

The Battle was at 4,000 feet, and Benjamin quickly dived to ground level while twisting from side to side to avoid the enemy fire. After some minutes they managed to shake off the 109s, but the rear gunner had been wounded by shrapnel. The Battle had been badly damaged, Benjamin having to put it down near the village of La Ferté Vidame. The wounded Hillyard was put

Above Abandoned Blenheim of 114 Squadron at Condé Vraux aerodrome, being examined by German troops. (*via R.C. Bowyer*)

Left Squadron Leader Charles Tait DFC, 103 Squadron, from Dundee. (*Mrs G. Tait*)

Below Roy Max, 103 Squadron, in Battle cockpit. (*R.D. Max*) into a French ambulance and then Benjamin and Armstrong proceeded to smash all vital parts of their downed Battle. They then set off towards Nantes, from where they managed to get back to England later that month.

Only two of four Battles from 12 Squadron managed to get airborne later that morning, and these, seeing few targets, bombed the aerodrome and road junction at Plessis–Grehan, the other bombing the Forêt D'Ivry. At 10 o'clock, 103 Squadron sent out three aircraft, and all returned safely.

By now the orders to leave were being received. At Houssaye, at 11 a.m. 150 Squadron sent all their serviceable aircraft off to England – to RAF Abingdon. Already the road party had left on their way to Nantes. They would go on to Brest and board a ship for Plymouth on the 16th. 88 and 142 were soon to follow.

The squadron had been ordered to fly directly back to England but then they were told to return to Houssaye to refuel. All personal equipment went on the road convoy and was never seen again. Alan Frank:

> When the sudden change of orders came they left an absolute minimal ground staff to receive us and turn the aircraft round and some transport to drive them off. But really the idea was they just refuelled the aircraft, then disappeared. The old Merlin engines were always having mag. drop trouble and on this particular occasion I was foolish enough to run it up after take-off, switched off one magneto and there was an absolute dead cut. LAC Smith, of our ground crew, said he had a screwdriver and a nail file with which he'd clean the points! This would not have been acceptable in normal circumstances but one just had to talk oneself into saying it was all right. We navigated ourselves home; luckily one chap had a Michelin Guide with which to take us across the Channel.

It was with some relief that the crews of the squadron found themselves back in England.

Alan Frank continues:

> Having landed back at Abingdon, everybody let their hair down, inevitably, and we had a fairly good lunchtime session. Came 4 o'clock in the afternoon, we were told we all had to

go off to Stradishall! I flew this Battle in some discomfort
and had quite some trouble in finding the place. It was the
only time I flew an aeroplane in an unfit state.

Pilot Officer A.D. Frank, 150 Squadron

At noon, on Souge airfield, 103 Squadron were ordered to fly
out their aircraft. As they were about to do so, the airfield was
raided. Several Battles were destroyed and a shelter trench was
hit and blown in. A Sergeant Dowling was killed and eight
other casualties were inflicted on men of 12 and 226
Squadrons.

It was unfortunate that the Germans had struck at this
moment. Only the previous evening had seen the departure of
the ground defences prior to the evacuation. 12, 103 and 226
Squadrons had a total of 48 aircraft on the airfield, and the
only defences available were a few Lewis guns. Two other
attacks followed and in all some 15 men were killed. Being a
fairly new airfield, it had little or no camouflage, and the
number of aircraft clearly visible made it a tempting target.

We were briefed to fly a raid, drop our bombs and then fly
straight on back to England. We were preparing for this
when a message came changing the orders. We were now to
fly our raid but then land back and refuel first. We returned
to the airfield safely and were busily refuelling the aircraft.
They were all dispersed around the airfield and I was up on
one wing because as most of the ground party had gone off
we had to do most of the work ourselves. We were using 40
gallon drums to get fuel into our wing tanks. Then we heard
the awful sound of unsynchronised engines as about six or
eight Dorniers came in. I leapt off the wing and hared to a
slit trench which was just behind. The aircraft, of course, was
completely loaded with all our personal belongings at this
stage because we were going off to England.

As I was running to the trench I remember looking back
and seeing the bomb bursts coming across the field towards
us. I landed on top of my WOP, as one bomb landed on
either side of the trench, another falling on the aircraft
unfortunately. The trench was filled in with soil but luckily
I'd fallen on top of this poor fellow who was moaning like
blazes beneath me and I was able to pull him out but the chap

next door was right underneath and by the time we'd dug him out – and we only had our hands – he was dead. My aircraft was burning gently and there was nothing we could do about it.

All the ack ack guns had gone because we'd been initially ordered to fly back to England. So the Germans, after bombing, just flew round and round machine gunning. There were then just two or three lorries left so three of us took one aircraft and flew it to another airfield.

Flying Officer R.D. Max, 103 Squadron

I remember the aerodrome being strafed and shot up just before leaving for England but luckily a cow saved my life. I lay down and whatever was going to get me got the cow.

Flying Officer J.R. Havers, 103 Squadron

No sooner had the first attacks on Souge subsided and the CO and Squadron Leader Tait were having a last look round, than another raid came. Both men were lucky to survive, when the trench into which they had dived, was near-missed by bombs and machine-gun fire. As they then moved off towards the nearby river, as the raid ended, they were spotted by one enemy aircraft which dived and strafed them. They took cover, one in the river, the other halfway up a tree!

The CO's carefully dispersed aircraft was hit by a stray bullet and set on fire. Only one staff car remained, which could not carry all the personnel still on the airfield. An inspection was therefore made of two unserviceable aircraft and although one was completely u/s, the engine of the second one did work. Despite holed fuel tanks and a severed main spar, Wing Commander Dickens flew it to Nantes with Tait and Roy Max in the rear cockpits.

Dickens and Tait later flew to England, via Jersey where the leaking fuel tanks had to be refilled, while Max and another pilot flew a reserve aircraft to England direct. The rest of the air party landed at Abingdon with the exception of Pilot Officer Barrett, who had to make a forced landing at RAF Shoreham, only just clearing the Channel. Flying Officer Max:

We had landed at a depot with a lot of spare aircraft about so we each took one and flew it back to England. The only problem was that the only map I could find was from an old calendar. Of course, I didn't know exactly where everything was and it was murder flying back and we had to make a detour around the Channel Islands. I didn't know where I was when I crossed the English coast so I had to land at the first airfield I saw and then having scrounged a map flew on to Abingdon. So that was our return from France. The other sad thing was that some of our chaps who had gone off went aboard the *Lancastria*.

Flying Officer R.D. Max, 103 Squadron

The main party of 142 Squadron had left at dawn for Rennes, followed at 1 p.m. by the rear party. The aircraft left at one o'clock too, 13 Battles setting out, although one had to force-land at Rennes. Three u/s aircraft were destroyed on the ground. The aircraft landed at RAF Waddington, while the ground personnel arriving at Brest on the 16th, boarded the SS *Vienna* for Plymouth.

RAF Finningley saw the arrival of 12 Squadron's aircraft, and they burnt at least one Battle (N2150) at Nantes when it failed to start. Thus by the afternoon of the 15th, all serviceable Battles were back in England, with the squadron's ground crews all on their way back by road and by sea.

2 Group, in the shape of 82 Squadron, had tried to mount a raid to the south of Rouen, led by Philip Sutcliffe, with his observer, Sergeant Scott and gunner, Sergeant George Whitehead in P6895.

Target was AFVs and motorised columns on roads to the south of Rouen. This was an abortive trip and we returned to base on account of lack of cloud cover, which we needed to guard against attacks by enemy fighters.

Squadron Leader W.P. Sutcliffe, 82 Squadron

The great adventure was over. The dream that had turned into a nightmare was finally over.

*

Very few RAF aeroplanes were still flying in France. 59 Squadron were still operating but they would soon leave.

On 15th June we went to Caen airfield, back to Le Mans, then to a place called Douvre and finally to Rennes. On the ground at one place – Rennes I think – we were dive-bombed, with a bit of nasty shooting-up and so on. At the end of it we came out of our slit trenches and saw a large muck heap disintegrate in front of our eyes. Out of it came two or three Frenchmen where they'd been sheltering from the nastiness! As one can imagine, they smelt, and not of the usual garlic.

The aircraft hangars were a shambles and burning furiously, so the Frenchmen, and ourselves, had been lucky.

On the 16th, we flew another one hour 55, round the Caen–Lisieux area, and later set off for another recce in the Alençon area, which is not very far from Le Mans, but the cloudbase was 500 feet, probably lower, so we returned to Rennes. Then we went off to Dinard to refuel, back to Rennes and then again to Dinard on the 17th. On this day I flew my final sortie in France, again round the area of Alençon. I recorded on that trip that the Hun columns were pouring through on a front of 20 miles. We were flying over them for a couple of hours and I remember thinking what a wonderful bombing target they would have made. There was no opposition, they were just pouring through. Luckily for us, we had no opposition either.

Group HQ then gave us orders to return to England. We were given a specific route to fly back to Odiham, crossing the coast just west of Southampton. I had some friends who lived in the New Forest and I headed in their direction, fairly low down. The first thing I saw on crossing the coast, with France in her mortal agonies, was a game of village cricket!

Meanwhile, our squadron Equipment Officer, Paddy Kearon (later an Air Commodore) – a mad Irishman, had headed out with the ground party. He collected together about 100 or 150 RAF vehicles and drove them steadily west, and when I saw him subsequently, he said he got as far as Brest and was then told to push them all over the edge of the docks into the sea!

Flying Officer G.H.D. Evans, 59 Squadron

The squadron lost a crew on the 16th, the pilot and gunner being taken prisoner, the observer reported wounded:

| P/O B. Everton-Jones | Sgt Taplin | AC F.V.W. Thake | R3818* |

At about 4.30 p.m. on the 17th, Air Marshal Barratt issued his last orders. He instructed Wing Commander A. Walters, who had commanded No. 67 Wing throughout the campaign, to cover Nantes and St Nazaire with his fighters until embarkation had been completed. Barratt himself left for England by air, at six o'clock, leaving Air Vice Marshal Douglas Evill in charge.

In their first major campaign, the RAF had come off second best. The AASF squadrons, especially the Battle squadrons, had been let down by their aircraft. Their comparatively small numbers too had been against them. They were simply overwhelmed by the mass of ground fire which they met, and by a numerically superior Luftwaffe. There can be no question about the courage the Battle and Blenheim crews showed in the face of this desperate fight to stop the German invasion. More often than not, the Battles were sent out in small formations, often in twos and threes, mostly without any escort, or when escorts were available, it was not properly organised they pressed on regardless. There was never any question about not carrying out their orders. It was simply a case of get on with the job in hand and try to get home again. That so many did get back is in itself amazing. That so many tried and failed is a testimony to their bravery.

The crews of 2 Group had equally shown spectacular courage. Their raids over France, again often unescorted, especially in the early days of the campaign, defy adequate description. They also had long flights to and from the target areas, crossing and recrossing the English Channel, often struggling back with damaged aircraft and wounded crews. They, like their comrades in the AASF, had had to test the doctrines of peacetime thinking, peacetime tactics and to see if they would work. They didn't. And they too paid the price.

> The crews of 107 Squadron owe their lives, to a great extent, to the magnificent leadership of Wing Commander Embry, who was an inspiring leader, and to the excellent formation flying we maintained. On one occasion, we were flying in two boxes of six, approximately parallel and we managed to fight off a formation of Me109s without loss.
>
> I always flew as No. 3 to Embry and was there on one occasion when a large portion of his port wing was blasted out by flak – he flipped under me but he did manage to land his

aircraft safely at RAF Hawkinge. I was not with him on his last flight with the squadron when he was shot down over France.

The discipline and morale of 107 Squadron was excellent throughout this period, but the standard of training of the replacement crews was low and lessened their chances of survival in the event of mechanical trouble or battle damage.

Our ground crews were marvellous and worked all hours to keep the aircraft in the air. They were always rather excited when we returned with battle damage, although it meant extra work for them.

All our targets came to us from France via many telephone channels so that information was usually long out of date. I think that the worst part of this time was sitting in the mess waiting for the telephone to ring and call us down for briefing. As for No. 2 Group Headquarters, we all felt very strongly that the AOC of the Group never bothered to come and visit us at any time.

Flying Officer R.C. Rotheram, 107 Squadron

The Blenheim crews and their leaders quickly learned. They had to in order to survive. The tragic myth of the unescorted bomber getting through should have been quashed earlier in the war. It also should have been obvious that an invading enemy would defend to the limit its advances by both heavy and light anti-aircraft guns and by fighters. The scene had changed as the campaign continued, but that was merely a natural progression of events.

As the battle moved into northern France after the breakthrough from Sedan, it was plain that fighter cover should be provided and in some instances this helped cut losses. From 20 May onwards it became regular practice to provide close escort to the Blenheims, although during the Dunkirk evacuation, the Blenheims merely had cover by patrolling fighters operating in the area, rather than direct escort. There were not enough fighters to go round.

From 5 June onwards, the battle had begun to move onwards, south across the Somme and the Aisne, out of range of Fighter Command operating from bases in southern England. Beyond Rouen, Fighter Command aircraft could not operate effectively, and by this time, Hugh Dowding was not letting any more of his preciously few fighters be sent into the bottomless pit that was the Battle of France. His thoughts, quite rightly, were on the coming Battle of Britain.

After the Air Component bases had been abandoned, the Blenheims had mainly to rely on the five overworked Hurricane squadrons of the AASF: 1, 73, 501, 17 and 242 (later increased to eight.) Casualties as a result rose slightly. The Battles, meantime, fought on, sometimes with fighter cover, often not.

However, after the first disastrous days of the invasion, there was a marked decrease in overall casualties due mainly to the following factors:

1. The abandonment of very low level delay-action bombing;
2. The extension and consequent weakening of enemy AA fire and fighter defences;
3. The fact that in the latter stages of the campaign RAF aircraft were not attacking the main German armoured thrusts:
4. The shorter distances to be covered by Bomber Command Blenheims in the period 20 May to 4 June;
5. The provision from 20 May onwards of closer fighter escort.

*

The overall losses by the AASF squadrons have always been difficult to assess because of missing records. Even the lists that have been produced from time to time have inaccuracies in them. One such list showing 137 Battles, 37 Blenheims and 55 Hurricanes as lost by the Advanced Air Striking Force, is open to question. Some of the daily losses shown on this list do tie in, others do not. By merely adding together losses shown in surviving records we have something in the region of 125 Battles lost in action plus many more destroyed during various evacuations of airfields. The AASF lost 13 Blenheims in action with others lost on the ground. Component recce squadrons lost over 30 Blenheims in action.

Two Group lost over 90 of their Blenheims in action. As always, aircraft numbers, while giving an indication of the severity of the attrition rate, take no account of the loss in lives. The true losses were from among the pilots, observers and air gunners of the Royal Air Force who daily took their Battles and Blenheims into the Battle of France.

According to one list of casualties, the RAF suffered the following losses:

Killed, Missing or Died of Wounds:
321 pilots, 359 aircrew, 277 ground personnel.

Prisoners of War:
115 pilots, 120 aircrew.

Wounded:
98 pilots, 86 aircrew.

*

France requested an Armistice on the 17th and the next day came the second great evacuation, this time from St Nazaire, Brest and other Atlantic ports. The sinking of the SS *Lancastria* with the loss of an estimated 5,000 lives was the most serious casualty of this evacuation. At least ninety personnel of 98 Squadron were lost in the sinking.

Many of the AASF squadrons' ground crews left France at this time, and Air Vice Marshal Philip Playfair left on the last ship to leave. Joe Gardiner BEM, who had been wounded with 150 Squadron back in September, had returned to the AASF towards the end in France.

> I was pushed over to 88 Squadron to help with the new boys coming in. There was apparent hope then of continuing the fight – '*Combat continuer*' to quote the words of the great General. We did carry on for a while after Paris fell. We were at Nantes at the time and we were still at it until the order came to get out. The ground crews and squadron personnel were to be evacuated on the SS *Lancastria*. Well, 124 of our chaps were lost on that ill-fated ship. We flew out. The last I saw of France then, was the pall of smoke over a burning St. Malo.
>
> *Sergeant F.H. Gardiner, 88 Squadron*

France surrendered on 22 June.

Probably the last raid was flown by 82 Squadron, on the 18th. Six Blenheims, led by Squadron Leader Sutcliffe DFC, attacked

AFVs on roads from Les Piève to Cherbourg, hits being observed on vans and motor cyclists.

The target was AFVs and motorised columns on roads south of Cherbourg. Bombs dropped on a column which was also attacked with front and rear machine guns. This was my last operation before being posted away from 82 Squadron.

Squadron Leader W.P. Sutcliffe, 82 Squadron

(Philip Sutcliffe had flown 12 raids during the period 12 May to 18 June.)

Then, as France was in her death throes, and immediately afterwards, 2 Group began to hit enemy occupied aerodromes. 15 Squadron bombed Boos aerodrome on the afternoon of the 19th, led by Flying Officer Hugh George (L8848). 40 Squadron went too. A number of German aircraft were destroyed on the ground, and a hangar was also hit.

Later 15, 40 and 82 Squadrons attacked Amiens aerodrome (Glisy), seeing many hits on aircraft and hangars, with huge fires being started.

Boos aerodrome was hit again, this time by 107 Squadron, the next day; Wing Commander Stokes took six Blenheims, in company with 12 of 110. (On the evening of the 22nd, 107 attacked targets in the Ruhr, but lost Flying Officer J.W. Stephens who had flown many of the raids into France. He was reported a prisoner of war.)

On the day France fell, 107 and 110 Squadrons attacked Boos again causing more mayhem with bursting bombs seen amongst aircraft and hangars under construction.

No. 40 Squadron were busy in the latter part of June. On the 22nd Squadron leader Batt flew a lone recce over Holland, but low cloud forced him to abandon this. Instead he made a shallow dive attack on Schipol aerodrome. On the 25th the squadron bombed Waalhaven aerodrome and two days later, Batt was out again, leading six Blenheims on a photo-recce op to St Valery.[1]

---

[1] F/Lt Robert Batt DFC failed to return from another recce on 9 July. His body and that of his gunner, Sgt Johnson, was picked up by HMS *Brilliant* and buried at sea. Sgt A. Spencer DFM was not found. Batt had been flying L8836, the Blenheim in which they had won their decorations in June.

That same afternoon six aircraft went to do the same around Boulogne and Guines. Flying Officer Bromley (R3811) was attacked and hit by Me109s and had to force land at RAF Hawkinge with his gunner, Sergeant Gamble, wounded. Gamble later received the DFM. One Blenheim failed to return, the crew being killed:

Sgt J.S. Morton	Sgt A.D. Kelso	Sgt J.C. Winston	R3778*

On the last day of the month, 107 went for Merville aerodrome. An attack was pressed home in the face of accurate AA fire. Three of the Blenheims had become detached from the others and were found by Me109s. All three were shot down. Pilot Officer D.A. Vinson had to make a forced landing at Manston, due to flak damage. (N6237). Those lost were:

S/L H. Pilling	Sgt F.A. Roche	Sgt H.T. Dennison	R3870*
P/O R.H.M. Bennett	Sgt A.E. Langford	Sgt D.S. Harrison	R3823*
P/O J.P. Quirke	Sgt D.C. Hawkins	Sgt K.E. Murray	L9467*

Only Roche of Pilling's crew survived as a prisoner, Bennett and his crew all died, Paddy Quirke and his crew were also taken into captivity.

*

This ends the story of the Battles and Blenheims' contribution to the French campaign in 1940. Many instances of courage had been rewarded already with decorations to pilots and aircrew. Other awards were announced over the following weeks.

Two men who had led a number of operations with 15 Squadron both received DFCs: Len Trent and Alan Oakshott.

In 18 Squadron, who had moved to West Raynham on 12 June, and was about to become a 2 Group Squadron, DFCs were announced for Pilot Officers M.P.C. Holmes, Arthur Hughes, Peter D. Smith, and James Roger Whelan. Holmes later became a fighter pilot and commanded a Typhoon squadron. DFMs went to Sergeant J.H. Strong and LAC J. Brown.

In August, DFCs were announced to three 21 Squadron pilots, the late Squadron Leader George Pryde, Squadron

Above Abandoned RAF aircraft depot in France with the wreckage of warfare. Blenheim fuselages and a Battle fuselage can be seen. The nearest wreck is TR-F of 59 Squadron. Far right a German car of the German Pioneer Corps can just be made out. (*via J. De Vos*)

Below Another picture of the same wrecked aeroplane. The two Blenheims behind the Battle in the foreground are P6922 of 53 Squadron which was wrecked in a crash on 5 April. The other is P4901. The Valiant Wings have been clipped. (*via J. De Vos*)

leader R.D.C. Gibson and Flight Lieutenant S.F. Coutts-Wood,[1] while DFMs went to Sergeants L.H. Lightfoot (AG), Jack Guest (AG) and Barnes (OB). 21 Squadron was to lose its CO, Wing Commander Bennett when five out of six Blenheims of the squadron were shot down by Me109s following a raid on Stavanger on 9 July. He was flying with Pryde's old observer, Sergeant A. Summers, and Coutts-Wood's gunner, Sergeant Burt.

No. 15 Squadron too received a number of awards. Trent and Webster, of course, had received DFCs, and DFMs went to LAC Robert Hunter and Sergeant Ray Stone. Later Alan Oakshot received the DFC. Trent's crew William Stephens and John Sutcliffe received DFMs. Before the end of the year, others in the squadron, prominent during May and June, were rewarded. Hugh George and Bob Gilmore received DFCs while DFMs went to Alfred Box, Sidney Readhead, Charles O'Donnell, Albert Taylor and Vernon Treherne.

Distinguished Flying Medals went to five of 40 Squadron's NCOs, Sergeants Neville, B.C. Wooldridge (OB), Gamble (AG), J. Corney (AG) and F.H. Jones (AG).

Ronald Rotheram of 107 Squadron received the DFC in July, and his navigator received the DFM. Others in the squadron too were soon decorated, including 'Flash' Pleasance and Wing Commander Stokes. Embry too, upon his return from France, received a second bar to his DSO.

It has already been mentioned that Alan Pitfield, who was killed in June, was to receive the DFC. Other 88 Squadron awards were DFCs to Flying Officer J.A.F. Maclachlan and F.W. Snell, while DFMs went to Corporal John L. Briggs, and LACs Leslie V. Davies and William H. Sturdy. Maclachlan was to later find fame as a fighter pilot. Over Malta he was wounded and lost his left forearm but continued to fly with a false hand. He was killed in action flying Mustangs in 1943 having added a DSO and two bars to his DFC to his decorations, and having shot down 16 enemy aircraft. Another 88 Squadron pilot to win later fame as a fighter pilot was Dudley Honor, who flew successfully in the Middle East, becoming a Wing Commander. Paul Rabone had flown 16

---

[1] Coutts-Wood was killed on active service later in the year.

sorties with the squadron in France, including one against the Maastricht bridges in May. He had had to bale out twice. He too became a successful day and night fighter pilot winning the DFC and bar before he was killed in action in 1944.

In 103 Squadron, DFCs went to John Havers and Dermot Kelly. Kelly was later killed flying Wellington bombers over Germany. DFMs went to Sergeant L.F. Waern (OB) and Sergeant Derrick Norrington (OB). Roy Max won the DFC in 1941. He later commanded 75 (New Zealand) Squadron in Bomber Command and received the DSO. BEMs went to the two NCOs in charge of A and B Flight ground crews, Flight Sergeants E.J. Partridge and W.H. Jennings, to Warrant Officer W. Cunningham, I/C the squadron's armaments, and to LAC P.S.P. Corrick, who during the squadron's various moves, had driven alone, towing the squadron's bomb train.

Some rather late awards went to NCOs of 150 Squadron later in the year. DFMs were awarded to Sergeants S.E. Andrews (pilot) (who had by this time been commissioned), Norman J. Ingram (OB), Henry R. Figg (WOP/AG), Ernest D. Martin (OB), and Clifford Cooper (WOP/AG). Martin and Cooper had been the crew to Walter Blom DFC.

Blom himself was killed on 27 June 1940. While the squadron was at RAF Newton, his aircraft caught fire when it was being bombed up. The aircraft blew up killing Blom, six other airmen with four more injured. Two of the men killed were Sergeants Gould and Franklin who were trying to release the bombs. It was the same Sergeant Franklin who had won the Empire Gallantry Medal in France for twice helping to deal with burning aircraft on the ground. For him the third time proved unlucky.

In July, 226 Squadron heard of the award of the DFC to Pilot Officer D.A.C. Crooks, and DFMs for Sergeants T.C. Davies and R.W.S. Green, who had flown many ops together in France. David Crooks later went onto fighters and so did another of 226's pilots, the Australian, Bob Bungay. He later won the DFC and commanded the first Australian Spitfire squadron in Europe, before his death in 1943.

On 19 June, Pilot Officer Clive Wylie of 59 Squadron, who had had such an adventure over and then in France in May, was killed in one of the final recce sorties. The casualties would continue to mount. The war had five more years to run. Britain and the RAF had lost this first round, but not the fight.

*

In life one has always to learn from one's mistakes or from experience. It seems clear that the RAF leaders had not remembered the lessons from the First War. They had forgotten that the bombers of that war needed fighter escort by the last year of that war. Then, DH4s or DH9 day bombers had been escorted closely by Sopwith Camels, SE5s, Bristol Fighters and Dolphins. With the advent of 'modern' bombers, all that seemed to be lost. The bomber will fight its way through. How they were supposed to out-run or out-gun modern single seat fighters such as the Messerschmitt 109s, has never been made clear.

New lessons and new experience in the early weeks of the Second World War should have warned these same leaders that the theory was not right. Even after the shattering losses between May and June 1940, Blenheims continued to be sent out, in daylight, and with no fighter escort. In July 1940, with 2 Group reeling from its casualties and still licking its wounds, it lost 31 aircraft, and included in the lost crews were no fewer than three wing commanders. And it was not just to targets in northern France that they were sent, but to places like Aalborg – in Denmark!

They went again to Aalborg in August, 13 of August. It was 82 Squadron that was assigned, the same squadron that had lost 11 out of 12 Blenheims on 14 May, led by Wing Commander E.C. Lart. Alerted by reports of the bombers crossing the coast, the flak gunners were ready. Five of the 12 Blenheims were shot down as they reached the target area. As the survivors turned for home, they were intercepted by Me109s of JG77 and five more were shot down. The last two Blenheims made for the coast where the 11th Blenheim was forced to make a crash landing.

A month earlier, on 10 July, Harold Pleasance had led a six aeroplane formation to bomb the airfield at Amiens/Glisy.

I have a very vivid memory of a sortie I did on 10th July. I led six Blenheims to bomb Amiens/Glisy airfield. As far as I can remember we had no fighter escort.

As we were on our bombing run over the target, at about 18,000 feet, we met a lot of very accurate flak. The black puffs were appearing in front of us – always an ominous sign! Several aircraft were hit and the formation broke up. At the same time we were attacked by a number of 109s. By then I had only one other aircraft with me and we dived steeply to try to get away from the fighters.

The aircraft with me broke away – he'd probably been hit, and I continued diving and turning down to the deck. There was still a couple of 109s with me, making passes at me. By flying at nought feet and turning like mad we managed to avoid them. The compass was going round in circles and I really did not know which way I was heading. After what seemed a lifetime, I saw the sea ahead and I dived over the cliffs to sea level, frightening myself and my crew fartless! The two 109s formated on me at a distance for a brief while, then the pilots waved their hands and disappeared.

We landed thankfully at Wattisham in a muck sweat a while later. I was the sole survivor of the six Blenheims I had led out three hours earlier.

Flight Lieutenant H.P. Pleasance, 107 Squadron

It took a long time but eventually, fighter escort for day bombing sorties by 2 Group became established. In fact, in 1941, although the tactics had changed somewhat, the Blenheims might be directly or indirectly, escorted by up to five fighter wings, when operating over France.

The pilots and crews of the light bombers of the AASF and 2 Group had fought bravely during the first year of the war. Many had fallen in dispelling the myth of the invincible bomber. That they did so, so valiantly, is a testimony to their courage.

We shall not see their like again.

Bibliography

One of our Pilots is Safe, William Simpson DFC, Hamish Hamilton, 1942.

The RAF in the World War, Vol 1, Capt N. MacMillan MC AFC, Harrap & Co., 1942.

The RAF in the World War, Vol 2, Capt N. MacMillan MC AFC, Harrap & Co., 1944.

Mission Completed, ACM Sir Basil Embry GCB KBE DSO DFC AFC, Methuen & Co, 1957.

Into the Silk, Ian Mackersey, Robert Hale Ltd, 1956.

2 Group, RAF, M.J.F. Bowyer, Faber, 1974.

For Valour, The Air VCs, Chaz Bowyer, Wm Kimber & Co, 1978.

Bristol Blenheim, Chaz Bowyer, Ian Allan Ltd, 1984.

The Bomber Command War Diaries, Martin Middlebrook, Viking 1985.

The Right of the Line, John Terraine, Hodder & Stoughton, 1985.

The Air Battle of Dunkirk, N.L.R. Franks, Wm Kimber & Co, 1983.

Venturer Courageous, James Sanders, Hutchinson NZ, 1983.

And Then There was One, AM Sir Gareth Clayton KCB DFC, (Unpublished M/S) from which an extract, in precis, was taken with kind permission.

Index of People